Teaching Transformed

Achieving Excellence, Fairness, Inclusion, and Harmony

Roland G. Tharp
University of California, Santa Cruz

Peggy Estrada
University of California, Santa Cruz

Stephanie Stoll Dalton
U.S. Department of Education

Lois A. Yamauchi
University of Hawai'i, Mānoa

Westview
PRESS

A Member of the Perseus Books Group

Renewing American Schools

Copyright © 2000 by Westview Press, A Member of the Perseus Books Group

Published in 2000 in the United States of America by Westview Press, 5500 Central Avenue, Boulder, Colorado 80301-2877, and in the United Kingdom by Westview Press, 12 Hid's Copse Road, Cumnor Hill, Oxford OX2 9JJ

Find us on the World Wide Web at www.westviewpress.com

Library of Congress Cataloging-in-Publication Data
Teaching transformed : achieving excellence, fairness, inclusion, and
  harmony / Roland G. Tharp . . . [et al.].
    p.   cm. — (Renewing American schools)
  Includes bibliographical references and index.
  ISBN 0-8133-2268-5 (hc) — ISBN 0-8133-2269-3 (pb)
  1. School improvement programs—United States.   2. Educational
equalization—United States.   3. Inclusive education—United States.
I. Tharp, Roland G., 1930–   . II. Series.
LB2822.82.T44   2000
371.2'00973—dc21   99-42077
                                                                                          CIP

The paper used in this publication meets the requirements of the American National Standard for Permanence of Paper for Printed Library Materials Z39.48-1984.

PERSEUS
POD
ON DEMAND   10   9   8   7   6   5   4   3   2

Contents

Tables and Figures

Tables

Figures

Acknowledgments

A diversity of teaching and learning activities, including both individual and collaborative, is both advocated and exemplified by this book. It is a genuine collaboration; no other form of activity could have produced it because it attempts to integrate theory, research, and practice in a broad range of domains into a unified design for transforming teaching. As in a well-designed instructional activity, we are an assemblage of very diverse individuals with individual strengths, which we both brought to the endeavor and sharpened through it. While there are certainly traces of our individual voices remaining in the final version, the ideas were fully negotiated and co-constructed. To the task, Lois A. Yamauchi brought scholarship and original research with Native American Indians and Hawaiians, Asian immigrant and Asian-American populations, and cultural-historical analyses of school-community relationships. Stephanie Stoll Dalton brought her broad experience teaching at-risk students (from first grade through high school); coordinating preservice teacher education in Preservice Education for Teachers of Minorities (PETOM) at the University of Hawai'i, Mānoa; and researching teacher development in pedagogy and instructional design. Peggy Estrada brought scholarship and original research on classroom relationships and their consequences for social and academic development and on teaching and learning in bicultural and multicultural classrooms. Roland G. Tharp has long studied and written about education and social science theory, particularly in the areas of cultural diversity and unity.

We have all worked in preservice and in-service professional development, frequently together; in classrooms of the University of California, Santa Cruz, and the University of Hawai'i; and in the field—in American Indian communities of the U.S. Southwest and Canadian British Columbia, in schools of northern California's Bay Area, and with multicultural populations and Native Hawaiians in public schools on Oʻahu, Hawai'i, Molokaʻi, and Kauʻai. This book is the result of those joint and individual experiences and of the generous assistance of many others.

We have worked and talked with so many colleagues of such quality that a complete list of their names is impossible. We can only mention by name or affiliation those who are closest in time or closest in the "final common pathway" to this manuscript. These include our colleagues in some extraordinary institutions: the Kamehameha Elementary Education

Program (KEEP); Preservice Education for Teachers of Minorities (PETOM); the National Center for Research on Cultural Diversity & Second Language Learning; and the Center for Research on Education, Diversity & Excellence (CREDE). That incomplete list spans thirty-seven years. To them, and to the many who came before: Thank you, living and dead.

Even the list of those involved in the specific activities of creating this manuscript is long. This book would not be, were it not for their contributions. First, the classroom teachers whose work is reported in this book. They have taught us and given this manuscript life: Cynthia Waters, Georgia Epaloose, Janet Anderson, Claire Asam, June Sison, Audrey Sirota, Jack Mallory, Consepción Martínez, Wendy Greenfield, Genie Praetzel, and Pat Minsloff; and the many teachers and mentors of the Santa Cruz New Teachers Project, Ellen Moir, Director. In this manuscript we have often used their real names. We have changed the names of students who appear in the transcripts of lessons even though they might be equally proud of their performances. But they were not aware at the time that they might be models for the future.

To the excellent scriptwriter, Ann Gibb, we are indebted for the editing and preparation of the entire manuscript. For the artwork and design, thanks to Liz Goodman and Jessica Dalton. Motivated by dedication to "the cause," many have worked at levels of detail far below their talents. We thank, for bibliographic scholarship, Ruth Soleste Hilberg, Maile Aki, and Valerie Amby; for audio and videotape transcription, Lilly C. Orellana and Ingrid Gaines; and for editorial assistance and advice, Barbara Imhoff and Barbara DeBaryshe.

Patrick Shields and Tracy Trevorrow contributed sustained engagement and encouragement in development of our ideas and of the manuscript. To their mother, Gabriel and Analisa Shields-Estrada provided constant interest and encouragement and infinite caring and patience.

For invaluable reflections on the manuscript we are deeply indebted to Jeannie Oakes, Catherine Murphy, and Lisa Churchhill. Blame nothing on them, but recognize that the work would have been lessened without them.

Roland G. Tharp
Peggy Estrada
Stephanie Stoll Dalton
Lois A. Yamauchi

I would like to learn.
Can you tell me how to grow?
Or is it something unconveyed,
Like melody, or witchcraft?

—Emily Dickinson

1 Introduction and Overview

The Goals of Activity and Teaching

All school reform has one final common pathway: instructional activity. Whether reforms concentrate on school finance, class size limitations, preservice teacher education, national standards and goals, teacher induction, community partnerships, or any other piece of education, nothing will have any effect on student learning except as it operates through the teaching-and-learning activities at the classroom level. It is ironic that so much reform agitation occurs at other levels while so little attention is given to that common pathway toward learning. Approaching reform at other levels is like moving granite blocks around the construction site, at great expense and effort, with no clear image of what the building should be. If we had a vision of the ideal classroom, perhaps we could begin to move policies toward its construction.

This book's purpose is to convey a vision of the ideal classroom for today's students and academic standards. That vision is attainable now. Its elements are virtually consensual across educational research and development professionals, the national standards movement, and the principal theorists of education and social science. But because its elements are most often argued separately, few have seen the vision and its implications: that if we would just do what we all know to be best, the American classroom would be utterly transformed.

We attempt here to assemble these elements, articulate the vision, illustrate it by examples, expose its dynamics, elucidate its effects, present its supporting evidence, and explore its potential for transforming teaching in the school of the future. Our work is at the "classroom" level; not restricted to the physical classroom box, but "classroom" in the sense of the organized instructional activities that may extend outside the school building and even into the community. The activities engaged in by teacher and students make up the common pathway that leads to educational success or failure. Our purpose is to present a system by which the pattern of activities can be designed to achieve simultaneously all the major goals of all branches of the school reform movement: academic Excellence, Fairness, Inclusion, and Harmony.

The Goals of Educational Reform: Excellence, Fairness, Inclusion, and Harmony

All school reformers are trying to get to better schooling, but we are a huge body, and it is not clear that we are marching to the same drum. Four goals—Excellence, Fairness, Inclusion, and Harmony—all shared at the abstract level, are emphasized by different groups, and it has not been clear that we have enough patience with each other even to find a shared rhythm. Often we are less a parade than a crowd in a square, swaying this way and that in response to rumor, fad, and big noises. Do our different goals actually constitute competing interests, even competing ideas of the good, so that national political debates must result in prioritizing, in winners and losers? This book proposes that schools made of the classrooms we will describe can achieve all four goals, simultaneously and maximally. Excellence, Fairness, Inclusion, and Harmony can make a music for marching and can play together to celebrate our shared arrival.

In retrospect, we can see that our current impetus for school reform began with the Civil Rights movement of thirty years ago and accelerated ten years later due to exploding immigration to the United States, which can also be seen as a part of the (post–World War II and still ongoing) migrations of world peoples in proportions not seen since the times of the movements of the Mongols and Huns. With the civil rights reforms, the United States accepted the legal and moral challenge of providing Fairness in education for all children; with the influx of so many more children of diverse cultures and languages, the challenge to teach effectively in harmonious schools became a crisis.

Fairness

Fairness began as the piercing fife-call to conscience of the Civil Rights movement; it became the rallying cry of the cultural revolution of the 1960s. The first effort to reform schools to serve minority students better was the movement to secure "equality." Making schools equal meant making them the same for all. Through busing, redistricting, or parental choice, schools were re-created in the image of the mainstream common tradition, a model never intended for a diverse student body. In the process, the traditional African-American school, a model with many merits and achievements, was virtually obliterated rather than drawn into the mix needed for true equity and Excellence. It is now generally agreed that "equality," in the sense of just-like-the-majority, was not Fair, did not adequately promote the value of Excellence in student academic learning, and has not produced Inclusion or Harmony. Fairness has since been sought through "equity," which accepts equivalence, understood in more complex ways than merely as sameness, and which recognizes that in shared schools, equity means that changes must occur for everyone, if everyone is to learn.

Parallel to the movements for Fairness and equity was the "cultural compatibility" movement that attempted to improve academic Excellence by specific tailoring of schools for particular cultural populations. This effort collapses in the complexity of the urban multicultural, multilingual classroom. Those classrooms are microcosms of the nation, and their small societies of twenty or thirty students illustrate one point the nation must accept: Some solution must be found that works for everyone. Thus Fairness is interwoven with Excellence, and we see now that Fairness in redistributing the limited benefits of unreformed schooling is not going to produce Excellence for anyone. Although that might be Fair across groups, it is not "fair" to any of our children.

Excellence

The competitions of the Cold War, global marketing, and exploding technological advances have driven American policy to insist on more able school graduates. There has been little or no resistance to that bugle call; Excellence in academic attainment as a national goal is embraced widely, as is its operational definition: U.S. test scores superior to those of other nations. As policy rhetoric that definition may suffice, but a more inclusive and detailed goal of Excellence is required for classroom reform. The national standards movement is steadily defining the elements of Excellence in each major subject matter at each grade level. In this book, and in the design of activities we propose, Excellence means the achievement of each student's full potential. Few students achieve their full potential in classrooms that are part of the common tradition. Reform for Excellence should mean a tide on which all boats rise, whether they are gifted, challenged, or average.

How does the goal of Excellence relate to the goal of Inclusion? Fairness has been extended to a broad diversity of previously excluded students; they now "count," both morally and statistically, even though school reform has not yet embraced pedagogies that will provide them with excellent academic attainment. To achieve national Excellence, shall schools race on, accelerating attainment for those who can grasp it, in our classrooms of the common tradition? Would prioritizing Fairness delay Excellence, while everyone "catches up?" As this book illustrates, there are ways to achieve both goals, but at the present time it is not uncommon to suppose that Fairness and Excellence are in conflict.

Inclusion

Another part of school reform has focused on including all students in the school's social and instructional opportunities. In schools of the common tradition, access to instructional opportunities has been by no means equally distributed across all students. Those who were "tracked" into "trade," "industrial," or "commercial" curricula were not offered higher-level academic subjects; special education students were excluded from contact with (or even observation of) their mainstream peers; children who were speakers of languages other than English were immersed in a new language where they could swim or drown. Many reform movements have beaten the drum of Inclusion: untracking, mainstreaming, bilingual instruction. Inclusion seems a natural ally of Fairness, and their advocates have often made common cause. Inclusion as a reform theme extends beyond the school building. Including families, community organizations, and industry in school programs and policy is a broader manifestation of this overarching value—that everyone has a stake in schooling, and everyone should have access and a voice.

As we demonstrate, a reliable program for Excellence means that Excellence will be best achieved by the broadest possible Inclusion because the base of Excellence will be broadened. In the absence of such a program, many frustrated teachers, parents, and citizens—who may truly endorse both Excellence and Inclusion—nevertheless see those goals as in conflict, believing that the broader the sweep of Inclusion, the more the "able" are dragged down, and that is hardly Fair. How do we resolve this conflict? Which way do we turn?

Harmony

Harmony is our label for the one overall value shared by school reformers, although it is not a common term and is not necessarily recognized as a common value even by its many advocates. If schools are to be fair to all, highly educate all, and include all in educational opportunities and discussions, then the achievement of some form of shared values and rules of relationships and process, some reconciled community of common understanding, become the more indispensable as they become more elusive. In this sense, the pleaders for multiculturalism and the preachers of English-only instruction agree: Harmony is paramount. They see very different routes to its attainment, the one emphasizing a shared language to build a shared national community, the other emphasizing a primary value of broad and generous tolerance of multiple perspectives. But these two disputants (and virtually all other social philosophers) agree that the Harmony allowed by some agreed-upon foundation of common values is indispensable to a civil society. We argue below that a Harmony of values is necessary and achievable at the classroom level and thus at the school level, and through those experiences, at the level of the next generation of adult citizens. Even if that Harmony can be achieved, where does it stand in the order of Excellence, Fairness, and Inclusion? Can all four goals together even make music, much less a march?

Can Schools Actually Provide Excellence, Fairness, Inclusion, and Harmony?

School reformers throughout the second half of the twentieth century have been concerned with issues of Fairness and Inclusion and have been frustrated with the apparently meshed gears of schools and social class. Two decades ago the social critic Michael Apple observed:

> Schools exist through their relations to other more powerful institutions ... combined in such a way as to generate structural inequalities of power and access to resources. Second, these inequalities are reinforced and reproduced by schools ... Through their curricular, pedagogical, and evaluative activities in day-to-day life in classrooms, schools play a significant role in preserving if not generating these inequalities. Along with other mechanisms for cultural preservation and distribution, schools contribute to what has elsewhere been called the cultural reproduction of class relations in advanced industrial societies (Apple 1979, p. 64).

Apple specifically negates the conspiracy assumptions implicit in some reaches of critical theory:

> This is not to imply that all school people are racist (though some may in fact be) or that they are part of a conscious conspiracy to "keep the lower classes in their place." In fact, many of the arguments for "community" and about curriculum put forth by some of the early educators, curriculum workers, and intellectuals ... were based on the best liberal intentions of "helping people."... [My argument] is that "naturally" generated out of many educators' commonsense assumptions and practices about teaching and learning, normal and abnormal behavior, important and unimportant knowledge, and so forth are conditions and forms of interactions that have latent functions (Apple 1979, pp. 64–65).

To these arguments, twenty years later, we continue to subscribe. Indeed, our purpose could be described as explicating those "educators' commonsense assumptions and practices" and—extending past the usual concerns of critical theory—proposing practical ways of transforming them, available to every educator from policy maker to classroom teacher, so that the unintended, latent functions are replaced by an educational outcome corresponding to our highest goals.

Analytically, the groundwork has been laid in the work of preceding decades. Structural social inequalities are reinforced in schools in a variety of ways. Social class differences in schooling opportunities and outcomes can be identified in features of selection, tracking, curriculum, ideology, and values and in exposure to and acquisition of "cultural capital"—the knowledge, skills, and discourse routines that operate the societal and economic levers of power. The daily lives of students "at risk of educational failure" are markedly different from those of the middle classes. Schooling of the common tradition is not fair. Its opportunities and activities do not include the needful. Excellence is differentiated. Under such conditions, how could Harmony be expected?

Critical theorists blame educational inequities on economic and political systems; discouraged and ill-supported educators blame it on families. Liberal social theorists, in eternal utopian tinkering, seek the ever-elusive perfect policy.

Simultaneously alive and potent, sometimes within the same person or groups, is an utterly opposed ideology that holds education to be the creator and sustainer of social change, the escape hatch from historical class and familial fate, the proving ground in which every girl and boy—of whatever means and whatever history—can prove and improve their gifts of character and intellect, thus realizing their potential and enriching the national future. It is this ideology that moves most educators to choose the life. Many of us from the lower and lower-middle classes are living proofs of this belief (certainly in the universities there are far more of us than is generally understood), living proofs that education does vault many into influence and comfort. But it must also be acknowledged that the optimism of many youthful educators declines during the course of their careers. The rock chafes on Sisyphus's shoulder.

We propose a resolution of this paradox. A signal gain in Excellence, Fairness, Inclusion, and Harmony can be achieved by an improved understanding of how human society operates in social relations, teaching and learning, and the design of classroom activities. In this book we describe the ways that "educators' commonsense assumptions and practices" can be transformed to achieve the highest potential of schooling. From the point of view of policy makers, there is a goal, a desired end state that can guide their constructions. For burning-out educators, there is a way to replace unintended "latent functions" with the opportunities for students that we all want to provide. And for critical theorists, there is available a liberation pedagogy. These solutions all turn on a few points of theory. The action consequences are available to every classroom.

Unified Reform

Can proponents of the four goals march together? When we answer "yes," the themes together can make a melody, our optimism rests in large part on the great progress made within these (sometimes non-communicating) camps. An extraordinary convergence of findings has emerged among the four fields: Fairness (the research fields of equity, cultural and linguistic diversity, and students placed at risk); Excellence (cognitive science and "sociocultural development"); Inclusion ("untracking," "mainstreaming," and "social organization"); and Harmony (multiculturalism, conflict resolution, moral and values development, and service learning). The congruence of their recommendations is extraordinary and allows a new design of the organization of activity and a reformed pedagogy.

This book is too brief to contain a thorough review of all evidence pertinent to all branches of school reform. We do attempt to review some of the crucial research and ideas that speak to the ways that classrooms can achieve Excellence, Fairness, Inclusion, and Harmony, all together and all successfully. If, as we claim, this can be achieved in the classroom, then we will all be in a position to create a school that enables such classrooms, and to create school systems, communities, and policy environments that allow such schools to prosper.

Our scope is the classroom, because the classroom contains the final common pathway through which all school structures and policy finally have their effect. That pathway is the instructional activity of teachers and students. The design and organization of that activity affords or restricts opportunities for learning and social development. Through that activity, school succeeds or fails, lives are opened, or lives are closed. All other aspects of education—policy, resources, administration, and leadership; laws and social values; programs and professional development; curriculum and evaluation—funnel through the activity of teachers and students, organized in the units we call "classrooms." We therefore focus also on the theory that can rationalize and guide the classroom's functions and design. Theory can reveal the regularities in psychocultural processes and sociocultural conditions that determine the working of classrooms. The same theory will reveal how classrooms contribute to duplicating current society, perpetuating the next generation in the image of our own, with its flawed Fairness, insufficient Excellence, systematic exclusions, and disharmonious consternations. Studying this theory can reveal the way these processes work and can guide us to make the changes we choose. Our calipers are delicate—one point on the classroom and the other on theory. But our drawings are proposals for the marching route for the entire endeavor. If education can come to agreement on a vision, a standard, for the patterns of activity in classrooms, then all other aspects of educational decision making, policy, and preparation could be guided by and evaluated on the basis of whether they bring us closer to that ideal envisioned condition.

Plan of the Book

The study of the design and organization of classroom activity is not yet recognized as the foundational element of education, although it is tantamount to the study of teaching and learning itself. In the theory of human development that organizes this book, activity is the basic framework of human ontology, and the pattern of activity (comprising actions, persons, interactions, settings, roles, and symbols) determines the outcomes of socialization and human development. Yet these concepts have barely penetrated educational policy discussions, nor have they had much effect on teacher education or on discourse among the general public. For that reason, we present an overview of the vision of the reformed classroom first, followed by the rationales for its elements and their integration. Chapter 2 presents the vision.

The presentation begins in Chapter 2 with portraits of two classrooms, one of the common tradition and the other of the transformed vision. In these brief sketches, the distinguishing features will be clear, and the remainder of the chapter discusses the primary elements of the reformed classroom. The intellectual architecture of the transformation consists of Five Standards for Effective Pedagogy, and Three Necessary

A Vision of the Transformed Classroom

Teachers and students are working together, on real products, real problems. Activities are rich in language, with teachers developing students' capacity to speak, read, and write English and the special languages of mathematics, science, humanities, and art. They teach the curriculum through meaningful activities that relate to the students' lives and experiences in their families and communities. Teachers challenge students to think in complex ways and to apply their learning to solving meaningful problems. Teachers and students converse; the basic teaching interaction is conversation, not lecture. A variety of activities are in progress simultaneously (individual work; teamwork; practice and rehearsal; mentoring in side-by-side, shoulder-to-shoulder, teacher-student work). Students have systematic opportunities to work with all other classmates. They all learn and demonstrate self-control and common values: hard work, rich learning, helpfulness to others, mutual respect.

Conditions for their enactment. The Five Standards represent the consensus of research findings across all populations, subject areas, and grade levels. They are standards for instructional practice within all classroom activity. We discuss these standards in detail, especially how they work to make each classroom Fair, Inclusive, Excellent, and Harmonious. To enact the standards it is necessary that every effective classroom achieve the Three Necessary Conditions. First, there must be multiple simultaneous activity settings. Second, the activities must be diverse in requirements, products, participants, and roles. In that diverse mix of activities, there will be opportunities for every child to receive the teacher's assistance in a context of intense, responsive, and sustained dialogue. Finally, a systematic, co-constructed, explicit shared value system must permeate every activity, so that each classroom is a living community of learners.

We devote Chapters 3 through 5 to a review of three bodies of research and theory that justify and explain the strength of the model and that guide its enactment. In Chapter 3 we present the first body of research and theory, introducing our core concept—the organization of activity—in the language of sociocultural theory and discuss how patterns of activity affect communities and classrooms. In sociocultural theory, the basic unit of analysis is the activity setting. Activity settings are the organizational structures through which society acts and through which it socializes its members. The activities in which children engage, and the language and problem solving that accompany them, are formative for their developing cognitions, perceptions, motives, and values. The critical task of schooling is the design and implementation of activity settings that are varied, interrelated, appropriate to task and participants, and involve students and teacher. There are regular principles that characterize both effective activity settings and effective patterns of the multiple activity settings of a classroom.

Sociocultural theory is essentially a theory of development (Vygotsky 1978): development of capacities, individuals, institutions, communities, and cultures. A theory of development is ideally suited to a study of education and to produce the heuristics needed for design and reform of pedagogy, classroom organization, and schooling. When designing a general theory of education (Tharp and Gallimore 1988), we pointed out that sociocultural theory provides a flexible, inclusive integrating lingua franca for social science's plethora of mini-theories and hypotheses, preserving the close fit between disciplinary theories and inquiries but uniting them into an overarching intellectual architecture. Likewise in this book, we draw on work that originated in many orientations. In addition to work in education itself, we draw on findings and analyses from cognitive science—(Bruer 1993); cross-cultural psychology (Hofstede 1980; Triandis et al. 1988); developmental psychology (Asher and Parker 1989; Ladd and Kochenderfer 1996); theology (Rubin 1991); literary criticism

(Bakhtin 1986)—and from various concepts from sociology, including propinquity and assortative mating (Tharp 1963), contact theory (Allport 1954; Slavin 1985, 1996), and organizational theory (Cohen and Lotan 1997; Epstein 1986, 1989). The detailed positions and their methods have been important for building the knowledge base; but none alone can discuss all relevant phenomena. Sociocultural theory provides a language that can allow these multiple participants to engage in a shared conversation.

Also in Chapter 3 we address the questions, Who shares activity with whom? Which students work with which others and which with the teachers, and how much, and when? Who decides? How are the people in the classroom sorted out? At every moment in the classroom, forces sort students into propinquity groups or affinity groups or preference groups. Other forces sort them into relationships with teachers or make teacher relationships unlikely.

Many of these forces are not of the teacher's making, although many can be modified by teachers through the planning and design of classroom activity. Many formal and informal patterns of activity are strongly influenced by policy set at a level far above the individual classroom. For example, "tracking" limits not only the content of instruction but also propinquity to peers and teachers, which in turn limits the possibilities of friendship and mutual influence. "Departmentalization" versus "team" organization of faculty and students have quite different consequences on possibilities for association, working together, and relationship qualities.

All these features apply forces that sort students into friendships, affinity groups, interest groups, and social preferences. The teacher may choose to use that force, for example by using affinity as the basis for self-selected cooperative work groups. Maximizing teaching and learning effectiveness will require that the teacher often create activity patterns that work against those forces, seeking to increase Excellence, Fairness, Inclusion, and Harmony.

In Chapter 4 we examine the research literature on instructional activity and interpersonal relationships; show how the patterns of classroom activity affect relationships; and demonstrate how those relationships affect social and academic Inclusion, Excellence, and Harmony. More than venue, more than furniture, more than actions, activity settings consist of people, and in the classroom, activity settings consist of various combinations of teachers and students. The nature of their joint activities determines the qualities of peer relationships and teacher-student relationships, and these relationships have profound consequences for the Excellence of learning or the lack of it.

Relationships participate in the social construction of knowledge, and quality of relationships (teacher-student, student-student) have direct, strong consequences on the attainment of academic Excellence. Activity patterns of collaboration, reflection, and active involvement foster positive relationship development (teacher-student, student-student), whereas other patterns do the opposite. Grouping may expand or restrict relationship opportunities. Collaborative activity groups, as opposed to lectures or other teacher-dominated activities, can expand relationship opportunities not only among students but also between teacher and students.

Before students ever arrive at school, they (and their families) already have been sorted into propinquity, affinity, and preference groups, and into certain relationships with teachers as well as peers. In Chapter 5 we review the theory and research on culture and education. The cultural and historical roots of current activity account for the ways that people interact with young learners, thus transforming them into culture members and perpetuating the culture for new generations. The historical, symbolic, value, and social dimensions of culture have played little part in the practice of education. Now we have a means of analyzing and improving education by responsiveness to the cultural context of students (Tharp and Gallimore 1988).[1] Sociocultural concepts allow us to analyze both cultural forces and patterns of activity characteristic of students' families, communities, or ethnicities and how they sort participants into certain activity settings and discourage others. Schools may work with these forces or work to modify them. Contextualizing classroom activity in the activity patterns of the community may empower students as it activates their repertoires and provides the comforts of familiarity. To allow these cultural forces to totally determine classroom activity settings may also limit learning, both academic and social. Therefore, there is a role for expanding students' experiences beyond the familiar, for expanding their repertoires and their range of achievements, and therefore their opportunities in a diverse society.

In short, the design of the pattern of activity in the classroom determines its critical capacities and either affords or limits a classroom's potential for children's development—intellectual, social, and moral. The teacher has enormous latitude in determining that design and its fruits. The most critical attributes of activity design affect what happens during activity, not merely its structures. Good structure, good "organization," alone will not produce academic Excellence, and good grouping alone will not produce Harmony. The instructional practice, the pedagogy within the activity patterns, is the key both to Excellence and Harmony.

In Chapter 6 we present a developmental analysis of the reformed classroom, a process for transforming any classroom from a unitary organization such as a rank-and-file seating for a teacher-led recitation script into a more differentiated organization containing varied, simultaneous, related, and appropriate activity settings. The steps for this development are discussed in a practical way, allowing a reader-teacher to move forward in reorganizing his or her own classroom in a series of five phases, culminating in the fully realized reform of Phase 5. That developmental analysis also provides a deeper discussion of the interacting dynamics of the classroom elements.

Finally, in Chapter 7 we review the reasons, functions, dynamics, and evidence for the efficacy of the Phase 5 classroom and consider how it can become the classroom of the future.

Notes

1. Cultural dimensions are being introduced into the practices of all the helping professions, such as community psychology (O'Donnell and Tharp 1990), child and family psychotherapy (Tharp 1991), and adult psychotherapy (Miltenburg and Singer 1999; Tharp 1999).

2 Transformed Classrooms: Description, Principles, and Criteria

TWO CLASSROOMS IN THE SAME SCHOOL, similar in student composition and curriculum. Both taught by dedicated teachers of unexceptionable professional and human values that have led them to request assignment to this urban, multilingual, multicultural school whose students share neighborhood, poverty, and need. Ms. Lee and Ms. Young are much alike, but as we visit their classrooms, we will observe sharp differences in patterns of activity and pedagogy.

From Our Files

Notice Taped to Door of Observation Deck

Kamehameha Elementary Education Program (KEEP)
From the elevated observation deck, visitors watch four classrooms of the transformed vision through one-way glass walls. On the entrance door to the observation deck, this notice was taped:

FIGURE 2.1   Notice Taped to Door of Observation Deck

VISITORS,

PLEASE ENTER WITH A HOST.

SEE SUSAN

Entering the rich complexity of a vigorous classroom, visitors tend to observe in terms of their own familiar concepts and can be oblivious to features and concepts that the classroom's designers consider crucial. A host can explain those concepts and guide some part of the visitor's attention to the classroom's purposes and rationales. We will serve as hosts for your observations of many classrooms, in repeated visits throughout this book, each visit focusing on different categories and concepts. For this first observation, we suggest that the reader consider especially Michael Apple's "conditions and forms of interactions that have latent functions"—the unintended effects of educators' common actions and assumptions.

From Our Files

A Mathematics Classroom of the Common Tradition

From her desk, Ms. Lee watches as her sixth-grade mathematics students enter and move to their accustomed seats, arranged in three long rows, with chalkboards on three walls and windows behind. The students are six African- and six Anglo-Americans, ten Latinos, and four immigrants from Southeast Asia. Half of the Latinos and the four Asian students have limited English proficiency. On this semester's standardized mathematics tests, their scores ranged from the 14th through the 66th percentile by national norms. The students gather with others of their ethnic group and chatter with one another in a mixture of English and their primary languages. When the bell rings, Ms. Lee passes out the previous day's homework, which the students examine while she writes a formula and a set of calculations on the side chalkboard. To illustrate a common mistake in the homework, she talks them through the solution, asking questions to which students call out answers. Some answers are answered in chorus, while for some only two or three students speak out, including especially Tara, who is able to answer all questions quickly and adroitly from her somewhat isolated seat in the back row.

Moving to the front board, where she has already written an extensive formula and calculations taken from the textbook, Ms. Lee lectures on the new material for the day, occasionally asking for student contributions. Primarily the same students reply; Ms. Lee is grateful for Tara. The demonstration/explanation takes twelve minutes. She then passes out a worksheet containing similar problems. (There is a list of categories containing sets of numbers, and the students are to represent the sets in three different types of graphs.) For a time, the teacher "floats," looking over the students' shoulders, occasionally giving instructions. After five minutes, she moves to the extreme right side of the room and chats with a group of boys whose work has been desultory.

(continues)

(continued)

The teacher talks with them a bit about their school basketball team, then tells them to get to work and goes to her desk, where she concentrates on grading homework turned in by the previous class.

The students continue, variously working or idling, occasionally whispering to one another; it is not clear whether the subject is mathematics or social gossip, but the noise level is low and the students are still. Tara has finished her worksheet and is apparently writing a letter. One boy takes his paper to the teacher with a question; she answers it, looks at the clock, and tells the students to complete the worksheet as homework. The bell rings. The students walk out in the same social groups in which they were seated.

From Our Files

A Transformed Mathematics Classroom

Down the hallway, another sixth-grade mathematics class is filling, and when the bell rings, the students (more or less in the same ethnic proportions) are already seated around five tables. The teacher, Ms. Young, quickly outlines the day's upcoming activities, referring to a schedule on the chalkboard that shows three different activities of fifteen minutes each and the goals for each of those activity settings. She reminds the students of the grouping for each activity, asks for questions, and clarifies that during the first "rotation" they will seat themselves with their "teams." The students sort themselves out at the different tables. Ms. Young joins one of the teams and begins an intense conversation with those six students about the concepts used in this week's lessons.

Ms. Young asks the students to bring out the data they have each gathered at home on height and weight of various family members. The students compare their various record sheets, and then Ms. Young asks the main concept question of the instructional unit: "What are some ways that we could represent these data?"

The students first consider lists, or groups, and then graphs of several types. "Which way would represent your data best?"

Students propose their own favorites; for each, Ms. Young asks "Why?"

After some animated discussion about the advantages and disadvantages of the various possibilities, the students agree on a bar graph. The group then practices using a bar graph to represent one student's data.

Meanwhile, the other teams are engaged in two other kinds of activities, either assembling the data they have each gathered at home on height and weight of various family members or designing a series of circle, bar, or line graphs to represent their group data once they are analyzed. The teams are of

(continues)

(continued)

mixed ethnic groups, the language is exclusively English, and the conversation is lively and loud.

After fifteen minutes, the students "rotate," staying with their teams but moving to different tables and different tasks. At Ms. Young's table, the concept-conversation is repeated; she asks those students who have already drawn graphs to discuss those representations and consider whether their original choices were the best. For the last fifteen minutes, the teams break up, and all students work on worksheets from the textbook. Seating at the tables is organized by primary language. Ms. Young rotates around the tables, sitting with the Spanish- and Hmong-speaking students for the longest time, questioning them to make sure their limited English proficiency does not hinder understanding. (This "sheltered instruction" gauges vocabulary and syntax to the students' level of comprehension.) The students frequently speak to one another in their first language, translating or explaining the concepts to one another. Ms. Young speaks neither Spanish nor Hmong fluently enough to teach in it, but she relies on the students to clarify issues among themselves and present to her their translation or concept problems.

At the end of the class, Ms. Young asks briefly about how the hour went and accepts a suggestion about a modification for tomorrow's concept-conversation with the other teams. She quickly reminds the teams of their production schedule, referring them to the week's printed schedule. The bell rings. The students move into the hallway talking to their team members about organizing their tasks, and although the talk is all in English, the ethnic mix is thorough.

Quality Criteria for Instructional Activity in Classrooms

Any pattern of instructional activity creates something. Ms. Lee's classroom will create a pattern of learning and a social structure that will perpetuate in her classroom the patterns of status, affinity, and differential achievement that exist on the streets surrounding the school. Ms. Young's classroom will create a pattern of learning and a social structure that will make each child more likely to develop his or her potential for achievement and democratic living, both in the classroom and beyond.

Designing and organizing instructional activity into an effective classroom community is the means by which teachers realize their goals and through which students learn academics and social values. By making decisions about instructional activity a teacher can provide for the highest goals for education or make them impossible to achieve. As a teacher approaches the point of decision, formulating a vision of instructional activity, how can he or she evaluate it? Are there general criteria to guide the design and organization of classroom activity? This chapter discusses several standards and criteria that, if met, will simultaneously achieve Excellence, Fairness, Inclusion, and Harmony.

Generic Principles for Effective Pedagogy

The first group of criteria was developed out of the study of effective teaching and learning and an effort to identify those conditions that maximize Excellence of achievement among students generally considered to be at risk for educational failure: the poor, the culturally and linguistically diverse, the isolated of the deep ghetto and the deep hills, the excluded, and the unfairly treated. In the "educational diversity" research community that studies these students and schools there exists a strong consensus supporting five principles. Once these were articulated, it became clear that there is an equally strong consensual subscription to them among the general educational research and development community. (This point will be elaborated with evidence in Chapter 7.) Because these principles are generally accepted as maximizing teaching and learning for all—the "all" that is fully inclusive—a central goal of instructional activity should be to maximize their enactment in the classroom.

These five generic principles do not represent "programs," although many effective programs exemplify them. They are not fads, propelled by the enthusiasts who sweep across education in apparently inexhaustible waves of huckstering. Instead, they are simply those principles on which educational researchers and program developers agree. Established by a thorough reading of the literature in research, development, and evaluation of educational programs for all cultural and social groups over a period of decades and across a wide range of settings, these five principles have emerged as consensus.

Scholarly review, consensus testing, and focused research detailing these principles have been conducted in major part by the researchers affiliated (formally or loosely) with the Center for Research on Education, Diversity & Excellence (CREDE) and its predecessors, the National Center for Research on Cultural Diversity & Second Language Learning and the Kamehameha Elementary Education Program (KEEP). The analytical and consensual process began (and continues) with an analysis of the entire literature produced by researchers and program developers working with majority and minority students in kindergarten through post-secondary classrooms. The principles are statements on which there is agreement about effective teaching across the widest possible range of diversity, grades, curricula, cultures, and language groups.

These principles are also generic across all subject matters. This claim must be phrased and read with great care. We know of no subject matter about which research and development evidence on pedagogy is not consistent with the principles as phrased here. However, the principles must be enacted differently in art than in mathematics, because every subject matter requires different concepts, tools, sequences, applications, and orders of proceeding. Teachers who seek to transform their teaching will find specific content-teaching guidance in the research and in the standards of each subject's professional specialty. We return to this issue later in this chapter, in the discussion of the teaching of complex thinking. Nevertheless, the generic principles articulated here can serve as quality standards for all subject matters, benchmarks to gauge the integrity of one's own classroom, and criteria to evaluate any classroom's design.

These principles are claimed only as current consensus, not a final or complete list of desirable elements. The consensus process consumed approximately ten years, with successive versions and explications of the statements being issued (Tharp 1989, 1991, 1994, 1997; Tharp, Dalton, and Yamauchi 1994; Dalton 1998a, 1998b; Dalton and Youpa 1998; Hilberg et al. in press). Simultaneously, a national program of oral presentations and discussions was conducted, in which criticism or exceptions were invited. These venues ranged from national television to small conferences to focus groups of parents and teachers.

Recently, CREDE has issued the principles in the form of Five Standards for Effective Pedagogy, with supporting indicators and examples (Dalton 1998a). There is high consistency between these five standards and those issued by other national standards groups, to the extent that they discuss pedagogy (e.g., for mathematics, National Council of Teachers of Mathematics 1991; for science, National Research Council 1996 and American Association for the Advancement of Science 1993; and for general teaching standards, the various publications of the National Board for Professional Teaching Standards).

Linder-Scholer (1996) notes that "standards" need not mean templates to copy or hurdles to jump. Standards can be understood in the original sense of the word: as banners guiding the way at the head of a procession. This meaning of standards emphasizes their broad base and consensual nature, a consensus about ideals and principles that must be enacted in local contexts through local participation. Clearly, specific strategies and activities to accomplish standards will vary from one local situation to another. All approaches, however, share the common intention of aligning teaching practices with the broad statements of the standards. Standards, in this vision, provide general guidance for teachers, schools, teacher educators, and others interested in pedagogy and its effects on learning. They are statements of ideals toward which teachers can strive and which they can reach through reflection, practice, interaction, constructive feedback, and continuous learning (Dalton 1998b).

Proponents of the Five Standards do not claim that they are comprehensive; instead, we assume that in the fullness of time and through the accumulation of data additional or refined statements will emerge. But for now, they are the best available criteria for pedagogy. They are sufficient, if thoroughly enacted, to produce cognitive development; school achievement; and classrooms characterized by Excellence, Fairness, Inclusion, and Harmony.

Not surprisingly, the principles are entirely consistent with natural teaching and learning, as practiced by *Homo sapiens* traditionally, in all informal community, cultural, productive, and familial settings since the dawn of time and on every continent. Schools of the common tradition, however, have not practiced such education. In fact, it is families and communities who have provided the activity, the conversation, the language development, and the shared context upon which the schools could depend. A dependable similarity between school and home is no longer present in our culturally and linguistically diverse nation. Schools must now provide the common experience, activity, language, and conversation that learners require, both for individual development and the development of a common, shared, and mutually endorsed community.

The Five Standards are expressed here in a particular theoretical language, that of the sociocultural perspective. Naturally, not all the research and development literature—from which the principles were derived—uses that terminology, and indeed, many writers whose work has contributed to the consensus write from other perspectives. Bruer (1993) provides an excellent treatment of instruction from the cognitive-science perspective, as do Cohen and Lotan (1997) from an organizational theory viewpoint and Horton and Freire (1990), and McLaren (1999) from a critical theory perspective. This, of course, increases the credibility of the consensus. Nonetheless, there are strong advantages to expressing the principles in a uniform theoretical language, because the articulations and interacting dynamism among the principles are revealed with the clarity of bones on x-ray.

The credibility of the consensus is also fostered by the degree to which the principles are supported by, and indeed deducible from, the tenets of sociocultural theory. The reader will see shortly that these empirical principles could equally well have been derived from the theoretical discussions in Chapter 3.

Powerful and consensual as they may be, a thorough enactment of the Five Standards remains rare. If we all agree, why do not teachers routinely enact them? Practice always lags behind research knowledge, of course, but there are other more pointed explanations. Classroom activity in the common tradition has been characterized as obeying a "recitation script," in which the teacher makes assignments (usually from text, also from lecture); the students then attempt to master the assignment on

The Five Standards for Effective Pedagogy

Standard I: Teachers and Students Producing Together

Facilitate learning through joint productive activity among teacher and students.

Standard II: Developing Language and Literacy Across the Curriculum

Develop competence in the language and literacy of instruction across the curriculum.

Standard III: Making Meaning: Connecting School to Students' Lives

Contextualize teaching and curriculum in the experiences and skills of students' homes and communities.

Standard IV: Teaching Complex Thinking

Challenge students toward cognitive complexity.

Standard V: Teaching Through Conversation

Engage students through dialogue, especially the Instructional Conversation.

Standard I: Teachers and Students Producing Together

Facilitate learning through joint productive activity among teacher and students.

their own; they are then required to recite facts from the assignment, either in writing or orally; and then the teacher makes the next assignment. This script produces a whole-class based, lecture-dominated, worksheet-flooded environment like that seen in the classroom of Ms.

Lee. It simply does not allow the enactment of the pedagogy Standards. Enactment of them—converting Ms. Lee's classroom into Ms. Young's— is tantamount to a radical change in the design of instructional activity and the human relationships in the classroom community. Such a transformation is long overdue.

Perhaps the recitation script's simple, repetitive, and uniform classroom formats were once efficient in creating expectations and skills useful for factory work. This impersonal, rigid, factory/bureaucracy model has been largely abandoned even by industry and bureaucracy, yet it continues to dominate in American schools, even while national and international commerce, communication, humanities, and amity now require high literacies, cognitive flexibility, problem-solving capacity, and interpersonal skills that can address projects of gargantuan complexity. Although all of its justifications are long dead, the old model lives on. Surely this new millennium requires a new schooling, with new capacities for thought, creativity, and problem solving, and with new values to accommodate our teeming, diverse, communicating, and rocketing planet.

As we discuss in theoretical terms in Chapter 3, sociocultural theory emphasizes that learning takes place best in joint productive activity, that is, when experts and novices work together for a common product or goal and during the activity have opportunities to converse about it (Tharp and Gallimore 1988; Wertsch 1985). The common motivation provided by a joint goal inclines all participants to offer and receive assistance, since it is in everyone's best interest that the goal is reached. Because providing assistance is the basic act of teaching, joint productive activity creates the conditions in which development will occur. Research evidence also clearly supports the role of the constructive, productive activity itself; while assistance is vital, the feature that nails down learning is applying that knowledge in productive action (Webb, Troper, and Fall 1995; Tharp and Gallimore 1988; Vygotsky 1978).

In natural (non-formal) settings even the youngest students, as well as mature adult learners, develop their competencies in the context of joint activity. Whether it is mother and child cooking together or leader and team producing together on the shop floor, shared ways of understanding the world are created through the development of language systems and word meanings that are used during shared activity. Schools of the common tradition do not work that way: There is little joint activity, particularly with teachers, from which common experiences emerge, and therefore there is no shared context that allows students to develop a common understanding with the teacher and with each other.

The classrooms of Ms. Lee and Ms. Young (pp. 14–16) offer a sharp contrast in the degree of working and producing together. Ms. Young sets tasks for her work teams that require collaboration in collecting, analyzing, and reporting their data. She works with them intensively, three times a week at least, focusing on their understanding of the task and the concepts, so that she is continuously able to assess and assist each group and each individual. For much of their work time, however, the students work and produce among themselves, frequently in collaboration.

The formal task of schools is to promote the development of discourse competencies, word meaning, and conceptual structures in a variety of content areas. This development requires shared activity in which the concepts take on meaning by creating an interface between "schooled" concepts and those of everyday experience. The student thus develops the capacity of using academic verbal thought for the solution of practical problems of the experienced world. This appropriation of the academic languages of school is the basic process by which a student becomes an educated person. To foster this appropriation, the learner must hear how the new conceptual language is used to describe and analyze immediate, shared experiences. This is why doing things together and conversing about it is such an essential condition for socialization and cognitive growth. This system is used consistently in the highest reaches of scientific and philosophical thought. It is the process used in the graduate seminar, the star in the crown of international education. Theoretical thought and discussion requires a continual freshening by example and a testing against sensory data. This constant connecting of "schooled" concepts and everyday concepts is the basic process of understanding the world used by mature "schooled" thinkers.

Although small groups of students working together may also acquire many of the benefits of joint productive activity, student discourse during tasks is not automatically nor reliably of the quality needed to produce high levels of conceptual understanding. Students may be taught quality criteria and metascripts for group discussion that elevate conceptual understanding (Swing and Peterson 1982; King 1990; Stacey 1992; Webb and Farivar 1994; Richmond and Striley 1996; Bianchini 1997). Participating with the teacher during activity in which he or she is available as guide, dialogical partner, and model is the most powerful experience by which students learn the criteria and metascripts appropriate for them to use in their collaborative groups.

Excellent work exists in the literature on "cooperative learning," some of which meets the criteria for joint productive activity and some of which does not. In U.S. classrooms, cooperative learning is frequent in first grade, then rapidly declines in frequency, until by high school it is quite rare. This is entirely unnecessary; joint productive learning activity is not only for primary school children. A recent meta-analysis demonstrates the robust effects of cooperative and collaborative small-group instruction at the undergraduate college level in mathematics, science, engineering, and technology courses. Improvements in academic achievement, attitudes toward learning, and persistence through courses and programs are of such impressive magnitude that the analysts recommend widespread implementation of such joint productive activity (Springer, Stanne, and Donovan 1999). Various features of cooperative learning are discussed throughout this book; in fact, cooperative learning is one of the chief contributors to the consensus principle of joint productive activity. We mention here only one of the better examples of the system, that developed by Cohen and her associates (e.g., Cohen and Lotan 1997), in which students work together on shared projects that require them to assist and learn from one another. Many inventive and effective examples can be found in Cohen's work, although the teacher's role is somewhat shadowy, appearing to float among a variety of student groups, commenting and questioning on an opportunistic basis.

While admiring that work, we add a different emphasis. Students and teachers should share a significant portion of classroom activities. Only if the teacher is also present sufficiently to share the experiences will there be the sustained, intensive discourse with a fully competent adult that maximizes development and creates intersubjectivity with that person. This is especially important when the teacher and the students are not of the same cultures. Joint activity between teacher and students helps to create a common context of experience in the school itself, vital when a shared cultural context is not present, and results in the creation of a harmonious set of values. The Cohen group is quite right in attempting to avoid the too-frequent problem of teacher participation: Teachers tend to dominate discourse and squelch student participation. But the technique of artful guiding of participation, without dominating the dialogue, can be mastered by teachers (Rogoff 1991; Tharp and Gallimore 1988), even novices (Dalton and Sison 1995).

Although joint, shoulder-to-shoulder work with teachers is rare in classrooms, we must not accept this condition as either desirable or inevitable. Being with a knowledgeable, experienced teacher is the richest learning opportunity for the student in the classroom:

> Learning by being with a knowledgeable partner is a more effective method of developing a particular language of thought than learning from books, classes, or science shows. The crucial aspect ... is that they provide the beginner with insights into both the overt activities of human productivity and into the more hidden inner processes of thought. While a polished teacher or an effective science exhibit can offer a lot of information about the content of a discipline, it is only through close collaborations that the novice is likely to learn what the mentor may not even know: how he or she formulates a question or starts a new project (John-Steiner 1985, p. 200).

Teachers who converse as they work alongside their students will provide that fountain of privileged information. It is the teacher who holds the knowledge of the concepts, lexicon, and ways of defining, analyzing, and solving problems of the subject matters at hand. The teacher provides the keys necessary for opening the doors of opportunity, the doors of future options. The fewer school-like repertoires children bring to school with them, the greater the need for that close interaction with an educated adult.

Estrada, Sayavong, and Guardino (1998) found that first- and fourth-grade teachers who engaged their students more frequently in joint productive activity rated their students' overall and language arts performance higher. This is discussed to a greater extent below under Standards II and V. In Chapter 4 we show that patterns of instruction that allow a rich mix of activity settings, in which teachers and students work productively together, have both academic and social benefits. In Chapter 6 we explain how to create such systems of organization.

Standard II: Developing Language and Literacy Across the Curriculum

Develop competence in the language and literacy of instruction across the curriculum.

Current literacy, cognitive, and educational research has revealed the deep ties among language, thinking, values, and culture. Language development is best fostered through meaningful use and through purposive conversation between teacher and students, rather than through drill and decontextualized rules (Speidel 1987a, 1987b). Everyday social language, formally correct academic language, and the languages of each subject matter are all vital for success in school and in life. So, language development at all these levels—informal, problem solving, and academic—is the overarching curriculum for the entire school day.

Certainly reading and writing must be taught as specific subjects, but they can also be taught within other subject areas, by fostering language expression and comprehension in the activities of each content area. Language development should be understood as learning and applying the specialized "languages" of science (Lemke 1990), mathematics, history, literature, and art. Effective mathematics learning is based on the ability to "speak mathematics," just as the overall ability to achieve across the curriculum is dependent on mastery of the languages of instruction:

> Science vocabulary is not a simple matter of a list of terms. Vocabulary learning, like language learning in general, is a complex process of developing relationships among ideas, terms and meanings (Fradd and Larrinaga McGee 1994). Appropriate use of key science terms is an indicator of

the precision and sophistication of understanding (AAAS 1993) (Lee and Fradd 1998, p. 16).

Teaching mathematics or science can be thought of as teaching a second language, and many of the techniques and principles of English as a Second Language (ESL) apply to these disciplines. The languages of science and mathematics also include sociolinguistic aspects: the rules and conventions of discourse, the metascripts of idea testing and communication (Palincsar and Brown 1989; Palincsar, Anderson, and David 1993; Lemke 1990).

Ms. Young (see pp. 15–16) illustrated Standard II in a number of ways. During her Instructional Conversations with the teams, her dialogue modeled, shaped, and reinforced the accurate use of mathematics concepts and set the standard for the use of the mathematics lexicon as the way for teams to plan their work and report it. Ms. Young also set up special conversational opportunities with the English Language Learners, participating with them in creating accurate translations and assuring that their understanding of the concepts was not weakened by problems in English. Simultaneously, this discussion assisted the development of English-language competence itself.

The most important condition for meeting Standard II is providing students with the opportunities to speak and write, practice language use, and receive the natural feedback of conversation. Joint productive activity provides an ideal opportunity for development of the language of the activity's subject matter. Language development, both oral and written, can be fostered by such simple strategies as restating, modeling, offering alternative phrasing, and questioning. Everyday language and academic language need continuous and integrated development. This is because academic language builds on and modifies everyday language and the thinking that it reflects. Academic discussion encourages students to move beyond everyday talk and use subject lexicons to express their understanding of concepts. Thus, the first rule of language development is to provide students with many opportunities to use varieties of language in appropriate forms.

Another visit to our two classrooms will be instructive if we observe through the lens of language development. Consider the raw number of communication surfaces present in the classroom of Ms. Young. In all her varied small-group activities, conversations among students abound, almost all on task, almost all in English, almost all using school vocabulary to express and refine thought. Even occasional social gossip is an opportunity for development of everyday social English competence. Ms. Lee is attempting to enlighten the classroom with her single candle through the one wall of lecture. In Ms. Young's classroom, every person in the room refracts and magnifies communication in a complex of planes and angles, illuminating every text and every task.

Standard III: Making Meaning: Connecting School to Students' Lives

Contextualize teaching and curriculum in the experiences and skills of students' homes and communities.

Students' developing understanding builds on two foundations: new academic material presented by the school and what they bring to academic topics in terms of everyday experience and knowledge. Effective teaching requires that teachers seek out and include the contexts of students' experiences and their local communities' points of view and situate new academic learning in that context (National Council of Teachers of Mathematics 1991). Students are willing to struggle with unfamiliar language and abstract notions in science, math, and other content areas when they are motivated by interesting activities they and their families value.

Typically, schools teach rules, abstractions, and verbal descriptions. They also teach by means of rules, abstractions, and verbal descriptions. Many cultural communities do neither. Schools must assist such students by providing experiences of how rules, abstractions, and verbal descriptions are drawn from the everyday world and how they are then applied to it.

Activities designed within units that are situated in problems and issues of students' everyday lives provide vivid opportunities for teachers to assist students to stretch their informal understandings to more abstract levels (Preston 1991). Interaction in the activities of contextualized units helps students map their informal understanding of how their world works onto the formal formulas, equations, abstract systems, and theories presented in classroom content instruction (Bruer 1993). From kindergarten to high school, curriculum that is designed around compelling practical problems provides opportunities for teachers and students to jointly design activities that have meaning, personally or in the larger context of group, class, school, or community.

Estrada, Sayavong, and Guardino (1998) found the use of contextualization extremely rare in culturally and linguistically diverse first and fourth grades. Nonetheless, when teachers did use contextualization, tapping into students' relevant individual and familial experiences always elicited more lively, attentive participation. Indeed, this strategy often brought a tangential or vague discussion back into focus. Students' responses often indicated a weaving of their palpable experiences with the more abstract, schooled concepts of the moment.

Ms. Young's design of the tasks for her sixth-grade mathematicians illustrates a simple but compelling way of situating the instructional goals of her lesson in the students' family contexts. She could have presented the goal concepts in highly abstract, decontextualized terms (equivalence of percentages and fractions; equivalence of alternative representational systems for mathematical relationships), or, as Ms. Lee did, depend on the textbook's word problems to give some surface gloss of pertinence. Ms. Young, however, had the students collect the data for analysis by measuring each member of the family, an activity that the students found very amusing and motivating.

Anchoring abstract concepts in the experienced world is a universal cognitive growth process, just as common in adults as in children. Hvitfeldt (1986) studied the classroom behavior of Hmongs in an adult education English class. However hard the instructor would try to use abstract and decontextualized examples, the Hmong themselves contextualized the instruction by promoting a warm, personal relationship with the instructor, by asking him personal questions, teasing, laughing, and joking with him. When the instructor would not specify context, the students themselves would relate it to a known personal event or community condition. When the instructor used fictional Hmong names in drills, the students invariably stopped the lesson to check with one another about who this person might be in the Hmong community. These adults forced contextualization on the instructor. Child students can seldom do so. The teacher and school therefore must provide contextualization.

Three levels of contextualization are discussed in the culture and education literature. At the first, or pedagogical, level is the necessity to invoke children's existing schema as they relate to the material being instructed (Au 1979). That is, the content of instruction should be drawn from, or carefully related to, the child's own environment and experience (Garcia 1991; Tharp and Gallimore 1988), much as Ms. Young did in her mathematics class.

From Our Files

Students in a Cambridge, Massachusetts, eighth-grade science class for Haitian immigrants decided to investigate a persistent and contentious school rumor that the water from the third-floor drinking fountain tasted worse than the water downstairs. The science class interviewed other students and analyzed the chemical properties of the water from each fountain. Bilingual teachers trained in science teaching by Warren, Rosebery, and Conant (1994) conducted these classes in the Haitian Creole language.

This study also illustrates another aspect of contextualized pedagogy, the use of students' characteristic ways of speaking to aid their engagement in the teaching/learning process. There are many studies illustrating this form of culturally compatible instruction, such as the use of the Hawaiian "talk-story" discourse pattern in the Instructional Conversation (Tharp and Gallimore 1988; Boggs 1985) and the use of African-American English features in classroom instruction (Foster 1992, 1995; Foster and Peele in press; Lee 1995). Chapter 5 covers this topic in detail.

At the second, or curriculum, level, there is uniform advocacy for instructional use of cultural materials and skills as the media in which goals of literacy, numeracy, and science are contextualized. Drawing on personal, community-based experiences affords students opportunities to apply skills acquired in home and school contexts (Garcia 1991) and use them as the foundation for developing school skills (e.g., Wyatt 1978–1979). The work of González and Moll (González et al. 1995) in studying the "funds of knowledge" in students' families and communities and using those funds as curricular bases for mathematics instruction is an excellent example of making instruction meaningful.

At the third, or policy, level, there are advocates for contextualization of the school itself. School learning is a social process that affects and is affected by the entire community. "More long-lasting progress has been achieved with children whose learning has been explored, modified and shaped in collaboration with their parents and communities" (John-Steiner and Smith 1978, p. 26). Readers can find excellent examples of this level of contextualization in McIntyre (in press), Andrade et al. (1999), and Lipka (1986, 1994).

All levels of contextualization that provide an anchor in personal, community, and cultural meanings appear to have this felicitous, if paradoxical, effect. The high-literacy goals of schools—verbal, analytical, and abstract knowledge, and cognition—are better achieved in everyday, culturally meaningful contexts. This contextualization utilizes child experiences and skills as a sound foundation for appropriating new knowledge. This approach fosters pride and confidence, as well as greater school achievement. A well-known summary of the research knowledge on educating language-minority children states: "Prior knowledge plays a significant role in learning in terms not only of where to start, but also of the actual meanings attached to new information" and "studies incorporating into the classroom features of learning and talking that are characteristic of the homes and communities of English-language learners have shown positive results" (August and Hakuta 1998, pp. 31, 38).

Standard III is crucial for promoting student participation and engagement and for establishing the vital connections between the known and the to-be-known. However, this Standard does not assert that "the known" is the goal and object of instruction, nor that learning should be confined to the languages, knowledge, and conventions of home, family, and culture. Far from it; the known is the bridge over which students cross to gain the to-be-known (Lee 1995). This bridging or connecting is not a simple association between what is already known and what is new; it is an active process of sorting, analysis, and interpretation (Beals 1998).

For discourse in some academic disciplines, such as mathematics and science, there is reason to believe that some cultural discourse styles are incongruent and that the ways of "talking" mathematics and language become for some students a prime goal of teaching (Lee and Fradd 1996a, 1996b). Contextualization is the route toward developing cognitive and academic complexity.

Finally, we should consider issues of contextualization in the multicultural, often multilingual, classrooms of the contemporary urban—and increasingly, suburban—United States. Students who do not share a culture in their homes and neighborhoods must find some of their relevant everyday experiences in the shared activities of the classroom itself. Creating a community is even more crucial for mixed-culture classrooms. School-based or school-organized activities can serve as the everyday level of experiences to which abstract school concepts can be attached. The science experiment on the school's water quality is an excellent example. Making instruction meaningful is achieved by connecting the experienced everyday world to new schooled ideas. The value of this connecting may be the most fundamental proposition known to psychology, justifiable in terms of the "priming" principle of cognitive science, of "contextualization" of sociocultural theory, even in nineteenth-century theories of associationism and classical conditioning. In educational research and development in culturally diverse communities, we emphasize the everyday experiences and knowledge of the home and community because they are so little invoked in schools of the common tradition and because they are powerful organizers of the mass of students' everyday experiences. But this does not mean that only "culturally valid" experiences can serve as effective domains of application. In multicultural classrooms, teachers can create shared experiences through activity-based and problem-oriented instruction, shared activities, and a vigilant seeking of opportunities to invoke and instructionally use students' individual experiences and knowledge, especially in teacher-student dialogue.

Standard IV: Teaching Complex Thinking

Challenge students toward cognitive complexity.

There is a clear consensus among researchers that all students, perhaps at-risk students especially, require instruction that is cognitively challenging; that is, that requires thinking and analysis, not only rote, repetitive, detail-level drills. This does not mean ignoring phonics rules, or not memorizing the multiplication tables, but it does mean going beyond that level of basic skills into the exploration of the deepest possible reaches of analysis and problem solving. When all students are expected to meet high academic standards and to devote serious effort to academic pursuits; when they learn how to engage in sustained, disciplined, critical thought on topics relevant beyond school; then there will be achievement gains for all students, including the disadvantaged (Lee, Smith, and Croninger 1995; Waxman, Padron, and Knight 1991).

Working with a cognitively challenging curriculum requires appropriate leveling of tasks, so that students are stretched to grow within their "zones of proximal development" (Vygotsky 1978), where they can reach higher performance with assistance from teachers and collaborating peers. Teaching complex thinking certainly does not mean drill-and-kill exercises; neither does it mean overwhelming challenges that discourage effort. Getting the correct balance involves striking the "productive tension" between support and challenge, between the pleasures of mastery and of moving beyond present accomplishments (Csikszentmihalyi, Rathunde, and Whalen 1993; Langer 1995; Applebee 1996). Designing activities that are more challenging will bring a marked advance in the excitement and gratification of the classroom day.

It is much easier to teach to routine, minimum standards, because challenging students toward cognitive growth requires that teachers challenge, assess, and assist themselves right along with the learners. The perceived cost of the effort to teachers in preparing cognitively challenging learning activities too often deters it. Yet this is the level of activity that can keep the profession (and individual teachers) vital. In addition, at-risk students, particularly those of limited standard English proficiency, are often "forgiven" any academic challenges on the assumption that they are of limited ability, or they are "forgiven" any genuine assessment of progress because the assessment devices don't fit. Thus, both standards and feedback are weakened, with the predictable result that achievement is handicapped. Although such policies may often be the result of benign motives, the effect is to deny many diverse students the basic requirements of progress: high academic standards and meaningful assessment that allows feedback and responsive assistance (Fradd and Larrinaga McGee 1994; Waxman, Padron, and Knight 1991).

Challenging and stimulating cognitive growth means encouraging students to review and question their own and others' beliefs and rationales. Activities for problem solving through dialogue provide an organizing structure for students to construct new understandings. Dramatic problems with real-life meaning can help students at any level to evaluate, revise, and reorganize their conceptual structures (Bruer 1993). The object of complex thinking is most often not to conclude with a correct answer, but to expand discussion and promote alternative solutions or perspectives (Langer 1995).

This is true across subject matters, but the route to the condition is different depending on content. Consider the following quotation from an article in the Journal of Research in Science Teaching:

> Much of children's learning during the elementary years, especially in science and technology, depends on their capability to inspect things and figure out how they work—that is, to make inferences about the function of a device from its structure. The importance of this kind of reasoning is emphasized in current science education reform objectives, such as those developed by the American Association for the Advancement of Science and the National Research Council. These objectives target the relation between structure and function as a central organizing theme for science instruction. (p. 3–4) ... the instructional challenge is to identify a means to encourage children to go beyond merely noticing empirical regularities or patterns, to search for explanations that would account for those observed regularities. Similarly, it is also important to encourage them to look beyond their existing favored conceptions about mechanism to consider patterns of data that may or may not be consistent with those theories. Coordinating these two forms of information—empirically observed patterns of regularity and ideas about mechanism grounded in theory—is cognitively more challenging than working only within either. Yet doing so is foundational for model-based reasoning, which emphasizes relationships—such as those between mathematics and mechanics, or more generally, between a model and the phenomenon being modeled in the world (Lehrer and Schauble 1998, p. 24).

Substitute the terms "metaphor" or "rhetoric" for "mathematics and mechanics" and the point remains valid and central to good teaching of literature. Whereas Lehrer and Schauble developed instructional activities involving bicycle gears and eggbeaters to reveal principles of mathematics, a teacher of literature must choose with equal care those instances of text in which general principles of the functions of metaphor can be observed and discussed. In teaching mathematics, Ms. Young (pp. 15–16) gave her teams a challenging task and, through dialogue, required them to engage in complex thinking to explore and choose among alternate ways of presenting the data they gathered on their families' measurements. Although she worked alongside them in many of their discussions, she did not provide answers, but rather provided assistance as needed through clarifying questions or by suggesting tools and resources. She also gave them practice in routine skills, but unlike Ms. Lee's assignments, those routine skills were then applied to the creation of a complex product.

Standard V: Teaching Through Conversation

Engage students through dialogue, especially the Instructional Conversation.

The fundamental principles of pedagogy are not different across subject matters. But enacting them in the context of content requires a thorough knowledge of subject matter and careful planning to match activity to appropriate cognitive challenge.[1]

The concept of the Instructional Conversation was first articulated in 1988, based on research and development work in the KEEP program begun in 1970 (Tharp and Gallimore 1988), and extensive research and development has been continued by the KEEP group and its descendants.[2] However, other groups, in apparently independent discovery, have contributed generously to the growing consensus for the primacy of place to be accorded to teaching through dialogue. Haroutunian-Gordon's (1991) work on teaching high school students through conversation; the work of Carol D. Lee (1993, 1995) on teaching literary interpretation through dialogue; Judith Langer's (1995) mature distillation of effective practice in literature instruction, called "envisionment building"; and Arthur Applebee's (1996) treatment of curriculum as conversation: All these, like KEEP, growing from the teaching of language and literacy, have made significant contributions to understanding the transformative power of teaching through conversation. Now, dialogic teaching is recommended for far more than literature and is equally powerful and appropriate for instruction in mathematics and science (Newmann 1996; Newmann, Secada, and Wehlage 1995; Lee and Fradd 1996a, 1998; Lehrer and Romberg 1996).

The Instructional Conversation affords several conditions essential for maximum learning. It provides the "grouping structures that create extended, intensive teacher/student relationships" advocated by Darling-Hammond (Darling-Hammond and Falk 1997). It provides the cognitive and experiential basis for relating school learning to the individual, community, and family knowledge of the student. It provides the critical form of assistance—dialogue—for the development of thinking and problem solving, as well as for forming, expressing, and exchanging ideas in speech and writing. Through this substantive conversation that builds on themes or principles, the teacher guides student participation through the questioning and sharing of ideas and knowledge (Newmann 1996; Newmann, Secada, and Wehlage 1995).

The concept appears to be a paradox: "Instruction" and "conversation" are often antithetical, the one implying authority and planning, the other equality and responsiveness. The task of teaching is to resolve this paradox. To most truly teach, one must converse; to truly converse is to teach. In the Instructional Conversation, there is a fundamentally different assumption from that of traditional lessons. Teachers who engage in conversation, like parents in their natural teaching, are assuming that the child may have something to say beyond the "known answers" in the head of the adult. They occasionally extract from the child a "correct" answer, but to grasp the communicative intent of the child requires the adult to listen carefully, to make guesses about the meaning of the intended communication (based on the context and on knowledge of the child's interests and experiences), and to adjust their responses to assist the child's efforts—in other words, to engage in conversation.

Through this conversation, the culture and knowledge of the learner will be clearly revealed. The assumptions, perceptions, values, beliefs, and experiences—all the subjective and cognitive components of cultural membership—will be present, thus allowing the teacher to be responsive, to contextualize teaching in the experience base of the learner, and actually to individualize instruction, in the same way that each learner is individualized within culture.

Teaching through dialogue is (in one way) already present in the cultural repertoire of most teachers, since that is the way they interact at home with their own children. In another way, the Instructional Conversation is an exquisite skill that requires much work to perfect. While good Instructional Conversations often appear to be spontaneous, they are not, because they are always pointed toward a learning objective.

In kindergarten to twelfth-grade schools, the Instructional Conversation is rare. However, there is evidence that it matters. Instructional Conversations raise reading comprehension scores, more so for students of limited rather than full English proficiency (Saunders and Goldenberg 1999). Teachers who engage more frequently in teacher-student dialogue and responsive assistance to students rated their students' overall and language arts performance higher than did teachers who less often used dialogue and assistance (Estrada, Sayavong, and Guardino 1998). More often teachers perform the "recitation script," in which the teacher repeatedly assigns and assesses, assigns and assesses (Tharp and Gallimore 1988; Hoetker and Albrand 1969), a pattern that cannot provide optimal learning experiences (Applebee 1996). The common, standard form of mathematics lesson illustrated by Ms. Lee is an example of this pattern. But when true dialogic teaching occurs, classrooms and schools are transformed into "the community of learners" that schools can become "when teachers reduce the distance between themselves and their students by constructing lessons from common understandings of each others' experience and ideas" and make teaching a "warm, interpersonal and collaborative activity" (Dalton 1989). Ms. Young achieves this environment, in no small measure because her classroom activity settings contain at least one Instructional Conversation every day, and as the schedule rotates throughout the week, every student has at least three opportunities of interacting with the teacher in true, sustained, intensive dialogue.

Nystrand and Gamoran (1991, 1992) report on the instructional effectiveness of this pattern of discourse, in which teachers ask authentic questions that take dialogue into new territory. Applebee says that transformation of questions and answers is a "reconstruing of the underlying conventions involving discourse" (1996, p. 108). Indeed it is. As we will see, the Instructional Conversation both communicates and creates these new conventions. The Instructional Conversation can only occur in a community of learners, and it is by means of that conversation that the community is created. The Instructional Conversation is the capstone of effective education.

The Five Standards are related and form one holistic view of education. That is, the Instructional Conversation is the best method for development of the language of instruction, which occurs best when contextualized in experience, ideally created in joint productive activity, which becomes the setting for the Instructional Conversation. Instructional activities that are cognitively challenging can be effectively designed only when each of the other Standards allows knowledge of the strengths and needs of the individual student.

These Five Standards distill not only the prescriptions drawn from sociocultural theory but also the uniform research and experience of those who have worked in monocultural majority and minority schools, as well as those that are multicultural and linguistically diverse. The Standards provide the basis on which (1) effective education for all can be achieved; (2) education in its broadest form can be built for all students, by adding to their community-based competencies; and (3) intersubjectivity among the largest number of students and teachers can be established, thus creating the climate in which the most support and attainment can be realized for the most students.

Necessary Conditions for the Effective Organization of Instructional Activity

In our train of reasoning, the organization of activity should foster the enactment of the consensus pedagogy standards. Therefore, quality criteria for activity organization are those that maximize the likelihood of those enactments. In fact, three conditions are necessary for the full enactment of the Five Standards: simultaneity, variety, and value consistency.

Simultaneous, Diversified Activity Settings

The first necessary condition rests on logical and real-world necessity. Joint productive activity with teacher and peers, and opportunities for the Instructional Conversation, require that classrooms employ multiple, simultaneous, and diversified activity settings. Although it is possible to have some teacher-student dialogue in single, undifferentiated activity settings such as whole-group instruction or seatwork, quality Instructional Conversation cannot take place with thirty students, or even with fifteen. If we are to organize groups of four to seven students, engaged in conversation with the teacher, then the balance of the students must be otherwise employed. If there is to be genuine joint activity, it cannot involve twenty or thirty students doing the same thing; rather, even when there is a joint class-wide project, for example writing a school newspaper, there must be smaller activity settings, devoted to parts of the newspaper, differentiated and simultaneous, to allow true joint participation with others.

Thus, we can see that diversified, simultaneous activity settings are a necessary condition for organization because such a system enables each of the five pedagogical standards to be employed. The smaller group size makes for quality joint productive activity, because smaller groups can work together more easily. Contextualization is made more likely, because smaller groups allow the teacher to invoke individual students' experiences. Language and Literacy Development is made more likely because the teacher can listen to individual students' contributions and provide growth-enhancing responses.

Cognitive Challenge is made more likely because the teacher can individualize instructional levels more sensitively. Instructional Conversation is made more likely because the teacher can concentrate on dialogue with a few students while the others are engaged in other joint productive activity. On the empirical level, Estrada, Sayavong, and Guardino (1998) found that with a single exception, all of the first-grade teachers who frequently used a number of Standards indicators also used such organization of activities.

Thus, the apparently most superficial difference between Ms. Lee's and Ms. Young's classroom turns out to be one of the most crucial. Whereas at any given moment there was only a single activity setting in Ms. Lee's classroom, Ms. Young and her class were operating at least three different activities concurrently in as many as five groups. Because the work teams were active and self-managing in activity that provided learning, Ms. Young was free to concentrate on intensive, sustained conversational teaching in small groups that assured full Inclusion of each student.

Classrooms can be transformed by a vision that includes many activities, all productive and functioning simultaneously. Ms. Young did it; preschools do it; the workplace does it; research institutions require it; and nothing prevents this condition from existing in classrooms from kindergarten to twelfth grade, except limitations of vision and imagination.

Diversification of Persons and Activity

If we accept the principle of multiple, diverse, and simultaneous activity settings as the basic classroom organization, a next question immediately arises. Who is in which of all these activities? An answer is offered by the second necessary condition: diversification (variety) of persons and activity. This criterion grows directly from the ideals of education for a democracy. The capacity of individuals to claim their rights and to discharge their obligations to the community rests on education that allows all students to reach for their maximum potential. This means that classroom opportunities to learn should be extended equally to every student, and opportunities to learn also include the opportunities to teach and assist peers.

1. Diversification provides for education—that is, for expanding experiences and capacities and relationships—and affords opportunities for new affinities and new learning.
2. Diversification builds on the existing varied strengths of all, ensuring Fairness and Inclusion and promoting Excellence.
3. Diversification, paradoxically, allows the emergence of an overall Harmony because an inclusive, common system provides the experience that builds intersubjectivity and affords the greatest development for all.

These points will be elaborated further in Chapter 4 and in Chapter 5's treatment of cultural differences and cultural compatibilities. A wide range of cultural expectations and preferences can be perplexing and frustrating in a multicultural classroom. Should schools provide activity settings that allow students to use and enjoy their own cultural preferences and competencies of goals, roles, and power? Yes. The evidence for benefits of such cultural compatibilities is very strong (August and Hakuta 1998). But should we also limit students' experiences to such activity settings? Certainly not, because in every American community students will need not only their group's own local competencies but also a diversity of others, especially those of the larger, mainstream national culture.

The answer to the question of diversity is ... diversity. Classrooms should provide some activity settings that reflect students' culture and some activity settings that expand students' awareness and competencies.

One expression of the diversity criterion is the simple goal of letting all students have consistent and systematic opportunities to work with all other students, as well as with the instructor. In Chapter 4 we discuss the felicitous effects such joint work has on the development of a broader range of affinities and social relationships, as well as academic achievement. The range of abilities and skills is so broad in even the ordinary classroom that it is of benefit to students to have some opportunity to learn from one another.

Consider this classification list, from which there are a variety of representations in every classroom:

- Teacher
- Peers
- Genders
- Affinities
- Status levels
- Cultures
- Performance levels
- Languages

Each student should engage in joint activity with the teacher and with peers, with both boys and girls, with peers of affinity and those of lesser acquaintance, with peers of the same and other cultures, with peers of similar and different performance levels, with peers of similar and different status, and with students who speak the same language as well as those who are learning it.

Likewise, the natures of activities themselves need to be diversified, for the same reasons. That is, the panoply of activities should require diverse competencies. This is possible to achieve. Judith Langer, discussing the range of activities appropriate in literature classes, writes:

> The envisionment-building classroom is likely to include a great variety of different writing activities: free-writing, quick-writing, brain-storming, journal entries, reading logs, oral readings, role playing, written and oral conversations, small group and whole class presentations, portfolios, artwork, essays, computer graphics and the like. Any given type of writing activity, however, can serve a variety of purposes, and an understanding of its role in students' thinking requires an understanding of its pragmatic intent—for the student as well as the teacher (Langer 1995, p. 140).

In the several activity settings of a classroom across the day or across the week, activities should be diversified so that each student can experience variety in four conditions:

- Power relationships
- Roles
- Individualism/collectivism
- Language codes

Each student should have opportunities to lead, to follow, and to collaborate; to occupy many different roles and positions of power; to experience the challenges and pleasures both of individual and collective goals and products; and to use informal, academic, and subject matter language codes.

Consistent Values

The values of the classroom culture should be expressed consistently in every activity setting. This third necessary condition emerges from both theory and practical considerations. Theoretically, we know that the components of subjectivity—systems of meaning, of understanding, and of values—are created by the use of language (and other semiotic systems) that are used and learned during joint activity. Whether or not it is consciously guided, this process does produce values. Things, words, and actions take on meaning, negotiated and evolved by participants. Willy-nilly, "rules" develop in activity. Teachers participate in this process, sometimes by default and passively, sometimes by exercising creative leadership.

Effective teachers understand the process and use it to develop values conducive to the goals of teaching and learning. Even the greenest teacher knows that maintaining "classroom management" or "deportment" or "good values" in the classroom is an absolute precondition for any effective instruction and must be in place before beginning more complex differentiation of activity settings (Hatch 1994). True even for classrooms of the common tradition, this is even more so for classrooms organized into complex, diverse, simultaneous activities, where most students, most of the time, are working under their own self-control and are not dependent on close teacher monitoring.

Certainly, the teacher (backed up at the school level) must have a systematic system of positive and negative sanctions that can ultimately enforce the classroom values and serve as a buttress for self-control. But an effective instructional atmosphere is one in which those back-up sanctions rarely need to surface.

The basic value presumption of a productive classroom community is that each member has important contributions to make and serious business to do and that teacher and students will do this together, making it work for each other. As the class develops that understanding, much else will accompany it: rapport, trust, and mutual respect. The teacher will learn from the students and be responsive to their needs and preferences. Students will accord this same respect to the teacher and their peers.

Only as such a community is built can the teacher move into a system of differentiated activity settings. If the classroom is to be productive, cooperative, and filled with appropriate talk and activity, with each person having equal access to opportunity and to others, then certain individual actions are necessary: helping—not interfering—with the work of others, caring and generosity, high standards, and mutual respect.

Common Values, Diverse Cultures

Within this general value prescription, there is enormous room for a diversity of values, drawn from the local community and families, individual teacher's preferences, task demands, subject matter activities, and developmental stages. Negotiating the values and rules for each classroom leads also to Inclusion of culturally specific concerns, even as it subordinates them to the greater unity. In this way, the values promote inclusiveness for all students, mainstream and non-mainstream. A test that can be used for the quality of the community values in a multicultural classroom might be: Will all the parents be able to recognize how the identities and interests of their children are maintained, as well as how the success of all is safeguarded?

The pedagogical and organizational standards advocated here allow students to use their natal (as well as previous school-based) experiences, competencies, and knowledge and to participate through joint activity and shared communication in the building of a common classroom/ school culture. This will create high levels of intersubjectivity, which can then be used for the steady growth of a common classroom value culture, which itself values and practices respect and assistance for all.

In fact, the emerging common culture in such classrooms tends to represent some features from the origin cultures, unique features co-constructed by the particular mix of students and adults and recognizable core "school" features. Thus diversification—and consequently, Inclusion—offers the best opportunity for allowing all, but especially non-mainstream students, to integrate their individual, varied repertoires into one integrated identity.

The Tower Community

Arturo's class meets in the corner "tower" of the building. He wrote:
In our Tower community, we have our own language as well as the languages we bring from outside (like Spanish and English) which helped us make our own language. So, for example, someone that is not from our classroom community would not understand what insider, outsider, think twice, notetaking/notemaking, literature log and learning log mean. If Ms. Yeager says we are going to "make a sandwich," the people from another class or room would think that we are going to make a sandwich to eat. Of course we aren't, but that is part of our common language (Fránquiz 1995, p. 31).

Conclusion

Can a teacher create such a value system? Is such a system even possible? Indeed it is, at every level of education. In the following pages, you will "observe" many such classrooms. They are possible because the necessary conditions—simultaneity, variety, and value consistency—allow the enactment of the Five Standards for Effective Pedagogy. The classrooms, in turn, create an authentic intersubjectivity, the common understanding and mutual respect upon which the ongoing creation of shared values depends. The co-construction of values is ongoing in the classroom as in every society and every age. Communities are not stable. New challenges, new complexities and perplexities, and new members require that even classrooms must continually reinterpret themselves and create solutions to emerging problems.

Value consistency will arise again and again as crucial in each topic to follow, from sociocultural theory, to instruction and interpersonal relationships, to culture and the classroom, and it will be the first order of business in the actual processes of developing the classroom in Chapter 5. The creation of a consistent, shared value system is crucial to the development of the fully reformed classroom.

We now move on from our direct observation and analysis. It is time to take out a set of conceptual tools that will allow us to critically examine and discern this transformation. Stepping back is a necessary step for understanding any complex reality, particularly one that is so utterly

From Our Files

Post-Observation Procedure

Kamehameha Elementary Education Program (KEEP)

A portion of every visitor's available time was reserved for post-observation discussion around a seminar table. Every attentive observer came down from the observation deck with questions, puzzlements, and challenges. Why are you doing things that way? What is the basis for such revisions of the common tradition? Is all this really necessary? Couldn't it all be done with much less fuss and more efficiency? Isn't a well-educated teacher with good intentions the only thing that really matters?

Only through this instructional conversation could seeing be elevated to understanding.

transformed from the common tradition. Many readers will never have seen such a classroom. There is wide variation in reactions of first-time observers to such drastically reformed teaching, whether of live classrooms or virtual ones, and even to their written descriptions. For some, the activity is so rich and complex that only confusion is perceived. Others may be blinded by the brilliance of a total conversion experience. To many, much of the transformed classroom will seem sensible, right on the surface, but much may not. Skeptics may question the necessity for some elements, or perhaps for the entire conception.

In Chapter 5 we return with full force to the classroom itself and present a systematic developmental analysis of how such classrooms are produced. For now, we adjourn to the seminar table. The next three chapters consider how and why these classrooms work, by discussing the basic theories and supporting research that undergird the vision of teaching that guides their transformation.

Notes

1. Many resources for ideas about instructional activity exist in the standards of the various subject matter professional organizations, as well as in many specialized scholarly and professional treatments, such as Designing learning environments for developing understanding of space and geometry, edited by R. Lehrer and D. Chazan. Hillsdale, NJ: Lawrence Erlbaum Associates, 1998.

2. Saunders and Goldenberg 1999; Dalton 1998a, 1998b; Dalton and Sison 1995; Echevarria 1995; Tharp 1994; Goldenberg and Patthey-Chavez 1995; Goldenberg 1992–1993; Rueda, Goldenberg, and Gallimore 1992; Saunders and Goldenberg 1992; Gallimore, Tharp, and Rueda 1989.

3 Activity in Theory and Classroom

I N SCHOOLS, AS IN LIFE, more is learned than is taught. In fact, the entire sum of the formal curriculum and all the purposive lessons of every teacher, coach, tutor, counselor aide, school board member, and visiting specialist all together make up only a small portion of the vast transformations of consciousness forming each child's education.

But schools do make minds. The vast termite hill of the school—with its society; its curriculum; its competitions, economics, intrigue, lessons, spectacles, laboratories, passions, work groups, lectures, homework, terrors, and occasional teaching—produces, at the end of it all, minds, "planes of consciousness," each created by the complex, mysterious, but comprehensible social world of the school. The unintended social interaction may have more consequence than the carefully planned. The unexamined effect is almost certainly more potent than the fully understood. The person of the teacher is a more comprehensive lesson than is his or her lecture. In schools, we learn how to be, as well as what to be. We learn how to value, to be fair or hateful, to be generous or argumentative or curt, and we learn all that from teachers as surely as we learn from them the list of "the pretty kings of France." And we learn these things by watching them, listening, silently trying on their behaviors, behaviors of which they are often unaware as they earnestly urge us on to memorize all their lists.

Our teachers are not all "teachers." We are taught by peers, older students, coaches, counselors, lovers, teammates, co-workers, and finally perhaps by our own students and children. We now understand that the developing mind is a set of transformations from the social world into the psychological world. Gradually building through the course of the twentieth century has been an intellectual perspective, a gathering force that has made clear a fundamental human proposition: What is now psychological was first social.

The Social Construction of Mind

Many theorists, researchers, and educators today subscribe to a "constructivist" view of cognitive development. That is, knowledge is not somehow poured into the "empty mind" of a learner. Instead, learners construct their own knowledge through their experiences with the material of the world and by observing how that material responds to their attempts to manipulate and explain it. No matter how carefully a word or idea might be presented by a teacher, understanding will be attained only through active use and experience of the word or idea. That is, knowledge is achieved through a new construction of meaning by students' individual acts. Psychology and education have always considered learning and development to be an individual matter. Due to genetics, and then to maturation, and then to personal accidents and opportunities, each person is given a life and constructs of it what he or she can. But there is another view, a growing awareness that this individual-psychological focus is too narrow; its blinders obscure the context in which the individual exists. In this broader view, we see individual development as situated in the external world that that individual inhabits. For humankind, that external world is profoundly social, cultural, and historical.

This new and vital set of ideas, emerging in the social sciences and humanities, accepts that view of the world and attempts better to understand education in terms of its social, cultural, and historical processes. Known as the "sociocultural" perspective, this point of view accepts the constructivist view of mental development, but with an additional emphasis. That is, while agreeing that a learner creates knowledge and understanding during and from activity, socioculturalists emphasize that the learner's interaction with materials and activity occurs primarily in a social context of relationships. In fact, that social context is the major matter of the activity itself. The social aspects of activity provide for role assignments, problem-solving approaches, interpretations of events, and the ways that events are valued or despised. In short, social activity provides for knowledge.

The sociocultural perspective is shared by a number of contemporary theorists. Although there are differences in emphasis, they have in common at least one intellectual ancestor, L. S. Vygotsky, and most writers acknowledge old and deep debts to Dewey and Bakhtin. More important, there are common positions. Knowledge is constructed through joint activity. As people (adults and children) act and talk together, minds are under constant construction, particularly for the novice and the young.

Activity and its results are like the timbers of the constructed knowledge, but words are the nails and bolts that hold it together and give it shape. This shaping and meaning of knowledge are provided by the words and other symbols that represented the activity as it flowed. Discourse, and visual symbols exchanged and interpreted during joint activity, are the primary methods by which the young are socialized into a new culture or into a new community of practice.

> "Any function in the child's cultural development appears twice, or in two planes. First, it appears on the social plane, and then on the psychological plane. First it appears between people as an interpsychological category, and then within the child as an intrapsychological category. This is equally true with regard to voluntary attention, logical memory, the formation of concepts, and the development of volition" (Vygotsky 1981, p. 163).

So even the higher order functions—language, attention, memory, concepts, the will, values, perceptions, and problem-solving routines—all have their origins in social interactions. Each begins as a way of acting and talking among people. Each is "internalized" or "appropriated" and thus becomes a way of interpreting the world and of thinking that guides an individual's future actions. The social interactions of early childhood become the mind of the child. Parent-child interactions are transformed into the ways the developing child thinks, as are interactions with siblings, teachers, and friends. The praises and punishments of the community become a child's value system. A child's interpretation of the world is drawn from overheard adult conversations.

This is true not only for early childhood; it is true for learning at every age and stage. Adult apprentices draw their new skills and understandings from participation with the mentor. New teachers, or new physicians, or new carpenters learn their new perceptions of economics, politics, and social responsibilities from engagement with their new communities of professional practice.

In schools, then, dedicated to the transformation of minds through teaching and learning, the social processes by which minds are created must be understood as the very stuff of education. Because if teaching and learning depend so heavily on the activities in which teachers and students are jointly engaged, then there is no more important task than organizing those activities to achieve our educational goals. More than mathematics, more than literacy, more than computer science, the organization of activity in school is its fundamental curriculum.

Activity Settings: The Basic Unit of Analysis

Because the pattern of activity has such profound consequences for the creation of mind, in sociocultural theory the basic unit of analysis is the activity setting (Vygotsky 1987; Tharp and Gallimore 1988; Gallimore et al. 1993). The activities in which children engage, and the language and problem solving that accompany them, are formative for their developing cognitions, perceptions, motives, and values. Activity settings are the organizational structures through which society acts and through which it socializes its young and new members. Values are communicated during activity by a subtle mix of instructions, incentives, tones of voice, and stories told; it is not only skills that are developed in activity, but attitudes, values, priorities, and responsibilities.

Activity settings can be simply and straightforwardly described, using the simple journalistic device, who, what, when, where, and why (Tharp and Gallimore 1988; O'Donnell and Tharp 1990). Briefly, the "who" of activity settings refers to the individuals present. "What" refers to the things that are done and the scripts, ideas, or routines that guide these operations. "When" and "where" are descriptions of the time patterns and the places of the activity. Finally, the "why" of activity settings includes a description of the motivations of the members, the meanings of the activities to the participants, and the activities' objectives.

Once these descriptive categories have been filled, several analytical categories can be employed to help us understand the dynamics within an activity setting. Of particular interest in this book are four variables that have profound consequences for the course of each activity setting and for their developmental consequences:

1. Individual or collectivist patterns of activity vary across cultures and communities and affect the ways that products are made, owned, and valued; the nature of incentives; and all forms of social responsibilities and relationships. Individualist cultures emphasize the rights and opportunities of individuals, who are assumed to be protecting personal interests and achieving personal goals. By contrast, personal goals in collectivist cultures are often subordinate to the interests of the collective or "in-group" (e.g., extended family, school, or work organization) (Hofstede 1980, 1986).
2. Roles that different members enact within the activity (e.g., teacher, student, boy or girl, expert or novice, leader, conciliator).
3. Power relationships among the members of the activity setting (who writes the scripts, internal power relationships, external power relationships, status; magnitudes of power differentials, the degree of acceptance of those differences).
4. Language codes and genres used during the activities, including primary (English, Spanish, Cantonese, Navajo), disciplinary (the languages of mathematics, science, literary criticism), and informal ("Ebonics," pidgin, street codes).

These four variables are powerful influences on the developing learner. Through activity settings, including those of the classroom, students adopt certain role expectations and not others. They come to expect certain power patterns and not others. They adopt certain genres of language and not others. If there are re-occurring, invariant patterns across many activities, students will learn, expect, and perform those patterns in future varying circumstances. If these conditions vary across different important activity settings, students will internalize flexibility; they will learn and expect different patterns for different circumstances. These four variables will be used as analytical tools throughout this book.

A second visit to the classrooms of Ms. Lee and Ms. Young (pp. 14–16) may be profitable, particularly if we guide our observations with the theoretical concepts just introduced. This will enable us to contrast the classrooms' academic and social interaction patterns and thus consider their potentials for cognitive and social development. Most obviously, the reformed classroom simply has more and varied activity settings; in our own coding system, five versus two.[1] More is likely to be learned because more activities are engaged. More is likely to be taught because the teacher is with the students more, engaging them in dialogue and providing assistance as needed. In terms of our four analytical variables, there are also sharp contrasts.

1. Individual or collectivist patterns: Ms. Lee used individual activity exclusively; Ms. Young used both individualist and collectivist (team) activity. The latter is particularly appropriate for this mix of students because the Hmong speakers and the more recent Latino immigrants may well be more comfortable in teamwork, as the Anglo students might be expected to be comfortable working individually. All had a turn at comfort and all had a turn to learn a new repertoire.

2. Roles: In the common-tradition classroom, Ms. Lee was the only "teacher"; in Ms. Young's classroom, team members who were more skilled at one or another part of the task were able to assist and thus teach others.

3. Power relationships: Ms. Lee closely held all power in her classroom activities. Ms. Young, in her reformed classroom, closely held the power in no more than one of the activity settings; in all others, power was distributed.

4. Language codes: In Ms. Lee's common-tradition classroom, English was used exclusively for the academic work, and other primary languages were used only sub rosa for social interaction. In Ms. Young's classroom, primary code language was used ad hoc for academic purposes, to strengthen both English-language and

mathematics understanding. In student-to-student exchanges, English was actually used more frequently in the reformed classroom.

Values and Activity in the Classroom

An additional analysis illustrates the way that classroom activity patterns develop values, not only for the classroom activity itself but also for students to carry into other activities and settings. During our visit, neither teacher directly articulated much about values, but much can be easily inferred. The reformed classroom certainly required both individual responsibility and cooperation. Teacher and students communicated through action (the mixed-ethnicity team assignments) an equivalent respect for all ethnicities and language speakers, and they communicated a respect for Spanish and Hmong by encouraging their use for clarifying the English and mathematics lexicon and concepts. Ms. Young modeled social responsibility and a valuation of hard work by diligently assisting all students throughout the entire classroom period. Finally, we note a small but significant detail: At the end of the class, by providing an opportunity for group evaluation of the class operation, she demonstrated a key mechanism for maintaining, and tuning, an awareness of the class values for conduct. Ms. Young asked for and accepted a student's suggestion for improvement of the next day's lesson. (We will see in Chapter 6 how the early stages of development of the classroom community focus systematically and extensively on values.)

Will this one mathematics class session change any student's life? Probably not, certainly not in isolation. Would one year of this class change students' lives, even if their other courses in science, social science, and literature were taught in the common tradition? It might well; and a school career in a social environment like that provided by Ms. Young can be expected to produce minds more complex, more able, more flexible, and more academically accomplished, with stronger and more harmonious democratic ideals, a more inclusive range of acquaintance and respect, and a social identity richer and more nurturing.

The purpose of this book is to explicate how this is so, both theoretically and practically.

Joint Activity, Assisted Performance, and Teaching

We began this chapter by saying that more is learned than is taught, and more is developed than is intentionally developed. So, students learn much from each other, media, trial and error, and all their activities, both work and play. Sociocultural researchers have studied the processes by which learners develop their thinking and understanding, by which they become new members of communities of practice. Often, learners do so by taking on some legitimate but peripheral role in activity, learning by observation and gradually adopting more active roles in activity settings (Lave and Wegner 1991). In the majority of cultures of the world, and certainly in traditional, pre-industrial cultures, this is the routine way in which children gradually learn all of the society's necessary repertoires. A routine and necessary aspect of this evolving membership into any new community is the appropriation of the speech genres (syntax, lexicon, paralinguistics, pragmatics) of the new community, whether this new community is that of shoemakers, dancers, mathematicians, philatelists, the Crips and Bloods, or the society-wide community of educated people.

In schools, however, there is an additional way that students learn, and that is through systematic, self-conscious, intentional teaching. Especially in intentional teaching situations, but even in other contexts, development and learning proceed most surely when assistance is provided that permits a learner to perform at a level higher than would be possible alone. Vygotsky described this condition as a zone of proximal development, which is the

> Distance between the actual developmental level as determined by individual problem solving and the level of potential development as determined through problem solving under adult guidance or in collaboration with more capable peers. The zone of proximal development defines those functions that have not yet matured but are in the process of maturation, functions that will mature tomorrow but are currently in an embryonic state. These functions could be termed the "buds" or "flowers" of development rather than the "fruits" of development (Vygotsky 1978, p. 86, italics in original).

The proximal zone, then, is different from the "developmental level" where individual, unassisted performance is possible. Vygotsky's distinction between assisted versus unassisted performance has profound implications for efforts to influence development and learning. Focusing on this proximal zone allows us to see where teaching and learning actually occur.

"We can therefore derive this general definition of teaching: Teaching consists of assisting performance through the [Zone of Proximal Development]. Teaching can be said to occur when assistance is offered at points in the [zone] at which performance requires assistance" (Tharp and Gallimore 1988, italics in original).

So long as the needed assistance is there, development and learning will proceed. Most often, we think of the teacher as the assistor, but to the extent that peers provide appropriate assistance, learning will occur. Most often, we think of the teacher or the peer assistor as more expert than the learner, but that is not altogether true either. Many times a group of learners will have different parts of the needed competence, so they can provide assistance to each other in different portions of the task. Vygotsky discusses children, but identical processes operate in the learning adolescent and adult (Tharp and Gallimore 1988, p. 31).

From this point of view, too, we see the importance of patterns of activity of teaching and learning in classrooms. The activity settings of classrooms need to be created so that when assistance is needed, it is present in each activity setting designed for learning. When the only activity setting of a classroom is a "whole-group teacher-led lecture," it is virtually impossible for the teacher to be aware of the assistance needed by each learner, much less actually provide it. In the activity setting of "individual seatwork," either the work must be at the practice level, where individual unassisted competence is already present, or the activity setting must be reorganized so that assistance is available when needed.

A primary message of this book is this: The activity settings of the classroom must include opportunities for the teacher to work with individuals or small enough groups so that genuine teaching by assisted performance can take place. Not in every activity setting, not at every moment, but some regular, dependable activity setting in which there is joint productive activity between teacher and students. Only in such a setting—in a joint activity or in the Instructional Conversation—can the student hear on display the fully mature language of the educated person, available in close dialogue so that appropriation can be accomplished by the learner. During that joint activity, assistance will be provided, and thus teaching will occur—not to mention the opportunities for building common values and perceptions between teacher and students through working and talking together. Joint activity and Instructional Conversation activity settings are feasible. We have observed them in the classroom of Ms. Young; we have seen their necessity in the Standards for Effective Pedagogy. They do not require unrealistic faculty-student ratios. They do require a coherent plan and a careful process to implement that plan. By the end of this book, the reader will be fully instructed in how to develop such a plan and process.

The Organization of Social Relationships

The complex world of social relationships is highly organized and highly predictable. Who interacts with whom? Who joins together in productive activity? Who provides assistance, and who gets it? These questions pertain not only to schools, of course, but to all institutions and domains. Each person has family, friends, associates, colleagues, rivals, fellow members, and a myriad of other relationships, and it is only among these relationships that joint activity occurs. These relationships are actually very tightly structured and—considering all the people on the planet—restricted to a tiny proportion of those who are theoretically available for interaction. So, a first principle of the organization of relationships is that they are restricted.

The second principle is that social relationships are highly stable. This great sorting out of people into all their complicated patterns of social relationships is actually orderly, predictable, and highly conservative. Certainly, changes happen. On an individual level, marriages dissolve, friends quarrel, jobs change, people move into new neighborhoods. But compared to all the possibilities that exist theoretically, the pattern of relationships is highly conservative, in that it tends to maintain, reproduce, and repeat itself. Changes in the patterns of relationship actually require major forces to disrupt them.

As an example, think back to your own high school days. Re-create in your mind the pattern of the "crowds" at your high school. Different decades and different parts of the world use different terms—the pattern might have been called "sets," "circles," or "cliques." But the phenomenon is pervasive.

When a teacher comes to a new school, or when the school changes over time, a useful exercise is to sketch the school's informal student social organization. (Much of the theoretical material in this section can be brought alive by sketching one's own high school crowd pattern.) What were your "crowds"? Nerds? Punks? Jocks? Bikers? Populars? Hippies? Socials? Mexicans? Pakistanis? Druggies? Remember how very little movement there was between groups? Individual friendships might change as your class aged and matured, but new choices tended to happen within crowds, not across them. The new girl or boy in school has a challenge indeed: first to figure out the pattern of relationships and then to negotiate a way in. As we all recall, this is no simple task.

Sketching the informal social organization of the school community will reveal the interaction and friendship networks that the students bring into the classroom. In fact, this information is so important that it should be gathered regularly. Sketches from members of all the crowds can be revealing. Although most students use the same labels for each other's crowds, some labels depend on the perspective of the informant. Labels used by a middle-class European-American student and those of a working-class Latino student might differ and have different connotations.

Figure 3.1 is a sketch made by an upper-middle-class European-American student showing the pattern of crowds at her California high school in the mid-1990s. She observed that it is a map both of the crowds and of the school grounds, because each of the crowds always assembled in the same area, before school and during lunch. Her middle-sized, comprehensive high school drew primarily from middle-class neighborhoods, with a few pockets of working-class streets. Perhaps 10 percent of the students were Latino, and virtually none were African Americans. Many of the crowd names are familiar, while others are perhaps specific to that time and place.

52

FIGURE 3.1 Social Map of High School "Crowds"

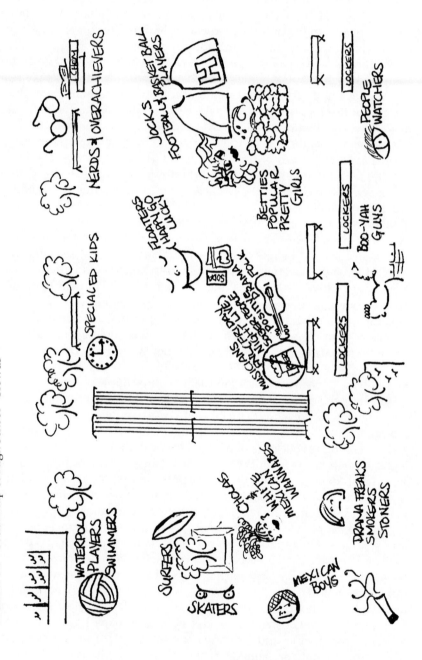

This social map reveals several principles of social relationships. A few Latino boys and girls were distributed in the other crowds, but notice especially the "Mexican boys" and the "Cholas," both predominantly poor or working-class Mexican heritage students. (Cholas and Cholos use the name for themselves; it usually denotes gang membership or identification and carries a distinctive hair, dress, and makeup style.) The "White Mexican Wannabes," girls who adopted Chola dress and behavior, were also from the poor neighborhoods. The wannabe label is an outsider's perception of a similarity almost certainly actually based on affinities emerging from shared lower–social class status. Notice also the "Special Education Kids," in their own crowd and on their own turf, in a special "track," even in the schoolyard.

Sociologists have made it clear that crowds tend to coalesce around certain predictable variables, primarily (1) amount of education of the parents, (2) amount of income of the parents, (3) neighborhood of residence, (4) culture and race, and (5) language spoken. The status of all of these defines social class. And that is the third principle of social relationships: They are organized primarily along social class and its components—income, education, race, culture, and language.

Friendship groups generally reflect the existing community social order. Certainly there are exceptions, but most friendships consist of the children of similar parents, with respect to language, social class, income, ethnicity, education, and aspirations. In fact, the exceptions to this rule are generally products of school-based social organizations that rigorously exclude affinities from their selection criteria. Sports teams, selected by athletic ability, include members from across communities, and the joint activities of the athletes produce "jock" crowds. Romantic attachments are also a leveling force that can operate across crowds, but strong pressures from the crowds and families usually restore the old order.

Recall again your own high school. Barring intervention by teachers or school policy, the crowds of the school were the de facto organization of its teaching and learning, because the crowd membership organized membership in academic activity settings as well as social activities. Existing friends provide assistance to one another in teaching and learning. The language of the crowds and the talk among its members provide the explanations and interpretations of the world. Crowd members' opinions and feelings about almost everything are more similar to each others' than to those of members of other crowds. The crowd shares values. The crowd perpetuates itself.

And unless the teacher works against it, these friendship groups spill into the classroom, providing the pattern of social organization of every room in the school. It may be invisible, particularly to teachers who do not pay attention to the school's patterns of relationships, but the schoolyard relationships are the ones that operate in the classroom, in homework, and in after-school activity settings.

In Ms. Lee's classroom, the ethnic/language groups walk together into her classroom, sit together, gossip together or help each other, roll their eyes together when bored with the lecture, walk out the door, down the hall, and into the next classroom, still together. The "map" of the school-yard is duplicated in the map of the classroom. This phenomenon is not restricted to sixth grade. Crowds in high school are simply the culmination of these sorting processes at work for years through elementary and middle school. They begin in kindergarten and are still in full force in master of arts teacher education programs in which we have taught.

How does all this work? How can teachers move against this conservative force when it is appropriate and work with this force when that is desirable? Providing the answers to these questions is the purpose of the remainder of this book, but before turning to those processes, it will be helpful to see how friendships form, which is merely another way of asking the question, How does it work, this social organization of activity?

Richard Rodriguez on Columbine High School

Public school. We used to know what that concept meant. Earlier generations understood, in a nation as individualized as ours, that we needed an institution, a school, where children would learn to regard themselves as people in common. [Today] the most balkanized region of America may well be the high school, inner city or rural, also suburban, middle class. In the cafeteria, the teenagers of America segregate themselves, each group with its own: jocks, skinheads, blacks, surfers, Latinos, nerds, etc.... An Italian friend of mine shakes his head. He says we Americans are always flattering ourselves by announcing our "individualism" to the world. But, my Italian friend says, you cannot be truly individualistic unless you have a strong sense of family or village. You can't become an "I" without a strong sense of "we." For all our American talk of individualism, my Italian friend says, we are merely the loneliest people on Earth....

It falls to the teacher, underpaid and overworked, to teach ... what public-school teachers have always tried to teach children, that they belong to a culture in common, speak a common tongue, carry a common history that connects them to Thomas Jefferson and Malcolm X. The ideal of public education is an extraordinary one, [but today], at a time when the American public school is open to all, many teachers settle for the sentimentality of "multiculturalism" (celebrate diversity!) instead of insisting on a communal vision ... imagine the task of today's public-school teacher. Everyday facing too many faces to know by name. Bodybuilders, pierced noses, shaved heads, brown skin, Calvin Klein

(continues)

The issue grows more important. Harmony is no longer a luxury when crowd antagonisms turn violent.

Social Relationships: The Dynamics of Formation and Change

In this section we examine how social relationships are formed and changed. These processes are potent, orderly, and predictable. Their effects are obvious, because the fourth principle of social relationships is that they are not randomly distributed. The school's friendship groups are highly patterned by social class, race, culture, and primary language. Yet none of these factors is a complete explanation because of the notable exceptions: The jocks in Figure 3.1 were an example in which social class membership does not determine group membership. In Ms. Lee's sixth-grade classroom, that same exception could also be seen. She gave some

---

(continued)

blues, black trench coats. At such a school, can we be surprised to learn that a sad little tribe, the Trench Coat Mafia, dressed like the Blues Brothers, published an ad in the yearbook that announced, "Insanity's healthy?" No one on the faculty apparently noticed or had time to remark. It turns out, something not nice was going on at Columbine High School. One father told CBS News that a football player used to look for his son in the hallways, pick on his son—a Jew—for being different. Meanwhile, elsewhere along the school hallway, two boys in black trench coats murmured Nazi tags to each other about football players.

You will say, of course, that high school is high school. It's always been the most conformist society of our lives. What is different now is that increasing numbers of high-school students come from families and neighborhoods that barely exist. They live surrounded by an architecture of impersonality and a technology of solitude ... after Timothy J. McVeigh's arrest in the Oklahoma bombing, a newspaper reporter, talking to his high-school teachers, found that none of them could remember the boy. As my Italian friend would say, you cannot become a true individual if you do not come from a "we."

Theodore J. Forstmann, a Wall Street financier-billionaire, and John Walton, the Wal-Mart heir, who have promised low-income children scholarships to private or parochial schools, announced that they had received replies from more than a million families. The rich, of course, long ago abandoned our public schools. Now the poor want out.... The question, now, is whether or not Americans will be able to embrace the idea of a public life—our responsibility to all children.[2]

special attention to the basketball players who were sitting together, including one Latino.

Some aspects of friendship patterning adhere closely to common sense. Primarily, relationships arise only between those people who have enough proximity to get to know each other. Sociologists refer to this restriction as a pool of eligibles, a concept used most extensively in studying mating, courtship, and marriage (e.g., Tharp 1963) but is equally informative in analyzing the patterning of any kind of relationship. The pool of eligibles is that restricted group, out of the world population of billions, from which relationships can actually be formed. What are the factors that draw members into the pool of eligibles? Common sense, in this instance, is dead right. A person can only be in the pool of eligibles for your friendship if you can get at him or her, if people are close enough to meet in the first place.[3]

Propinquity

Propinquity—the simple fact of being close together—is overwhelmingly the most powerful force in the formation of pools of eligibles. Think of a young man intending to raise a family in his small hometown. He must find his wife from a pool of eligibles that may number no more than thirty—out of a world population of millions of young women! We can understand how sociologists argue that propinquity accounts for 99.99 percent of the variance in sorting out not only marriage, but also all social relationships. Socioeconomic class sorting—sorting by race, culture, and/or language—has its first effect on propinquities, because streets, neighborhoods, districts, and even cities are sorted by these variables, so people in the same class, race, or culture are those who live next door to one another, whose children know each other, and who are likely to be going to the same school.

Out of the pool of eligibles, established so strongly by propinquity, the crucial choices are made. Actual friends must be chosen from the pool of eligible friends; a specific student must choose his actual mentor from the three or four eligibles of his art department faculty.

In fact, the initial formation of relationships is determined, in overwhelming degree, by this very simple fact of propinquity. Physical closeness in daily life—in residence, or work, or transportation, or classrooms—establishes the pool of eligibles from which friendships must be drawn. Associates, whether friends, colleagues, lovers, or even spouses, can come only from a pool of eligibles who are in contact with one another. Within that pool, factors such as physical attractiveness, perceived similarity, and social attention make relationship formation more likely. But even with these factors present, even among that subset of the pool of eligibles who are mutually attracted, the development of affinity is not assured. The young man and woman who travel on the same bus every day, even if they like each other's looks, do not necessarily "get to know each other." That takes something more. That something more, which will enormously raise the odds of making friends, is shared activity. Figure 3.2 illustrates how the processes work in the Great Cycle of Social Sorting.

Joint Productive Activity

The extraordinary influence of propinquity is that, although it does not guarantee it, it increases the likelihood of joint activity among members of the pool of eligibles. Joint productive activity is the most reliable and potent force influencing the development of affinities. That is, among the conditions that increase the likelihood of affinity development, joint productive activity (in and of itself) is the strongest and most reliable.[4]

Why is that so? In the first place, when people work together toward a common objective or to produce something together, two rare conditions emerge that have the most profound consequences for building relationships (just as for building cognition, as we discussed in Chapter 1). First, common motives are created, at least within the bounds of the shared activity and its settings. When a play is being mounted by the theater company, neither the actors, the designers, the director, nor the stage crew will succeed unless the play succeeds. Individual goals are

FIGURE 3.2 Great Cycle of Social Sorting

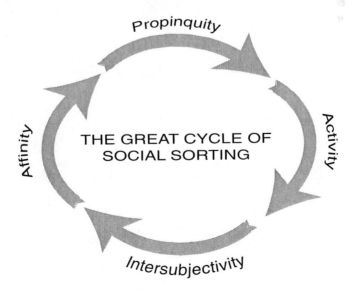

therefore subordinated to the group goal; the play itself is the thing. When a work crew carves a canoe, whatever else goes on in that complex undertaking, the canoe must be seaworthy and admired by the community, or no individual participant will be satisfied. Under that rare condition of common motivation, much of the competitive irritant in human relationships is dropped, and the conditions for Harmony are increased.

The second rare condition of joint productive activity is that it creates subject-subject relationships, rather than subject-object relationships (Leont'ev 1989). Because participants want the same thing, it becomes possible to experience empathy with them, to imagine that they want as you want, to feel together the pleasures of progress and the disappointments of setbacks. This condition, so different from experiencing the other as an object to be manipulated for one's own purposes, allows joint participants to understand and experience the other as one much like the self, a fellow worker, one with feelings and aspirations like one's own.

Thus working together for a common objective is not one among an infinite and casual variety of social arrangements, but rather an existential condition with unique powers for human transformation. But it should not be thought of as mystical. There are understandable processes involved in the transformations that take place during joint productive activity. Shared psychological transformations of understanding and valuing result in intersubjectivity; those in turn produce the transformations of affinity that produce ramifying consequences in social relationships.

For some time, it has been understood that—all else being equal—affinity is increased by frequent interaction (Zajonc and Marin 1967). However, we are now able to provide a more detailed description of this development. Affinity does not flow directly from interaction, but rather is mediated by the developing condition of intersubjectivity, which in turn is a probable consequence of joint productive activity. During shared activity, common meanings, understandings, and values are developed.

Intersubjectivity

As a term, "intersubjectivity" is admittedly awkward and off-putting, but we can find no adequate synonym for the concept, which is indispensable to an understanding of the human world. If its simple, surface meaning is kept in mind, the power of the concept will become immediately apparent. It refers to "subjectivity," of course; that is, the world-as-experienced, the subjective experiences of perception and interpretation and meaning and value. This subjective world is distinguished from the "objective" world as it is presumed to exist independent of human interpretation: the scientifically understood world of objects, agreed-upon facts, and events as-they-happen, a level that exists independent of anyone's individual perceptions or values.[5]

Many philosophers, and certainly sociocultural theorists and educators, emphasize that human events are always interpreted and valued and that these subjective, mental phenomena are crucial to understanding our actions. After all, we act in terms of our interpretations of events more than on the objective features of those events. Can we ever really know the objective features, independently of our interpretations of them?[6]

Intersubjectivity refers to shared subjectivity, between and among people. Intersubjectivity is present when people perceive things in the same way, interpret them in the same way, value them in the same way, use the same categories of understanding, respond in the same way, and expect the same response back from the world.

How are intersubjectivities created? It is during joint productive activity that these shared word meanings, concepts, motivations, beliefs, and expectations are acquired. The activity setting is the social process common to the participants from which cognitive processes and structures of meaning develop. The mind itself is created during joint activity, through (1) the use of signs and symbols, primarily language and visual symbols, (2) which establish the subjective purposes and meanings of the activity, (3) by using common cognitive strategies and problem solving. During joint productive activity, members who are more knowledgeable use language and visual symbols as they assist novices. Peers themselves develop word meanings and discourse routines during their cooperative work. The denotative, connotative, and affective components of word meaning are acquired in discourse accompanying action. Thus words, flags, badges, gestures, images, tunes, and the full panoply of symbols are the stuff of subjectivity, and accepted common meanings of words, signs, and symbols among people is the condition of intersubjectivity. When working together and talking about the purposes and meanings of the activity, strategizing and problem solving together, these aspects of interaction influence each participant and foster emotional and cognitive commonality. These common meanings, values, and discourse become the binding structures of the life and culture of every community, including schools. When we discuss the "appropriation of the language of the community," this is what we mean. The process of socialization into school or into criminal gangs or a religious community (Rubin 1991) or any other community consists of an increasing intersubjectivity mediated by the appropriation of the new code of language, sign, and symbol.

With intersubjectivity—when the world is taken in the same way—the conditions for felt kinship are created. In fact, intersubjectivity is the direct, proximal determinant of affinity, although it cannot be easily manipulated by a direct approach. Our sociocultural perspective emphasizes that joint productive activity, accompanied by a rich semiotic exchange, provides the language and other symbols that allow interactors to interpret the world in the same ways, express that understanding

in mutually understood symbols, and thus develop the sine qua non for
affinity: the experience of knowing the world in the same way. Nothing
is more magnetic.

To the degree that intersubjectivity is present, values are shared, and
goals are alike, more cooperation is possible, and thus more Harmony. One
of the joys of life is the achievement and the experience of intersubjectivity.
This dimension of joint activity serves as a reward to its members because it makes activities memorable, worthwhile, and gratifying to group
members and thus motivates them to continue participation in the group
(Tharp and Note 1988).

Deviant, alienated, non-participating members of a community almost
certainly signal a lack of intersubjectivity with the larger unit that defines
them as deviant, a failure to define the situation in the same way and to
accept the same process for problem solving, the same goals of the organization, the same values, and each other on the same basis.

Because of emerging intersubjectivity, participants tend to develop
more differentiated and pronounced feelings toward one another. To the
extent that they are positive and reciprocal, these feelings are likely to enhance developmental processes (Bronfenbrenner 1979). The development
of intersubjectivities is a consequence of profound importance for individual development, for a satisfying community life, and for the perpetuation of culture. Thus individual identity—the intramental, cognitive,
value-laden self-hood—arises in the social plane and is made individual
through the internalization of communication and shared activity. In a
way, psychologically, each of us becomes those people with whom we
work, talk, share, and grow.

Intersubjectivity is the condition of, if not a synonym for, Harmony.

Affinity

So, the condition of intersubjectivity establishes affinity. By affinity we
mean a felt kinship, and an inclination toward relationship. Affinity is not always a factor in the development of relationship, and indeed some work,
community, and even family relationships proceed with no sense of this
felt kinship or even of liking (Berscheid and Reis 1998). But this choosing
of one another on the basis of our inclinations—what we call friendship,
liking, love, "us"—feels like the final determinant of relationship choices.
Youth "hang out" with each other on the basis of affinity; teachers and
students support each other on the basis of a felt kinship; we choose who
we will work with, talk with, be with. When affinity is present, relationship formation and maintenance are facilitated (Berscheid and Reis 1998).
When affinity is present, a way will be found to be together. Is it not pleasurable to be with those with whom no complex discussion is necessary

because a nudge in the ribs and a roll of the eye is enough to produce total agreement?

So affinity is not only the end of the great circle of relationship development, it is also its beginning and its perpetuation. Affinity leads to propinquity, either new or continued. Thus, the force line intensifies. In childhood and adolescence, affinities are often volatile, but even when short lived, they are powerful determinants of activity and behavior. Those related to each other by inclination will somehow manage to bring themselves close enough together to maintain relationships. Thus affinity produces a new round of propinquity, with its activity, intersubjectivity, intensified affinity, and still more concentrated propinquity, and the great, conservative cycle of social sorting rolls on, rolls on.[7]

Teaching-learning relationships are no exception to these processes. To whom a learner attaches is first a matter of propinquity. Which teacher is assigned? Which other children are in the Blue Group? Who rides the bus? Who is in the vocational track? Who is there to choose from?

When affinity can be used to bring a teacher and a student together, it is certainly desirable. In graduate and professional schools, the sorting out of advisees and advisors, mentees and mentors, depends to some measure on felt affinities. In many traditional cultures, affinity is allowed to work as a major sorting principle. Young Pueblo Indians observe potters from a distance, until the natural attraction of a potter to child and of the child to the potter (or her pots!) results in a voluntary mentorship pairing (John-Steiner and Osterreich 1975). In primary and secondary schools today, little shopping for teachers is available to students. But in other teaching-learning relationships, particularly with peers, affinity is the basis of almost every voluntary association. But those affinities must be understood as the consequence of the rolling force line: propinquity, activity, intersubjectivity, affinity, propinquity, activity, intersubjectivity, affinity ...

Changing Patterns of Relationship for Improved Teaching and Learning

In discussing schools, we mentioned that in the absence of specific school-organized intervention, friendship groups determine the groupings for teaching and learning activity. The same diagram that depicts the schoolyard's friendship groups also represents the social organization in each teacher's classroom. This looks and feels like a pattern of friendship, based on the students' affinities. The students draw towards others with whom they feel comfortable, others like themselves. In fact, the students experience all these patterned relationships merely as affinities: They are with each other because they like and choose each other. They are unlikely to be aware that they choose each other due to propinquity, joint activity, and intersubjectivity. In any event, affinities determine the ways students group themselves in classrooms, given choices; if there is no pattern of diversified activities in classrooms—if there is only a whole-group organization, or if grouping is only by performance levels—the affinities will operate outside the classrooms so that whatever teaching/learning is conducted by peers will be within the existing friendship structure. Just as in Ms. Lee's classroom, these friendships tend to mirror community affinity structures, based strongly on social class and race. The great wheel is thus conservative, not only for affinities but also for the cognitive processes and development upon which social and economic success will perpetuate itself into the next generation.

Affinity as the Basis for Organizing Instruction

Although affinities are a powerful and predictable force in the classroom, they are often invisible to the participants themselves, be they teachers or students. To use the dynamics of affinities for the goals of education, educators need to understand that there are two strong functions of affinity: the security function and the conservative function. First, affinity grouping allows for the comforts, securities, and support of friendship in the learning environment, a condition that teachers must ensure, if not by existing affinities, then by other means.

Correcting this situation was an unusual instance in which the teachers changed patterns to allow affinities. At an institutional level, many private schools, colleges, and universities go to great lengths to provide for a basic structure of reliable affinities, through clubs, designated residence halls, and other voluntary associations. Rush week for sororities and fraternities is an intense concentration of activity settings designed to test for immediately available affinities among members and potential members and to

From Our Files

At a university elementary school, to which students travel from all over a large city, African-American parents complained to the school that the few African-American students in the school were separated in different classes. Thus the children had no opportunity for mutual support and identify formation, because they were never allowed to organize into their own affinities.

sort incoming students quickly into the Greek houses most likely to coalesce into immediate affinity groups.

Such voluntary affinity associations are very attractive both to students and their families because they provide social support, but also because of the social conservatism that results. To a certain degree, youth and their families want the support provided by associating with students like themselves, and they also want some protection against their children becoming too much like the children of someone else.

However, the conservative effect of the affinity force is also problematic. Strict affinity grouping is antithetical to an expanding inclusiveness. Because it tends to continue and reproduce the status quo, including the present affinities, it runs counter to the general intention of education, which is for expansion, growth, change, and experimentation, and counter to the educational reform agendum of Inclusion. All of us as students depend on the encounter with new teachers—others unlike ourselves—to expand our knowledge and sensitivities. Likewise, a part of education is to expand students through their contacts with students unlike themselves.

Even when we intend to counter this conservative force, it is almost impossible to affect affinities directly, as every teacher or parent knows who has tried to talk a young person out of a felt affection. What forms of intervention can successfully, and with good effect, counter the force of affinity?

Changing Intersubjectivities Directly

Likewise, a frontal attack on intersubjectivity is likely to be a poor tactic. Although schools can provide sermons and urging and interpretations, that kind of persuasion has limited power to provide new explanations, values, and interpretations of events. This does not mean that intersubjectivity cannot be intensified and directed, which after all is the main purpose of primary socialization in families and communities. Educators must work consistently at building the intersubjectivities of the community of school and classroom. Success will depend on imbedding the teaching of interpretations and values into joint activity as interpretations of shared experiences.

Intersubjectivity, and its contents, are vital elements of an effective school, and profoundly important for effective teaching and learning. Although values and meaning of events cannot be forced solely by preachment and proscription, they can be fostered when valuation and interpretation are provided before, during, and after joint activity.

As we discuss in Chapter 6, a complex and effective patterning of instructional activity absolutely depends on developing a sense of community values in each classroom. These values are the "handles" by which a

From Our Files

A Native American school was determined to institute more traditional tribal values into the conduct codes and values of their classrooms and schoolyard so that students would treat the teachers and each other with the patience, respect, and courtesy upon which their traditional institutions depended. The faculty and community leaders organized a set of rule statements and sanctions and presented them to an all-school assembly of students. Even though this kind of exhortation was culturally familiar, only some classrooms actually saw student improvement. These were the classrooms in which the teachers, in the following weeks, organized discussions of the new values in terms of ongoing events as they occurred in the classrooms themselves. This assisted the students to construct a shared understanding of the new ways in which they were to relate to one another and to the teachers.

good classroom is carried. And as sociocultural theory teaches, intersubjectivity develops by learning meaning through activity.

Changing Propinquity, Building Joint Activity

Thus intersubjectivity is a consequence of effective joint activity, and affinity flows from intersubjectivity. And those who feel the world in the same way seek each other out, and so affinity leads to propinquity. Might it be possible to work directly on propinquities, and by merely rearranging seating assignments and schedules, put students together in new ways so that the wheel would veer and move down a new road? Of course, propinquity is the primary condition, because it is difficult to engage in joint activity unless the participants are close enough in space and time to allow them to work and talk together. So propinquity is a necessary condition to create new relationships, but not sufficient in and of itself.

A clear example is available to us at the societal level. The desegregation policy interventions of the 1960s changed propinquities but have had limited impact on affinities among the races. Desegregation did not provide for joint productive activity among the races at the neighborhood, housing, school, or classroom level. Propinquity interventions were necessary, but were not sufficient, and cannot succeed until or unless joint productive activities are organized to create the intersubjectivity of seeing the world in the same ways across races. For the same reason, little consequence should have been expected from President

Clinton's "conversations about race" initiatives of 1997–1998. Talk alone, separated from joint activity, lacks the conditions that produce intersubjectivity, and thus will not increase affinities.

"Prejudice ... may be reduced by equal status contact between majority and minority groups in the pursuit of common goals. The effect is greatly enhanced if this contact is sanctioned by institutional supports ... and if it is of a sort that leads to the perception of common interests and common humanity between members of the two groups" (Allport 1954, p. 281, quoted in Slavin 1985).

Allport's "contact theory" is well summarized in that quotation, and Slavin has used "contact theory" to explain the good effects on interracial group relations of classroom cooperative learning groups. That is, cooperative learning creates "sanctioned," "equal status" conditions, and they are "the sort that leads to the perception of common interests and common humanity" (Slavin 1985, 1994).

Slavin also points out that Allport's theory provided much of the theoretical rationale for the early work on improving race relations, post–Brown vs. Board of Education. It is unfortunate that social science had

---

From Our Files

Re-Segregation Under a Desegregation Plan

There are several neighborhoods in this urban school district. Its European-American middle- and upper-middle-class students often attend private schools. The multicultural student population of the public schools tends to be from poor and ethnic/racial minority backgrounds. Under court-ordered desegregation, the district uses busing to maintain the percentage of any single ethnic or racial group under 45 percent in any school. Is this integration?

One of its schools has many observations in our files. In this African-American neighborhood, Latino students are bused from one neighborhood and Chinese-descent students from another. Once at school, staff assign Latino children to Spanish bilingual classes, most Chinese-descent children to Chinese bilingual classes, and most African-American students to Afrocentric classes. (Some multicultural classes exist—in response to parent requests.) Each ethnically specific program largely succeeds in its goal: to value its own culture. The cost is re-segregation. Before school, lunch hour, and recess are the times that students from different ethnic/racial backgrounds are together, but predictably, they sort themselves out by affinity. The school leadership wonders why all the friendship groups are ethnic groups.

not yet perceived the conditions that create "equal status" and the "perception of common interests and humanity": namely, joint productive activity. Had it done so, desegregation might have been much more successful in producing Excellence and Harmony. Desegregation has been too often implemented only by enforced propinquity. Merely pouring diverse students into the same school, no matter how sanctioned or by whom, will not produce the harmonies of intersubjectivity. That requires working together. School- and classroom-based joint productive activity among diverse students has almost never been provided by desegregation plans.

One need look no further to understand why desegregation as a policy failed to achieve the goals of Excellence, Fairness, Inclusion, and Harmony. Simply putting students in the same building or on the same schoolyard achieves nothing, except perhaps more divisiveness. Students simply have insufficient common experience to develop shared values and common interpretations of the world. To achieve the goals of Fairness, Inclusion, Harmony, and ultimately Excellence, schools and classrooms must supply the common experience of students working, talking, and producing together.

Conclusion

Joint activity is itself the single most sensitive and flexible point for school intervention in instruction and thus the most powerful means of affecting educational outcomes. To work together is to teach and learn together and to understand the world together. The effective design of instructional activity produces education through action, talk, work, and relationship. Social, intellectual, and community growth are enabled or crippled by patterns of joint productive activity. This is the route of reform taken by Ms. Young. Her classroom contains a variety of activity settings in which participants work together toward a common goal. Her work-team memberships cut across social class, language, racial, cultural, and crowd affinities. By scheduling extended, intensive conversations and activities with a variety of groups, she creates the conditions in which intersubjectivities can be created between herself and the students; she is closely present to assist them in advancing development of knowledge, cognitive processes, and language. And the odds are high that when her work teams walk down the hall together, some of those affinities will last into the next class period and beyond, into the schoolyard and community.

When the teacher or school takes control of the design of instructional activity, it can be expected to work against the affinity force. The specifics of the counterforce will vary according to the teacher-designed pattern. For example, a teacher may be concerned to broaden the interests and sensitivities of her computer nerd and art students and so assure that they work together in analyzing a history assignment. Another teacher may want to emphasize unity in the school community and assure that during the course of every week each student has some joint activity with members of each other ethnic group.

The most reliable quality criterion for instructional activity is that it should be patterned to produce diversity: of task, groups, roles, power, and language genres and codes. Diverse students have diverse strengths and diverse needs. Students, like teachers, have much to learn from one another, and expanding joint activity beyond existing affinity groups can enrich these opportunities.

In the next chapter we discuss the ways in which affinities, produced during joint activity, not only move the classroom toward greater Fairness, Inclusion, and Harmony, but also maximize academic Excellence.

Notes

1. The Activity Setting Observation System (ASOS). For a guide to observation and coding, see Tharp et al. (1998).

2. Richard Rodriguez, "Littleton Signals Death of the 'Public' School." Copyright © 1999 Pacific News Service. Richard Rodriguez, an editor at Pacific News Service, is the author of Days of Obligation.

3. Will "virtual propinquity" be developed by the explosion in distance communication by electronic means? Early indications are that virtual propinquity is frequently enough to induce joint activity, but because it depends on the richness and subtlety inherent in face-to-face communication, intersubjectivity does not reliably develop.

4. This point will become critical when, in Chapter 6, we consider what a school or a teacher can do to create new affinities.

5. Notice that the description of the activity setting contains both objective features (time, place, person, action) and subjective features (motives, explanations, meaning). The fullest description of the world must contain both, as the world consists of both.

6. Whether or not there is a single objective reality, independent of observing and perceiving, is called into question on the metaphysical level by post-quantum mechanical theories of physical science.

7. Of course there are exceptions, when relationships leap across the great cycle. War, sexual intoxication, natural disasters, and "miracles" of accident can bring people together in vital relationships that violate the predictability of social sorting. But it is the rarity of these "mutations" that makes them of such interest in literature, film, and fantasy.

4 Patterns of Instructional Activity and Relationships

ALL LEARNING THAT GOES INTO MAKING US WHO WE ARE—what we know, how we know it, how we solve problems, what we value, our goals—occurs first within the social plane. Through the processes of communication and shared activity, what we learn becomes our own, individual and psychological. School learning is not an exception to, but rather another instance of, this process. Major relationships within the school setting—teacher-student relationships and peer relationships—constitute a crucial social plane in which students' minds are created. These relationships exert their influence primarily through the assisted performance and the development of intersubjectivity made possible by joint activity and shared communication. Classroom relationships characterized by these qualities increase the potential for academic Excellence and classroom Harmony. To the extent that all students participate in such relationships with other students and with their teachers, the potential for social and academic Inclusion and Fairness is increased.

By the time children and adolescents enter classrooms, much has already been decided about the possibilities for their social and academic associations. School policies and personnel have selected their teachers and classmates. In turn, within classrooms, teachers determine with whom students will interact, when, where, how, and why. Absent teacher intervention, students will cluster themselves on the basis of existing affinities. In fact, much grouping by teachers, particularly by academic performance level, will result in the same clusters because school success co-varies so strongly with the affinities and crowds of the schoolyard that reflect the community social order. Actively or passively, then, in classrooms teachers determine whether students' interactions will be primarily with others like themselves in socioeconomic status, ethnicity/race, primary language, academic performance, or gender.

Similarly, teachers determine the nature of the activities in which students will interact. Will this interaction occur mostly in single, undifferentiated activity settings, in diversified, simultaneous activity settings, or will it vary? Will it involve individual, cooperative, or interdependent goals, incentives, and products? Will the interaction be recitation or activity based, teacher scripted, or co-constructed? Will students have opportunities to make decisions about what they learn and how? Will the interaction be characterized by equal status participation or will it be predetermined by the status characteristics students bring to the activity setting?

We will demonstrate that who is present in activity settings as well as the nature of the activity will affect with whom children and adolescents form relationships, the nature of those relationships, and their educational consequences. It will matter if students rarely have opportunities to work with others different from themselves, if their associations are restricted only to their existing friendship groups. It will also matter if they never or rarely have opportunities to talk and work together with peers and their teachers. These decisions about patterns of instructional activity will make a great deal of difference in whom children and adolescents "select" as friends and in the qualities of those relationships. These friends will serve as models, teachers, and companions. As such they will be primary sources of learning and influence. Similarly, instructional activity patterns will affect students' relationships with their teachers and the potential for teachers to become mentors, role models, and adult friends. All of these decisions will be involved in creating the conditions for Excellence, Fairness, Inclusion, and Harmony.

Propinquity: Affecting Inclusion, Fairness, and Harmony in Peer Relationships

Creating Propinquity in Schools

Propinquity is a major force in the formation of relationships. One of the primary ways in which we help create peer affinities is by determining propinquity; that is, who will be nearby and available to students during schoolwork. Although most of our discussion focuses on patterns of classroom instructional activity, we attend to school patterns of organization briefly because the parameters for some aspects of classroom activity are set by school-level policies.

At the school level, propinquity is created by the criteria used for assigning students to classrooms, the size and number of classrooms, and policies regarding the regrouping of students and teachers for academic and social purposes (Estrada 1997; cf. Hallinan and Williams 1989; Slavin 1987). Some schools try to maximize the heterogeneity of students in classrooms across a number of characteristics such as ethnicity, academic performance, primary language, behavior, and gender. Other schools use primary language or English-language proficiency as the main criterion for classroom assignment. After these initial groupings are made, school staff may use other student characteristics as well. In secondary schools, academic performance is often the primary criterion for grouping students into formalized tracks (Oakes 1990). Regrouping of students across classrooms is practiced by some elementary schools for a variety of reasons (Estrada 1997). For example, sometimes students are regrouped for primary language instruction in reading and/or mathematics. In other instances, students are regrouped for the purpose of integrating ethnic and language groups. Propinquity is also affected by the organization of nonacademic activities such as extracurricular activities that encourage or limit participation based on students' interests or talents (Hansell and Karweit 1983; Karweit 1983; Epstein 1989).[1]

All of these policies affect with whom children come into contact and whether these contacts are like themselves or different in ethnicity, primary language, academic performance, gender, and behavior. Estrada (1997) found three patterns of school-level organization in nine culturally and linguistically diverse elementary schools. At one extreme the school pattern of organization resulted in complete integration among different language and ethnic groups throughout the day. At the other extreme there was segregation throughout all or most of the instructional day. In the middle of the continuum, one pattern resulted in a moderate amount of contact among different groups.

These decisions about heterogeneous and homogenous arrangements of students will have profound effects for Inclusion, Fairness, and Harmony among students. When school policy groups students in classrooms or tracks primarily with others like themselves, they are significantly limited to forming friendships within specific pools of relatively homogenous students (Karweit and Hansell 1983). A study of the effects of racial distribution on cross-racial friendship selection in fourth- through seventh-grade classrooms (Hallinan 1982) found that both European-American and African-American students chose the most same-race best friends and the least cross-race friends when their racial group was in the majority. When classrooms were more racially balanced, both sets of students increased their choices of cross-racial best friends. Using data from a large-scale study of secondary schools, Karweit (1983) found that 75 percent of friendships were among students in the same curricular track. In a sample of sophomores and seniors from the High School and Beyond national longitudinal survey, Hallinan and Williams (1989) also found that students' friendship choices were less likely to come from different tracks. These researchers found that disproportionate assignment of ethnic/racial groups to different tracks was a factor in reducing cross-racial friendships.

Tracking also affects propinquity by limiting the opportunities of noncollege bound students to become involved in extracurricular activities that provide a context for the formation of peer relationships (e.g., Hansell and Karweit 1983). The rate of participation in extracurricular activities is higher for college track students than for non-college track students (Schaefer and Olexa 1971, cited in Karweit 1983). Karweit's (1983) analysis of the High School and Beyond data on sophomores and seniors suggests that this difference is at least in part a consequence of track placement. This line of research indicates that creating extracurricular activities that draw on varied interests and talents is an important, but only partial, intervention for increasing propinquity among diverse students.

Creating Propinquity in Classrooms

Within classrooms, propinquity among students is created by seating assignments and configurations (permanent assignments, rotating assignments, rank-and-file configurations, pod configurations); the number, diversification, and simultaneity of activities (all students engage in one activity, different students engage in different activities); the size and number of the groups (whole group, small groups, pairs); the criteria used for grouping (academic performance, primary language, gender); and rules about movement (rigid, predetermined, fluid, spontaneous) (Estrada 1997). By placing students near or far from one another and encouraging or limiting movement among students, these factors create propinquity for certain students and prevent it for others.

Seating arrangements most obviously create propinquity within classrooms. Traditional rank-and-file seating restricts propinquity in general, whereas other forms of seating such as desk pods or table groupings increase it. To the extent that we allow students to choose where they will sit within these seating arrangements, we reinforce the conservative Great Cycle of Social Sorting because they will tend to choose to be near those they perceive to be similar to themselves (e.g., Epstein 1986, 1989). In contrast, heterogeneous seating assignments work against this force. Clearly, the latter pattern will enhance Inclusion, whereas the former will limit it.

Grouping practices are among the most powerful creators of propinquity (cf. Hallinan and Sorensen 1985). In these practices, too, we can chart the conditions affecting Inclusion. To the extent that we consistently group students homogeneously by characteristics such as academic performance, primary language, gender, or behavior—or allow them to choose their groups based on existing affinities—we limit their opportunities for propinquity with diverse others. This in turn limits their opportunities for developing relationships with students unlike themselves and concomitantly expanded repertoires. In upper-elementary school classrooms, for example, researchers found that ability grouping affected friendship choice (Hallinan and Sorensen 1985). Membership in the same ability group increased the probability that students would become best friends. Over time, the density of best-friend choices within ability groups increased, and the overlap between ability groups and cliques increased. Similarly, Hallinan and Smith (1989) found that the greater the number of reading groups organized by ability, the greater the number of cliques within a classroom. Ability grouping apparently partitioned the students into formal groups that fostered close-knit, exclusive friendships.

Conversely, to the extent that we group students heterogeneously for some instructional activities, we increase propinquity and opportunities for the development of student relationships among diverse students. A study of two upper-elementary classrooms showed that providing more opportunities for students to interact in racially mixed, small groups yielded more cross-race peer interactions in the lunchroom (Nickerson and Prawat 1981). Importantly, the key difference among these classrooms was the extent to which they provided cross-race propinquity among students. The classrooms had similar distributions of African-American, Latino, and European-American students, and positive teacher-student interactions and peer interactions characterized both.

Diversified, multiple, simultaneous activity settings that involve a variety of student groupings and a relatively small number of students (i.e., two to seven) are likely to provide propinquity with a greater number of classmates. As students engage in a number of activity settings with a variety of classmates, propinquity increases. In contrast, single, undifferentiated activity settings such as seatwork or whole-group instruction offer propinquity only to those classmates who are in students' immediate vicinity.

Providing propinquity in some consistent way to students who differ in terms of ethnicity, language, academic performance, and gender is a critical feature of a pattern of instructional activity that lays the foundation for Inclusion, Fairness, and Harmony in peer relationships.

From Our Files

Affinity Without Intervention

In this kindergarten, students are middle and upper middle class, mostly of European-American background. Most students entered in the fall with estab-

(continues)

(continued)
lished friendships, many family or preschool based, although a few were less well acquainted. Ms. Roberts, the responsive and warm teacher, expected that they would soon find their places in the classroom society.

Each day begins with Morning Circle, in which children self-select spots with friends, usually in a gender-segregated pattern. At the end of Circle, each child chooses from a rich variety of activity workstations. Friends with friends, boys with boys, and girls with girls choose together. Ms. Roberts experiences each day as filled with child satisfaction; she maximizes student preferences.

In January, the mother of a student who entered school with few established friends confides: "Eddie is upset. He came home from school the other day and said, 'Jacob is the most popular boy in class, and it all got figured out in the first week! I never get to sit by him because Andy (Jacob's best friend from preschool) always sits by him.'"

Throughout the year the same pattern prevails. Children self-select friends for activities in a pattern that replicates the affinities that entered the classroom in September. As the school year progresses, the original affinities become more close knit and exclusive, forming identifiable cliques that function during playground as well as classroom activities. Students like Eddie become aware of the social status hierarchy and the difficulty of breaking into these friendship groups. The affinity pattern also becomes more gender segregated and stereotyped, with girls taking over the dramatic play area and boys taking over the building area during free choice time. Most of the children are happy, so Ms. Roberts is happy.

In sixth grade we revisited this elementary school. The affinities, in classroom and playground, had remained remarkably stable. They continued to reflect the social sorting of the parents and neighborhood. Even Eddie had found his place in the social status hierarchy.

From Our Files

Affinity with Intervention

This kindergarten is similar in many ways—filled with similar students and a warm and responsive teacher, Ms. Mann. Here, too, many children entered with established friendships. Ms. Mann begins her day similarly with Morning Circle, followed by a rich variety of activities.

The key difference is that Ms. Mann assigns the seating arrangements and groups based on her academic and social goals and on ongoing observation of students' current capabilities, talents, behaviors, and challenges. Ms. Mann regularly reconfigures groups. When problems or conflict arise among peers, Ms. Mann designs specific activities for those children to work on together. Over time, these children often become friends.

As the year progresses, students have opportunities to work with all other students. During free-choice time, when students self-select their play partners, a group of boys and girls have their heads bent over a challenging puzzle of the

(continues)

> *(continued)*
> world, discussing strategies for figuring it out. ("I'll do the corners. That makes it easier.") Later one of the boys joins a pair of girls who are at the art table. Another group of boys and girls puts on a play about the Little Red Hen in the dramatic play area. In the building area, boys and girls create a city with rail transportation. Friendships do not strictly mirror the pattern of affinity that entered in September. Friendships are relatively fluid and nonhierarchical, and they cross gender lines.

Instructional Activity: Affecting Inclusion, Fairness, and Harmony in Peer Relationships

Although propinquity makes joint activity more likely, it does not guarantee it. Although this point has already been made in Chapter 3, it bears repeating: Joint activity, accompanied by shared communication, is the more proximal determinant of affinities. It is through the conversation, the negotiation, and the "figuring out" that occur when students (and students and teachers) work jointly on instructional activities that the conditions for Inclusion, Fairness, and Harmony are laid out. Joint activity provides the common experience of participation and collaboration so that common interpretations—intersubjectivity—can develop. When students represent different cultural backgrounds this kind of activity is indispensable. Although status is in part imported into the classroom, classroom activity settings provide opportunities to create, maintain, or change status (Cohen 1986, 1994a). In activity settings a developing intersubjectivity is formed about which characteristics in oneself and classmates are important. Students come to know the criteria by which to select and judge one another. Thus, they come to value certain characteristics and not others.

Schools and teachers create opportunities to engage in joint activity and shared communication by determining the nature of the instructional activity settings in which students participate; that is, what students do, how they do it, and why. The nature of instructional activities in classrooms is created by the kinds of goals, products, incentives, and expressions that drive the activity (e.g., individual, collective); the roles that teachers and students perform (e.g., learner, teacher, leader, follower, collaborator); the power relationships among the participants (e.g., provision for or lack of shared decision making and student choice); and the language codes that teachers and students use (e.g., academic, informal, primary, second language).

Teacher decisions about these features of activity settings matter. Instructional activities that involve collective or cooperative goals, products, incentives, and expressions, for example, require joint activity and shared communication that individual learning does not. When power is shared and the roles of students are more fluid in instructional activities, the potential for increasing shared communication is greater than when they are not. For example, when students discuss and share decisions and responsibilities about how to proceed or about the solution of a problem, compromise and negotiation are required. Instructional activities involving the use of primary and second languages as well as informal and academic languages for all students provide opportunities for more inclusive participation. On the other hand, individual activities promote the development of accountability, individual responsibility, and self-reliant problem solving.

Patterns of instructional activity, then, either afford opportunities for propinquity and joint activity with peers or preclude them.[2] Key to affording such opportunities are patterns of simultaneous, diversified instructional activity settings. Teachers and students work toward a variety of integrated goals and tasks within the same instructional time unit (e.g., in literacy classes, toward the goals of vocabulary development, creative writing, and literary analysis, sometimes working individually and sometimes collaboratively) under a variety of simultaneous configurations (teacher-led small group, cooperative small group, pairings, individual). Such patterns afford students opportunities for inclusive participation with their peers in joint activity and set the conditions for Harmony and Fairness. Such patterns also provide students opportunities to develop repertoires required for success in individual activities.

Several features of simultaneous, diversified activity patterns are key. First, in such patterns students can actively participate in joint activity and engage in sustained meaningful dialogue with their peers because the groupings can be made small enough (i.e., two to seven students). Systematically working and producing together means that students will get to know their peers both academically and socially. In this common context values can be articulated, negotiated, and created, thus giving rise to intersubjectivity and Harmony.

Second, patterns of diversified, simultaneous activity settings allow the roles and power relationships among students to be more varied and fluid. With a wide variety of goals and configurations, students can more readily take the roles of collaborator, teacher, and/or leader, rather than strictly the traditional role of "student." Similarly, teachers can more often offer students appropriate decision-making opportunities about academic activities.

Third, such conditions allow students to work toward a variety of goals, expressions, and products. That is, teachers can provide opportunities for peers to work toward collective goals, expressions, and products—key to meaningful joint activity and dialogue—while also providing opportunities for interdependent and individual work.

Fourth, such patterns of activity increase student opportunities to both demonstrate and acquire competencies and interests that serve as points of connection with other peers. This is true because success in this pattern of instructional activities is likely to require a greater variety of capacities (cf. Hallinan 1976). Without such opportunities, the students who already possess recognizable school-like competencies and repertoires are those who shine and maintain or acquire status. Those who do not already possess such competencies appear less able and less desirable as friends.

Finally, patterns of diversified, simultaneous activity increase student opportunities to bring to bear relevant previous knowledge and experiences grounded in school, family, and the community and to demonstrate present competencies. It is the connection between what is already known and what is being learned, the weaving of everyday concepts with schooled concepts, that represents the highest form of learning (Tharp and Gallimore 1988).

From Our Files

Opportunities for Excellence, Fairness, Inclusion, and Harmony

It is language arts time in this two-way Spanish bilingual immersion first grade. Throughout the day, Ms. Gomez implements the Five Standards for Effective Pedagogy and their Three Necessary Conditions.

The seating arrangement consists of five tables where Ms. Gomez has assigned students heterogeneously by performance level, gender, language, and behavior, and there is lots of diversity among them: 40 percent European American, 60 percent Latino, mostly working class or poor, with a few from middle-class backgrounds. Approximately 40 percent of the children are English Language Learners. Spanish is the language of instruction during 85 percent of the day.

Each heterogeneous table group has a leader, a writer, and a materials person, and the student in these roles changes each week. Students carry out these roles in a variety of activities throughout the day.

At the beginning of the language arts block, Ms. Gomez calls students to the rug and reviews each of the five activities that will occur simultaneously. In the teacher-led, small-group reading activity, Ms. Gomez groups students homogeneously by performance. The groups change often, based on ongoing, criterion-referenced reading assessment. In the remaining activities, student groups are heterogeneous by performance level, gender, language, and behavior.

In the small-group guided reading lesson, Ms. Gomez and her students work and produce together, conversing about what the new story topic might be, reading the story together and individually, discussing the theme, and doing follow-up activities. During these Instructional Conversations, *Ms. Gomez*

(continues)

(continued)

elicits students' previous knowledge and experience, and she continually assists students toward more complex levels of understanding.

In the Poetry Center, Ms. Gomez creates student opportunities for leading, collaborating, and individual work. After leading students in a shared oral reading of the poem "February," the leader questions students about the months of the year, then selects another leader. Finally, students read and illustrate the poem in their individual poetry books.

In the Word Center, too, Ms. Gomez creates opportunities for leading, collaborating, and individual work. Using a posted chart of this week's spelling words, the leader creates each word with magnetic letters and dictates the word to the other three students. Rather than take over the task when the leader flounders, fellow students offer assistance such as, "Look at the word," and subtly directing their glance to the word chart. Afterward, students give each other practice tests or work individually.

At the Writing Center, students work individually, completing several pages of their 100s book. (I would like to have 100 _____ [e.g., flowers], but I wouldn't like to have 100 _____ [e.g., elephants].) Students share ideas and talk socially, but mostly they are productive.

At the Library Corner, students also work individually, listening to a book about love, then reading other books from the library. As they finish a book, they record in their reading logs the author, title, and what they liked. Ms. Gomez also allows Buddy Reading.

Within four twenty-minute, daily rotations occurring four days a week, every student in Ms. Gomez's class has an opportunity to work and produce with her and with a variety of peers, in a variety of activities, both jointly and individually, and in a variety of roles. During free-choice time, students self-select activity partners in a pattern of heterogeneity similar to their instructional groupings. In addition to enacting the values of Excellence, Fairness, Inclusion, and Harmony in each activity, Ms. Gomez reinforces and clarifies these explicitly in her daily dialogues with students.

In contrast to this scenario, patterns of single, undifferentiated instructional activity such as seatwork or whole-group instruction diminish the opportunities outlined above. Activities that exclusively emphasize individual goals, expressions, and products diminish opportunities for the joint productive activity and dialogue that are so necessary for students to learn from and about one another. They also deprive students of other instructional venues in which to exhibit their existing competencies and previous knowledge. Under such circumstances, students lack opportunities to learn from one another and know one another. They are left to select friends primarily on surface features of perceived similarity, and the Great Cycle of Social Sorting repeats itself once more. That secondary students from different racial/ethnic groups often express fear of, dislike of, distrust of, and discomfort with one another (e.g., Phelan, Cao, and Davidson 1994) demonstrates the lack of intersubjectivity and affinity that we would expect from a school life characterized by separate activity settings.

The work of Cohen and her colleagues (e.g., Cohen 1994a; Cohen and Lotan 1995; Cohen, Lotan, and Leechor 1989) is consistent with this theoretical view. These researchers have documented a number of classroom status inequalities based on academic, peer, and societal standing. These differences result in different participation rates for low- and high-status students. The Cohen group has studied ways to improve equity, individual student learning, and the overall intellectual quality of group products. Among the conditions required for the success of the intervention strategies are the use of a curriculum requiring a broad range of intellectual abilities (not restricted to conventional academic skills) and a high rate of interaction among students, so that peers can witness the competence of low-status students on a variety of tasks.

Affecting Number of Friends and Isolation from Peers

When patterns of school and classroom activity afford more propinquity, joint productive activity, and shared communication among peers, we would expect higher levels of intersubjectivity and affinity to develop among the participants. The available evidence is consistent with this view. In such environments, children and adolescents select more friends, and fewer are isolated from one another. Much research pertinent to this issue has examined the effects on friendships and peer relationships of participatory versus less participatory school and classroom environments. According to Epstein (1983c), participatory school and classroom environments are characterized by activity settings that permit and encourage frequent student interaction and provide opportunities for shared decision making about academic activities among students and between teachers and students. Teachers often allow students to choose among alternative activities, converse and assist each other, work on shared projects, and monitor their own progress. These activity settings often occur in learning centers or project areas that provide opportunities for working in small groups that change often, based on mutual interests (Epstein 1983c).

A number of studies indicate that in more participatory school environments, children and adolescents report having more friends (see Epstein 1986 for a review). Stevens and Slavin's (1995) two-year longitudinal study comparing cooperative classrooms with traditional classrooms found that students in cooperative classrooms listed more friends than did their counterparts in the traditional classrooms. In a longitudinal study of sixth, seventh, ninth, and twelfth graders, significantly more students were chosen as best friends in high participatory schools compared to low participatory schools in three of the four grade levels examined (Epstein 1983c). In the high participatory schools, adolescents more often had reciprocal friendships and their choices came from a wider set of peer contacts.

Even within the same school, differences in opportunities to participate in school activities affect the number of friends students have. Hansell and Karweit (1983), for example, found that college-track students participated in more school activities and had more friends than did non-college track students. There is also some evidence that clique formation is affected by the activity patterns of classrooms. In one study, fewer cliques occurred in open elementary classrooms than in traditional classrooms. Hallinan suggests that less exclusive, more fluid friendships can be formed in more open settings (Hallinan 1980, cited in Epstein 1986).

The evidence regarding isolates is similar to that for number of friends. Fewer isolates occur and friendship is more evenly distributed and less hierarchical in more participatory school and classroom environments both at the elementary and secondary levels. In a cross-sectional sample of fifth- through eighth-grade classrooms and a longitudinal sample of fourth- through sixth-grade classrooms, Hallinan (1976) found fewer social isolates in open classrooms (defined as having functional grouping rather than rigid homogenous grouping, prolonged student interaction, and student choice regarding activities and materials) than in more traditional classrooms. Friendship choices were more uniformly distributed in open classrooms, but more hierarchical in traditional classrooms. In addition, there were fewer asymmetric friendships in the open classrooms.

Similarly, high participatory secondary schools and classrooms appear to have fewer isolates and a less hierarchical peer structure (e.g., Epstein 1983c). An interesting intervention, conducted more than fifty years ago in a diverse sample of low-income students, reduced the number of social isolates drastically by changing the organizational structure of a high school homeroom from whole group/individual to small groups working toward common goals. Teachers gave social isolates particular responsibilities that would highlight their competencies and make peers notice them (McClelland and Ratliff 1947).

Affecting Friendship Selection Criteria

The research on participatory school and classroom environments also demonstrates that when patterns of instructional activity afford more propinquity, joint productive activity, and shared communication among children and adolescents, they less frequently use similar surface features and status characteristics (gender, race, school performance) as selection criteria for friends (see Epstein 1989 for a review). Students in high participatory secondary schools chose friends from more diverse socioeconomic backgrounds and achievement levels (Epstein 1983a). In the same study, low–socioeconomic status students in high participatory schools selected more high–socioeconomic status friends. Similarly, in these settings, students with no plans for college more often selected friends with college plans.

Epstein (1989) suggests that participatory environments provide children and adolescents with many opportunities for interaction and group work that may promote the selection of friends based on their interests, goals, ideas, helpfulness, or other characteristics rather than on traditionally defined status characteristics. We add that it is the joint activity and accompanying dialogue that allow students to discover these characteristics about one another and then to develop common interests, goals, ideas, and ways of problem solving and seeing the world—that is, intersubjectivity. Moreover, such activity settings allow students to demonstrate competencies that may otherwise go unnoticed.

The cooperative learning literature demonstrates even more clearly that patterns of instructional activity that provide for increased propinquity, joint productive activity, and shared communication among diverse peers can affect student friendship selection criteria. Learning activities that involve meaningful, sustained, cross-race contact among students have a positive effect on the development of such relationships. Much of this research is based on Allport's contact theory (Allport 1954). As discussed in Chapter 1, Allport's analysis omitted the crucial role of joint activity in creating that humane perception. Slavin's work, and that of others in cooperative learning, has provided an implicit improvement to contact theory; sociocultural theory explains it.

In reviews of the literature, Slavin (1985, 1995) gathered overwhelming evidence that cooperative learning involving racially heterogeneous groups has a positive effect on interracial friendship. In the 1985 review, sixteen of nineteen studies showed the positive effect of cooperative learning on intergroup relations. As a whole, the studies show that when students work in ethnically mixed, cooperative learning groups, they gain in cross-ethnic friendships. In addition, the evidence indicates that the friendships are long lasting and tend to be close, reciprocated friendship choices rather than distant or unreciprocated choices. In one of the few longitudinal studies of cross-ethnic friendship, Slavin (1979) found that cooperative learning involving ethnically heterogeneous groups at the secondary level increased cross-ethnic friendship. The effect remained significant a year later. Moreover, many of the cross-racial friendships made during the cooperative learning intervention were formed between students who had never been in the same cooperative group.

There is also evidence that positive cross-ethnic and cross-gender relationships formed in cooperative learning groups generalize to structured and unstructured activities within the classroom and to other activities in school and at home. For example, in a study of fourth and sixth graders, Warring et al. (1985) compared the effects of individualistic learning with several forms of cooperative learning on cross-ethnic and cross-gender choice for a number of school and home activities. All cooperative conditions involved ethnically and gender-heterogeneous groups. Students in cooperative conditions reported more cross-ethnic choices than those in the individualistic conditions for structured classroom activities. Students in the cooperative-controversy condition (members of a learning group each teaching a point of view within the group and coming to a consensus about a solution) also made more cross-ethnic choices for unstructured classroom activities. Students involved in intergroup cooperation versus intergroup competition made more cross-ethnic choices for structured class activities, unstructured class activities, out-of-class activities, and activities in the home.

The findings for cross-gender choices were very similar. Compared to students in the individual conditions, those in cooperative conditions made more cross-gender choices for structured classroom activities, unstructured classroom activities, and out-of-class school activities. Students involved in cooperative debate (members of a learning group competing to see who can best teach a point of view and provide information within the group) also made more cross-gender choices for home activities than did students involved in cooperative controversy and individual activities. Students involved in intergroup cooperation versus intergroup competition made more cross-gender choices for unstructured class activities and out-of-class school activities.

Slavin (1985) concludes that cooperative learning involving ethnically heterogeneous groups increases positive relations among such students in part because it meets a number of the requirements of Allport's theory for reducing racial prejudice, including equal status among participants, institutional endorsement, and increased perceived similarity. The institutional endorsement comes from teachers' acts of bringing together the racially or ethnically heterogeneous groups, and the cooperative learning methods create a new basis for perceived similarity among dissimilar students. The assignment of students to teams automatically gives them a common identity, according to Slavin. We would amplify this view to say that it is the joint productive activity and shared communication resulting from collectivist goals, products, and incentives that provide the conditions for the development of intersubjectivity leading to the possibility of affinity among diverse students. Without such activity involving collaboration and dialogue, these students have insufficient common out-of-school and in-school experiences to serve as a basis for intersubjectivity and affinity.

According to Slavin, "situational equal status" is achieved by bringing together students in the same grade level. Researchers who have documented classroom status inequalities among students and their effects on participation rates (e.g., Cohen 1994a; Cohen and Lotan 1995; Cohen, Lotan, and Leechor 1989) heavily dispute this notion. Cohen has documented that low-status children tend to participate less in classrooms, including in heterogeneous small groups, unless active steps are taken to counteract self and peer low-competence expectations (Cohen 1986, 1994a). This is a critical issue because participation is related to achievement gains.

Our own view is that the two sets of data both contribute to an understanding of how activity affects relationship formation and achievement (see Slavin 1996 for a review of the research on cooperative learning and achievement; see Cohen 1994b for a review of productive small groups). Cohen's data do not upset the strong case for the effects of ethnically heterogeneous cooperative groups on cross-ethnic friendship, nor for that matter the case for achievement gains under cooperative activity. Cohen (1986), for example, states that just by talking and working together with other students, low-status students will improve their performance. Similarly, Slavin's data do not undermine Cohen's well-documented case. Both types of strategies are likely required to maximize the achievement of low-status and/or low-performing students. In Chapter 6 we address practical issues of creating these effective patterns of instructional activity and student participation in instructional activities.

To summarize thus far: Propinquity, established by grouping or some other means, has powerful consequences on the probabilities of establishing relationships. But the nature of the activity itself within the groupings, particularly the provision of joint activity and dialogue, dictates the attributes of those relationships.

Affecting Patterns of Peer Affinities

When patterns of instructional activity afford more propinquity, joint productive activity, and shared communication among diverse peers, we would expect the overall pattern of peer affinities to be less hierarchical and less tied to academic status. Nickerson and Prawat (1981) found that providing more opportunities for students to interact in racially mixed, small groups yielded less racial bias on their ratings of classmates as work and play partners. Schuncke (1978) found that in ability-grouped classrooms versus cross-grouped classrooms, peer ratings of how well students could get others to do things (social power) and how well students were liked (affect status) mirrored academic status hierarchies, particularly for males.

A longitudinal study of two third- and two fourth-grade classrooms provides further evidence (Bossert 1979). In classrooms characterized primarily by recitation and homogenous grouping by ability, peers developed stable, homogeneous peer groups based on academic performance. In these classrooms, rigid status hierarchies developed based on academic performance. In classrooms characterized primarily by multitask activity (that is, simultaneous, diversified activity settings) and more fluid, heterogeneous grouping, friendships were changing and fluid, independent of academic performance, and based on similar interests.

Bossert suggests, and we would agree, that it was the activity itself that shaped both the teachers' and the students' behaviors. First, in recitation classrooms, homogenous grouping provided propinquity for some students and precluded it for others. The few small-group activities in the recitation classrooms involved homogenous groupings of students for reading or mathematics instruction. Occasional, special project groups were also organized by ability level. So, to the extent that students were engaged in common activity and communication, it was usually with others similar to themselves in achievement level. Second, in these classrooms, students rarely had opportunities to work and talk together productively. More often students performed single, teacher-led activities; they responded primarily to the teacher; and their performance was individual and public. Such activity provided both teachers and students opportunities to quickly assess who was understanding the material and who was not, easily leading to the development of academic status hierarchies. Finally, recitation activity promoted teacher control and a reliance on high-achieving students to demonstrate knowledge of the material. Contrary to their perceptions, teachers gave more attention and assistance to higher-achieving students. In summary, the recitation classrooms created a system of primarily individualistic participation, performance, goals, incentives, and products, and they segregated students by performance levels.

In contrast, multitask activity classrooms more often provided propinquity among diverse students, and they provided students with more opportunities to work and talk together in a variety of instructional activities. In these classrooms, students were involved in numerous activities at once, some of which involved collaboration (independent reading, small-group and independent projects, artwork, crafts). Students often exercised choice in activity and completion based on interests. Performance and performance evaluation were not primarily individual, nor so often public. Finally, teachers tended to assist the poorer performing students the most. Again, the activity itself provided teachers and students with opportunities for some behaviors and not others.

Other studies indicate that patterns of instructional activity involving simultaneity and diversification have a favorable effect on peer relationships.

Rothenberg (1982), for example, found that compared to classrooms in which students tended to perform the same tasks during the same period, those in which students engaged in simultaneous, diversified tasks fostered positive peer relationships that were not characterized by cleavages and static status hierarchies. This study of eight elementary classrooms found that in classrooms with high proportions of multitask activities (more than 38 percent) the status structure closely matched actual work and play interactions. In contrast, classrooms with high proportions of recitation and common worksheet assignments had clear sociometric stars who came primarily from the high-performing reading group and interacted only with small numbers of peers from the same reading group. Similarly, other researchers have reported that classrooms with multiple learning centers in which students have substantial authority in accomplishing their tasks promote more fluid, interdependent, supportive peer structures (and increases in student achievement) (Rosenholtz 1982).

Affecting the Quality of Peer Relationships

Patterns of instructional activity involving high levels of collective goals, products, and incentives that provide for joint activity and shared communication have a positive effect on qualitative aspects of peer relationships. In an intervention study that changed the activity and goal structure of a set of third- through seventh-grade classrooms from individualistic-competitive to cooperative, researchers found that peer relationships in the restructured classrooms were characterized as more prosocial and less conflictual than those in the non-restructured classrooms (Hertz-Lazarowitz and Sharan 1984). These findings are consistent with our prediction that high levels of intersubjectivity result from high levels of joint productive activity and shared communication. Moreover, these researchers found that during interaction on non-academic tasks led by someone other than the teacher, students from the restructured classrooms acted more prosocially toward peers who were not members of their study group. In two small-group experimental settings, these students were less selfish, less competitive, more cooperative, and more helpful than were students in a traditional setting. The positive peer-related behaviors these children and adolescents learned in one setting apparently generalized to another with a different substantive focus and different peers.

Similarly, in two studies involving large samples of fifth through ninth graders, Johnson and Johnson and their colleagues examined students' attitudes toward schoolwork and each other. Students who liked working cooperatively and perceived that the positive goal was related to interdependence were more likely to believe that their classmates cared about how much they learned and facilitated their learning, cared about and liked them as persons, and were friends and liked each other (Johnson and

Johnson 1983; Johnson et al. 1985). Students who reported participating in cooperative learning groups half or more of the time reported experiencing more help and academic encouragement from peers (Johnson and Johnson 1983). Over a seven-month period of cooperative learning experiences, there were increases in students' reports of responsibility for ensuring that all group members learned the assigned material, resource interdependence with classmates, classmates' caring about how much one learns and wishing to assist, classmates' caring about and liking one as a person, and belief that classmates are friends and like one another. Students also reported less alienation from classmates and school (Johnson et al. 1985).

Overall, these findings indicate that we can expect peer relationships created within classrooms to reflect the values and relationship qualities of those classroom cultures. There is also some evidence that students' behavior toward other peers will be based on these values and qualities.

From Our Files

Classroom Activity That Re-Creates the Status Quo

Although Ms. Birk has a pattern of varied, simultaneous activities (small-group guided reading, writing, listening, independent reading), few activities involve students working and producing collaboratively. In the independent activities, students typically sit together in groups but work on similar individual tasks. English Language Learners often get different tasks than the English speakers.

In this transitional Spanish bilingual first grade, about half of the students are European-American English speakers from middle- and upper-middle-class families. The other half are Spanish-speaking, English Language Learners primarily from poor backgrounds.

During the language arts block, Ms. Birk instructs both English and Spanish speakers in their primary languages. Ms. Birk provides all other instruction in English, including all Circles and whole-group activities. For all of the language arts activities, Ms. Birk groups students homogeneously by performance level and language.

As a consequence, English and Spanish speakers rarely have any meaningful contact and virtually never collaborate. During outside play, many of Ms. Birk's students play alone or in gender-segregated groups. Cross-ethnic play is rare.

From Our Files

Classroom Activity That Creates Inclusion, Fairness, and Harmony

Ms. Price instructs both English speakers and Spanish speakers in their primary languages in reading and writing. In this transitional Spanish bilingual first

(continues)

(continued)

grade, half of the students are of Mexican descent, half are European American. Most are from working-class families. By using Spanish and English on alternate days for whole-group activities such as Circle times, instructions, transitions, and mathematics instruction, Ms. Price develops both languages in all students. In these venues, both English speakers and English Language Learners respond, either in their own or their second language. Ms. Price encourages both receptive and productive language by accepting all student speech while responding in the language of the day.

During Centers, Ms. Price creates a pattern of varied, simultaneous activities (small-group guided reading, writing, listening, math, science, computers) and implements the Five Standards and their Three Necessary Conditions. In the mix of activities students produce individual and collaborative work in small groups, in pairs, and independently. For small-group guided reading, Ms. Price groups students homogeneously by performance level based on ongoing criterion-referenced reading assessment. In the remaining activities, student groups are heterogeneous by performance level, gender, language, and behavior. At the Science Center "bilingual buddies" (one English speaking and the other Spanish speaking) collaborate regularly, using Spanish one day and English the next, on tasks such as labeling body parts on a model.

In both the academic and social domains, Ms. Price emphasizes independence and interdependence, mutual aid, and caring. Before Centers begin, Ms. Price elicits from students what they are to do if they need help. ("Try to figure it out yourself; Ask three students to help; Come back to it.") Ms. Price ends with, "I see twenty teachers here today. You are all teachers, so while I am teaching reading, go to one of your other teachers for help."

The shared values that Ms. Price and her students have developed guide them in their daily interactions. On one occasion during singing/poetry Circle, Ms. Price jokingly tries to bring Kurtis into compliance, "Don't jump Juan's bones, Kurtis." After initially smiling and desisting, Kurtis begins to cry. Immediately, Ms. Price retraces her actions and their consequences, "Kurtis, did I hurt your feelings and embarrass you? I just wanted you to stop. I was trying to make a joke, but it wasn't very thoughtful of me, and I apologize." Spontaneously and simultaneously, four to five children, both girls and boys, of both Mexican and European-American descent, surround Kurtis with comforting words, hugs, and strokes. Quickly, Kurtis recovers and the activity continues back on track.

Activity-based relationships teach students how to relate to one another and how to be friends.

The literature reviewed thus far indicates that patterns of instructional activity that increase propinquity, joint productive activity, and dialogue among diverse peers create the conditions for Inclusion, Fairness, and Harmony among peers. Students are less frequently isolated; they have more friends; they select friends less often on the basis of traditional status characteristics; and their friendships are more fluid, interdependent, and supportive both academically and socially. In addition, heterogeneous grouping of students in cooperative activities can increase cross-ethnic and cross-gender friendships.

Substantial proportions of simultaneous, diversified activity settings rather than single, undifferentiated activity settings characterize these patterns of instructional activity. Students work in a variety of configurations, including small groups, pairings, and individually, toward a variety of instructional goals. Heterogeneous, more fluid grouping of students is used, although homogenous groupings may be used for specific purposes.

Several other features of these complex patterns of activity also bolster opportunities for meaningful joint activity and dialogue. First, the roles that the participants perform are relatively fluid. Providing students with opportunities to converse with and assist each other on shared projects means that students are not only students but also collaborators and teachers. In these settings, other roles, such as that of "expert," are more fluid. Power relationships among participants appear to be more equitable, with opportunities for students (and teachers and students) to engage in shared decision making about instructional activities. Finally, these patterns of instructional activity appear to include substantial amounts of collective goals, products, and incentives.

It is clear that the patterns of instructional activity described above provide propinquities that go against the conservative Great Cycle of Social Sorting. Teachers do not systematically and consistently segregate students by academic performance or any other characteristic that simply imports society's social order based on class, gender, and ethnicity/race. Some implementations of cooperative learning include activity settings for the express purpose of increasing student participation with diverse others. Other groupings bring students together based on mutual interests.

In summary, diversification of the persons with whom students work and of the activities in which they engage promotes Inclusion and Fairness and provides a common school experience that fosters the development of a shared set of values, goals, and standards on which Harmony rests.

Peer Relationships, Friendship, and Academic and Social Excellence

The quality of students' relationships with peers affects students' achievement of social and academic Excellence. These relationships exert their influence primarily through the assisted performance and development of intersubjectivity made possible by joint activity and shared communication. To the extent that peer relationships are characterized by these qualities, the potential for learning and academic Excellence is increased, as is the potential for social and academic Inclusion, Fairness, and Harmony.

Current research suggests a number of preliminary generalizations, despite some variations in findings. First, having friends, making friends, and being accepted by peers is usually better for achievement than having no friends (e.g., Asher and Parker 1989; Ladd and Kochenderfer 1996; Epstein 1983b). That is, children who have no friends or are rejected by peers tend to do less well in school academically and socially, whereas those who have friends and those who are accepted tend to fare better (e.g., Ladd 1990; Ladd and Kochenderfer 1996; Epstein 1983b). In a study of young children, Ladd (1990) found that those who formed more new friendships in kindergarten tended to gain in school performance by the end of the school year. Those who maintained prior friendships had better attitudes toward school at both the beginning and the end of the school year. Those who were rejected by classmates early in the school year had less favorable perceptions of school, higher levels of school avoidance, and lower levels of scholastic readiness by the end of the school year.

A more recent study of these issues showed that students who reported being well liked by their classmates and having greater numbers of friends in the fall of the kindergarten year tended to have positive attitudes toward school in the spring of the kindergarten year (Ladd and Coleman 1997). Students with greater numbers of mutual friends grew to like school better over time. Students who reported higher levels of peer support and lower levels of loneliness tended to like school better both in the fall and in the spring. In a study of third through sixth graders, researchers found that poorly accepted children tended to perform more poorly in school (Asher, Hymel, and Renshaw 1984). Finally, in a longitudinal study of middle and high school students, academic outcomes were better for students who chose some friends, even if they were low scoring, than for those who chose no friends (Epstein 1983b).

Researchers consistently report that poorly accepted children and those without friends feel lonelier than those who have friends or are accepted by peers. Poorly accepted children are also more likely to be victims of peer aggression (Perry, Kusel, and Perry 1988), and rejected children's social status is least likely to change over time (Coie and Dodge 1983). In a study of third to fifth graders, poor acceptance by peers, lack of a friend, or having poor-quality friendships all contributed to loneliness (Parker and Asher 1993). Similarly, children whom peers infrequently nominated as friends, and those whom peers rated low as playmates, were more likely to be lonely than their more well liked counterparts (Asher, Hymel, and Renshaw 1984). Compared to popular, average, neglected, and controversial children, rejected children tend to report greater loneliness (Asher et al. 1990).

Second, low peer status does not bode well for later functioning, particularly for school persistence (Parker and Asher 1987). In summarizing the literature, Asher and Parker (1989) concluded that low peer acceptance early in school is most consistently related to later dropping out. They reported drop-out rates for low-accepted children as two, three, and even eight times higher than for other children. On average, these rates equated to a 25 percent drop-out rate for low-acceptance children compared to an 8 percent drop-out rate for other children. Consistent with these data, in a longitudinal study, students who were neglected by peers in fifth grade had higher levels of truancy in high school. Those who were rejected had higher levels of juvenile delinquency (Kupersmidt 1983, cited in Ladd and Kochenderfer 1996).

Third, the qualities of friendships matter. On balance, having supportive, harmonious, satisfying relationships tends to be positively related to socioemotional functioning as well as to school performance and attitudes. In an extensive review of the literature, Savin-Williams and Berndt (1990) concluded that children and adolescents with such relationships typically report positive self-esteem, a good understanding of other people's feelings, and relatively little loneliness. Also popular with classmates, these children and adolescents have positive views of classmates and exhibit socially appropriate behavior. They typically behave appropriately in school, are motivated to achieve, and often receive high grades.

Similarly, in a short-term longitudinal study of kindergartners, Ladd, Kochenderfer, and Coleman (1996) found that students who reported higher levels of validation and aid from best friends tended to report increases in perceived social support from classmates. Those who reported higher levels of aid from best friends showed improvements in their attitudes toward school. In contrast, boys who perceived higher levels of conflict with their best friends tended to exhibit several forms of school maladjustment, including higher levels of school loneliness and avoidance and lower levels of school liking and engagement.

At the middle school level, adolescents who perceived their friendships as supportive had higher achievement test scores, report card grades, and behavior ratings from teachers (Berndt and Hawkins 1987; Miller and Berndt 1987, both reported in Savin-Williams and Berndt 1990). They were also more involved in school and placed more value on what they learned in school. In a longitudinal study of seventh and eighth graders, Berndt and Keefe (1995) found that students whose best friendships had more positive features in the fall (i.e., intimate self-disclosure, prosocial behavior, and self-esteem support) increased in their self-reported involvement in school by spring. Conversely, students whose friendships had more negative features (i.e., conflict and rivalry) self-reported as increasingly disruptive in school.

In a longitudinal study of social support during the transition to middle school in a sample of poor, urban youth, Estrada (1996a) found that young adolescents who were more satisfied with support from their best friends at the end of elementary school tended to perform better academically (on the California Test of Basic Skills and on teacher ratings of scholastic competence) at the end of the first year of middle school.

Fourth, friends' performance in and attitudes toward school condition how the qualities of friendships are associated with academic Excellence. In a series of studies, Cauce and her colleagues found mixed results. Two studies showed a positive association and two showed a negative association between support from friends and educational functioning. In a study of mostly African-American, low-income high school students in three inner-city schools, support from friends (amount of helpfulness) was negatively associated with grade point average and absenteeism (Cauce, Felner, and Primavera 1982). For European-American, middle- to upper-socioeconomic status middle school students in two suburban private schools, support from friends was negatively related to school competence (Cauce, Hannan, and Sargeant 1987). For African-American, low-socioeconomic status seventh graders, however, emotional support from friends, number of reciprocated best friends, and friends' school achievement orientation were all positively associated with both students' grade point averages and achievement test scores (Cauce 1986). More recently, Cauce and her colleagues again reported a positive association between support from friends and school competence in a sample of African-American seventh and eighth graders (Cauce et al. 1994).

We agree with Cauce's interpretation: Support from friends occurs within the context of peer group values, which explains whether it is negatively or positively related to school competence (Cauce and Srebnick 1989). In the 1986 study, Cauce measured peer group values by asking students how important it was to do a number of things to be well liked by peers (e.g., "Be a good dancer"; "Be a good student"). Of these students, 96 percent thought that being a good student was at least somewhat important and 70 percent said they would most like to be remembered at their school for being the best student, underscoring that peer support functioned within a school-achievement-endorsing value context. Consistent with this view, in a multiethnic sample (African American, European American, and Hispanic American) of second- and fifth-grade children, support from friends was positively related to both achievement test scores and grade point average when friends had positive attitudes toward school achievement (Levitt et al. 1995).

Finally, in secondary school, having friends who endorse schooling seems to be a critical factor in school achievement. Epstein (1983b) found that those middle and high school students who were initially low scoring on measures of mathematics and English achievement, satisfaction with school life, college plans, and self-reliance—and who had high-scoring friends—had the highest gains in these academic and affective domains a year later. Initially high-scoring students who had high-scoring friends also gained. However, initially high-scoring students with low-scoring friends lost ground on these measures. Initially low-scoring students with low-scoring friends remained low.

In a longitudinal study of a large multiethnic sample, Steinberg and Darling (in press) reported that peer crowd influence affects school achievement beyond parental influence for all ethnic groups. For some ethnic groups, such as European Americans, parents and peers were more likely to have shared achievement-endorsing values, whereas for others, such as African Americans, parents and peers were more likely to be in conflict. All parents almost uniformly endorsed school achievement, whereas African-American peers more often did not. In addition, at school African-American students had the most difficulty of all ethnic groups in gaining access to school-achievement endorsing crowds. From our perspective, the diminished possibility of propinquity and joint activity with other students in such crowds diminishes the possibility that these students can maintain or develop achievement-endorsing attitudes, values, and behaviors in school. The effects of allowing the Great Cycle of Social Sorting to function within the school context come into high relief.

Given this state of affairs, what are schools to do? Clearly, most teachers would choose supportive, achievement-endorsing friends for their students. The obvious answer is that teachers need to create classrooms in which achievement-endorsing attitudes, values, and behaviors are developed within the everyday activity settings of the classroom. Classrooms in which all participants, including the teacher, create a common classroom culture of Excellence, Fairness, Inclusion, and Harmony by working and talking jointly on meaningful products will have maximum potential for developing achievement-endorsing values and behaviors among all of their members. If certain students are consistently given less-challenging tasks and less-effective pedagogy, are not provided with success experiences, and/or are left out socially, the chances for developing these characteristics are slim and the outlook grim.[3]

Propinquity and Activity: Affecting Inclusion, Fairness, and Harmony in Teacher-Student Relationships

In the formation of teacher-student relationships, as in the formation of peer relationships, propinquity is a precondition. In schools, teachers and students are in each other's presence and so some kind of teacher-student relationships will exist, however slight. The nature and quality of those relationships will vary depending on a number of factors.

Creating Teacher-Student Propinquity in Schools

At the school level, propinquity is created among certain teachers and students by the criteria used for assigning students to classrooms, the size and number of classrooms, and the policies regarding the regrouping of students and teachers for academic and social purposes (Estrada 1997). In addition, proximity to teachers is in part created by whether students are organized into self-contained, core, or departmentalized classrooms. Self-contained classrooms provide the greatest potential for proximity to one teacher, whereas departmentalized classrooms provide the greatest potential for proximity to a greater number of teachers. The available evidence suggests, however, that in this instance more is not always better for the development of quality teacher-student relationships.

Creating Teacher-Student Propinquity in Classrooms

In classrooms, propinquity among students and teachers is created primarily by the number, diversification, and simultaneity of activities (all students engage in one activity, different students engage in different activities); the size and number of groups teachers directly instruct (whole group, small groups, pairs, individuals); and whether the teacher instructs all students in the classroom (English and/or English Language Learners). Diversified, multiple, simultaneous activity settings increase propinquity among teachers and students when used as vehicles for systematically working with small groups of students. Delivering instruction primarily in single, undifferentiated activities, such as whole-group instruction or seatwork, restricts propinquity to those near the teacher. If teachers do not instruct students at all in some or most content areas, propinquity is limited. Such is the case, for example, when teachers systematically instruct particular achievement-level or language groups and not others.

Creating Instructional Activity in Classrooms

Among teachers and students, just as among peers, propinquity makes joint activity more likely but does not guarantee it. Joint activity, accompanied by shared communication with teachers, is again the proximal determinant of affinities. As in the case of peers, teachers can create or restrict opportunities for students to engage in such activity and communication with the teachers themselves by determining the nature of the instructional activity settings in which they participate. As mentioned earlier, the nature of instructional activities in classrooms is created by the kinds of goals, products, incentives, and expressions that drive the activity (e.g., individual, collective); the roles that teachers and students perform (e.g., learner, teacher, leader, follower, collaborator);

the power relationships among the participants (e.g., provision for or lack of shared decision making and student choice); and the language codes that teachers and students use (e.g., academic, informal, primary, second language).

Teacher decisions about these features of the activity settings in which they are engaged with students matter. When teachers and students create collective expressions and products and work toward collective goals and incentives, joint productive activity and dialogue between teachers and students are required, whereas they are not in individual work. When teachers share power with students in instructional activities and provide fluidity in the roles of teacher and student, the potential for increasing dialogue between teachers and students is greater than when they do not. For example, when teachers and students discuss and share decisions and responsibilities about how to proceed or about the solution of a problem, or when students are involved in the selection of topics of study, collaboration, negotiation, and compromise with teachers are required. Finally, instructional activities involving the use of primary and second languages as well as academic and informal languages among teachers and students provide opportunities for more inclusive participation.

As with peers, patterns of instructional activity either afford students opportunities for propinquity, joint activity, and dialogue with teachers or preclude them. And, here again, key to affording such opportunities are patterns of simultaneous, diversified instructional activity settings. Recall that in these patterns of activity teachers and students work toward a variety of goals under a variety of configurations, simultaneously. Such patterns afford teachers opportunities for effective assessment and assistance and students opportunities for inclusive participation in the currency of the classroom: academics and social relationships. Because these patterns provide these opportunities for teachers and students, they create the conditions for Excellence, Fairness, Inclusion, and Harmony.

Several features of such patterns are key. First, teachers and students can actively participate in joint activity and engage in sustained meaningful dialogue because the groupings can be made small enough (two to seven). In school, linguistic signs and symbols function as the primary mediators of activity. When teachers and students work and produce collaboratively, the greatest opportunity exists for the development and transformation of the mind: the development of cognitive processes and structures of meaning. Through purposeful and meaningful dialogue with students, teachers can assess and assist students toward more complex understandings and mental capacities. It is in this context that students can most effectively develop and appropriate the languages and concepts of the specific subject matters. Through this same process of working and talking together teachers' and students' values, goals, and standards are articulated, negotiated, and created. Thus, joint productive activity provides the context for maximizing academic achievement and intersubjectivity among teachers and students.

Second, patterns of diversified, simultaneous activity allow the roles and power relationships between teachers and students to be more varied and fluid. With a wide variety of goals and configurations, students can more readily take on the roles of collaborator, teacher, and leader, rather than adhere to the traditional role of "student." Teachers also can assume a variety of roles beyond that of traditional teacher and authority figure. Moreover, teachers can create more fluid power relationships by increasing student opportunities for appropriate decision making about academic activities.

Third, such conditions allow students and teachers to work toward a variety of goals, expressions, and products. In small groups teachers and students can work collaboratively toward collective goals, expressions, and products, key to meaningful joint activity and dialogue.

Finally, patterns of diversification and simultaneity of activity provide students more opportunities to demonstrate their present competencies to teachers, acquire new ones with the assistance of teachers, and become better acquainted with their teachers. Recall our assertion that such patterns are likely to require a greater variety of capacities to succeed. For teachers, systematically working and producing together with their students means that they will get to know their students in an up-close and personal way, both academically and socially. Consequently, they will be able to assess and assist their students more effectively. Without such opportunities, the students who tend to succeed and to maintain or acquire status are those who already possess recognizable school-like competencies and repertoires. Those students who do not possess these qualities may appear, to teachers, to be less able and less enjoyable as students.

In contrast, patterns of single, undifferentiated instructional activity such as seatwork and whole-group instruction with a preponderance of individual goals, expressions, and products virtually eliminate opportunities for the joint productive activity and dialogue that are so necessary for teachers and students to learn from and about one another. Many teachers truly believe that their large-group, lecture-and-discussion activities provide real conversation with students. Although teachers have that dialogic experience, only a small number of students do; those are the confident, competent students who need it least. It is simply not possible to have inclusive dialogue and collaboration under circumstances in which teachers and students are both limited in their capacity to teach and to learn and to develop intersubjectivity and affinity for one another. Not only will Inclusion suffer, but so will Fairness; Harmony will be on the surface at best; and Excellence will be achieved only by a few.

Estrada, Sayavong, and Guardino (1998) examined patterns of language arts instructional activity in twenty-seven culturally and linguistically diverse first- and fourth-grade classrooms. Using a live observation tool, they focused on key features of pedagogy; the extent to which teachers used multiple, simultaneous, diversified activity settings; and the extent to which they diversified persons within activity settings. Compared to classrooms with patterns of single, undifferentiated activity, in classrooms where teachers and students were engaged in a variety of activities simultaneously (small reading group with teacher, reciprocal reading group with peers, pairs in writing conferences, individuals working on reference skills), teachers tended to rate their students' overall performance in school and their language arts performance higher. Teachers who more frequently produced and worked together with their students, engaged them in dialogue, assisted them responsively, and provided modeling and demonstration also rated their students' overall performance and language arts performance more highly.

Bossert (1977) found that in classrooms characterized by a whole-group, recitative pattern, teachers dominated instructional activities, controlling the flow of questions and answers and using high levels of control over student behavior, often by means of desists (requests to stop an activity that violates classroom rules). Bossert points out that in this pattern of activity the requirements for student attention are high, with inattention often leading to student misbehavior that tends to spread. All teacher and student behavior is public, so teachers must constantly monitor the behavior of all students and reprimand all transgressions in the same manner to meet the demands of equity. Finally, because the teacher initiates and maintains the activity, instruction often comes to a halt while the teacher exerts control over misbehavior. Estrada, Sayavong, and Guardino's (1998) findings agree. In this pattern of activity the roles of teacher and student are rigid, the teacher maintains power, and control is exercised through authority rather than personal connection or mutual understanding. Thus, opportunities for meaningful joint activity, dialogue, and intersubjectivity are greatly diminished, if not precluded. These conditions are not conducive to Inclusion, Fairness, and Harmony in the classroom.

In contrast, Bossert (1977) found that in classrooms characterized by both multitask (multiple, simultaneous, diversified activity settings) and class tasks (all students doing the same task such as a worksheet or math assignment), teachers less often dominated instructional activities, with students often able to initiate and organize projects. These teachers provided students with more freedom and choice and spent much less time monitoring and controlling student behavior. Although these teachers did not tolerate interruptions during discussions, they did not require constant attention and raised hands from their students. Bossert points out that in this pattern of activity the behavior of students is less public,

---

From Our Files

Ms. Lee Revisited

With Ms. Young and Ms. Lee, the contrasts come to life as well. In the pattern of single, undifferentiated activities that Ms. Lee offers, there are few if any opportunities for working, producing, or talking together either with the teacher or with other students. In the whole-group venue, mostly the same high-performing students participate. The pattern is repetitive, the range of activities restricted: quick review of homework with teacher at the front; introduction of a new topic via lecture, perhaps with demonstration and limited student participation; assignment of new work to be completed individually at students' seats; more homework. The conventional roles of "teacher" and "student" dominate. Power and decision making are vested in the teacher. The use of a variety of language codes is limited. Instructional goals and products are almost always individual. How and when will students who do not already know the answers learn them, so they too can participate? How and when will Ms. Lee come to know her students, academically and socially? How will students who do not have contact outside of class come to know one another academically and socially? How will Excellence, Fairness, Inclusion, and Harmony be fostered?

---

so some misbehavior may go unnoticed by both teachers and students and therefore may sometimes self-correct. Teachers were relieved of the burden of constant monitoring and reprimanding, and students were less likely to be influenced by peers' misbehavior so they could proceed uninterrupted with their work. In addition, these teachers were able to provide more individual, personalized assistance to students who were misbehaving or were off task. Teachers more often matched their responses to the individual needs of students. This pattern of instructional activity provides for more fluidity in the roles of teacher and student, more sharing of power among teachers and students, and more responsive assistance to individual students. Thus, opportunities for meaningful joint activity, dialogue, and intersubjectivity are greatly increased. Likewise, these conditions are more conducive to Inclusion, Fairness, and Harmony in the classroom.

Propinquity, Activity, and the Quality of Teacher-Student Relationships

When school and classroom instructional patterns afford more propinquity, joint activity, and dialogue among teachers and students, we would expect higher levels of intersubjectivity and affinity to develop

---

From Our Files

Ms. Young Revisited

We can see that in the pattern of activity Ms. Young offers, the potential is much greater for the development of these educational goals. Ms. Young and her students work, produce, and talk with one another routinely. Opportunities are greater for more fluid roles and power relationships. Language codes vary from academic to informal, from English to primary languages. The activities themselves offer students diverse venues in which to exhibit and expand competencies. Students produce both collaborative and individual products. Moreover, student groupings are both heterogeneous and homogenous, making it possible for Ms. Young to tailor her instruction and activities appropriately and for students to work with familiar peers and stretch themselves to do so with unfamiliar peers.

---

among teachers and students. The available evidence supports this view. In a study of middle and high schools, Epstein and McPartland (1976) found that students tended to report more positive reactions to their teachers if they reported participating in more open classrooms (fewer restrictions on student movement and interaction, more alternative activities for meeting student interests or needs, and greater student responsibility for selecting assignments and supervising progress).

Similarly, in two studies involving fifth through ninth graders, Johnson and Johnson and their colleagues found that the more students liked working cooperatively with other students and the more they perceived positive goal and resource interdependence, the more likely they were to believe that teachers liked them, cared about them and how much they learned, and assisted their learning (Johnson and Johnson 1983; Johnson et al. 1985). Students who reported participating in cooperative learning groups half or more of the time reported experiencing more caring and affection from teachers and more fairness in grading. When patterns of instructional activity afford opportunities to work and talk collaboratively with relatively small numbers of students, teachers and students can come to know one another and teachers can assess and assist their students more responsively and effectively.

There is also indirect evidence from studies of school-level organization that patterns that afford more propinquity, joint activity, and dialogue among teachers and students yield higher levels of intersubjectivity and affinity among teachers and students. These studies have documented the deterioration in teacher-student relationships as students move from self-contained classrooms in elementary school to departmentalized classrooms in middle and junior high schools. The evidence indicates that the quality of teacher-student relationships suffers after the transition to middle school, particularly in those schools with traditional departmentalization. McPartland (1991) examined this issue in a large national study using the National Education Longitudinal Study of 1988 survey of eighth graders. Three measures of teacher-student relationships were used. One assessed whether students got along with teachers and whether teachers showed interest in them; another assessed whether the teaching was good and whether teachers praised or "put down" students; and the third assessed whether students talked to teachers about academic, personal, and career questions or concerns. McPartland found that departmentalization had negative effects on all three measures of teacher-student relationships for middle school adolescents from all socioeconomic levels. Interdisciplinary teaming ameliorated these effects.[4]

Other researchers have also documented deterioration in teacher-student relationships after the transition to junior high school. Consistent with McPartland's findings, Berndt and Hawkins (1988) found that students who entered a more traditional junior high perceived their teachers as less supportive than their teachers from the last year of elementary school. In contrast, those who moved to a team-taught, less traditional school perceived their teachers as equally supportive. Feldlaufer, Midgley, and Eccles's (1988) sample of middle-class European-American students reported that their mathematics teachers after the transition to middle school cared less about them, were less friendly, and graded them less fairly than their counterparts prior to the transition. In one of the few studies that included a substantial number of minority adolescents, Hirsch and Rapkin (1987) found that students reported decreasing positive reactions to teachers over a one-year period spanning the end of the last year in elementary school through the end of the first year in junior high.

Consistent with these studies, in her longitudinal study of the transition to middle school among urban youth, Estrada (1996b) found a drastic decline in students' perceptions of teacher support between elementary and middle school. In elementary school most students reported seeking and receiving satisfactory support from their teachers, particularly emotional support and informational support for learning. In contrast, by the end of the first year of middle school students could be described as unsatisfied with the support they received; their reported frequency of seeking social support from teachers was quite low. There was a significant decline in frequency of and satisfaction with support between the spring of the last year in elementary school and the late fall of the first year of middle school, then another significant decline by the following spring. After the initial adjustment to middle school, students may view teachers as even less accessible, and their satisfaction with teacher support appears to go from bad to worse.

Our interpretation of these results is layered. We know propinquity makes joint activity more likely but does not guarantee it, and that joint activity accompanied by dialogue is the more proximal determinant of affinities. Although propinquity with a greater number of teachers is increased with departmentalization, it involves brief contact with many students, thus placing some very real constraints on the possibilities of relationship development (e.g., Braddock and McPartland 1993). Opportunities for joint activity and shared communication with teachers over meaningful academic tasks diminish. Although the latter may not be a necessary part of departmentalization, it appears to be a common condition in middle school. Both middle school teachers and students appear to view the school culture as more performance focused and less task focused than their elementary school counterparts (see Midgley, Anderman, and Hicks 1995 for a thorough discussion of this topic). The focus on individual performance appears to permeate instructional practice, assessment, and recognition in middle school, where teachers also tend to emphasize control and discipline and to provide fewer opportunities for student decision making and autonomy. This is particularly inappropriate because middle school students are entering a developmental stage of heightened needs for autonomy, greater cognitive capacity, and greater social maturity.

In our view, then, the typical middle school's departmental organization and conventional teachers' roles conspire to produce undesirable and unnecessary patterns of instructional activity. Compared to elementary school, the roles for teachers and students are narrowed; there are fewer opportunities for engaging in multiple roles; there are more individual goals, products, and performances; and power is less shared in instructional activities. These conditions are not conducive to developing teacher-student affinities.

Teacher-Student Relationships and Academic and Social Excellence

Teacher-student relationships and their qualities make a difference to the academic and social functioning of children and adolescents. The available evidence indicates that the quality of teacher-student relationships makes a difference to students' achievement-related performance, behaviors, attitudes, and motivations. In a study of kindergartners that examined teacher-child relationships, Birch and Ladd (1997) found that students whom teachers viewed as more dependent tended to perform more poorly academically, have more negative attitudes toward school, and engage the school environment less positively. Students with whom teachers reported conflictual relationships also tended to perform more poorly in school, have more negative attitudes toward, and engage the school environment less positively. Teachers tended to rate these students as liking school less, avoiding school more, being less self-directed, and being less likely to accept teachers' authority and to comply with classroom rules and responsibilities. In contrast, students with whom teachers reported more closeness tended to perform better academically, liked school more, and were more self-directed.

The quality of teacher-student relationships is also implicated in future school functioning. In a longitudinal study, a positive relationship with a kindergarten teacher was associated with higher levels of competence behaviors and lower levels of problem behaviors by the end of first grade than was predicted on the basis of adjustment early in the kindergarten year (Pianta, Steinberg, and Rollins 1995). A conflictual teacher-student relationship was strongly associated with a downward trend in adjustment. Students who were initially at high risk for special education referral or retention, but who were not referred or retained, had less conflictual, closer, more positive relationships with their kindergarten teachers. Conversely, their counterparts who were referred or retained had more conflictual, less close, more negative relationships with their kindergarten teachers.

The evidence from studies of older students is similar. In a study of secondary schools, students reported that caring, empathic, supportive relationships with teachers fostered in them positive attitudes toward school and themselves as students (Lucas, Henze, and Donato 1990).

Midgley, Feldlaufer, and Eccles (1989) found that changes across the transition to junior high in students' perceptions of their teachers' supportiveness were related to changes in their valuing of mathematics. Using a measure of teacher support that focused on caring, friendliness, and fairness, these researchers found that when young adolescents moved from elementary school teachers they perceived to be low in support to junior high teachers they perceived to be high in support, they reported higher levels of intrinsic valuing of mathematics. In contrast, these adolescents reported sharp declines in both their intrinsic valuing of and perceived usefulness of mathematics when they moved from elementary teachers they perceived to be high in support to junior high teachers they perceived to be low in support. In the latter group, declines were more pronounced for low-achieving students than for high-achieving students.

Similarly, in a study of suburban European-American middle school students, Goodenow (1993) found that teacher support (i.e., a sense of being included, liked, and respected) was consistently, positively associated with students' expectancies of success and valuing of English, mathematics, and science. Fraser and Fisher (1982) found a positive association between teacher support and eighth and ninth graders' enjoyment of and leisure interest in science. Teacher support was also positively related to students' ability to generate scientific conclusions and generalizations. Trickett and Moos (1974) found that teacher support was positively related to high school students' academic interest and feeling of security in the classroom.

Finally, in her study of the transition to middle school, Estrada (1996b) found that students who were more satisfied with the support they received from teachers in the spring prior to the transition tended to have higher grades in the late fall of the first year of middle school. Similarly, students who were more satisfied with the support they received from teachers in the late fall of the first year of middle school tended to have higher grades and to be rated by teachers as better behaved in the following spring. Students who were more satisfied with the support they received from teachers in the spring of the first year of middle school also tended to rate themselves as better behaved and as having better attitudes toward school.

Conclusion

Taken as a whole, the literature reviewed indicates that in schools and classrooms where the patterns of instructional activity afford opportunities for propinquity, joint productive activity, and dialogue among teachers and students, both students and teachers report better-quality relationships, and the quality of these relationships is related to students' achievement of academic and social excellence. When teachers and students participate in activity settings that afford opportunities to work and talk collaboratively over meaningful instructional tasks with relatively small numbers of students, teachers and students can come to know one another and teachers can assess and assist their students more responsively and effectively. Such a pattern of activity also provides students with more opportunities to exhibit their present competencies to teachers and to acquire new ones. Finally, meaningful joint activity and dialogue provide not only the medium in which teachers assist students (and students assist each other), make decisions, and create products, but also the medium in which values are created. Therefore, joint activity and shared communication become the medium for developing intersubjectivity about the particular endeavor and more broadly about the larger shared enterprise of school learning. As intersubjectivity increases, so does the potential for the development of affinity.

In this chapter we have delineated how patterns of instructional activity help to create peer relationships and teacher-student relationships and how those relationships matter to the academic and social functioning of students. We have outlined how certain patterns of activity are more likely to create the conditions for Excellence, Fairness, Inclusion, and Harmony and how others are not. We also have shown what it is possible to achieve when teachers work against the Great Cycle of Social Sorting for at least a substantial proportion of class time. In the next chapter we address culture as another important force to consider in the creation of effective patterns of instructional activity.

Notes

1. Propinquity is also affected by other school conditions, including architectural features, equipment and supplies, and demographic factors (Epstein 1989). We focus our discussion on those conditions over which teachers have more direct control.

2. As discussed in Chapter 2, patterns of instructional activity also afford or preclude other features of effective pedagogy.

3. It is important to note that the study (Cauce 1986) in which the vast majority of students endorsed school achievement involved low-income, inner-city students attending a school participating in a school- and classroom-level intervention that focused on the development of academic and social competence (see Comer 1980 for a discussion of the Yale Child Study Center Primary Prevention School Project).

4. McPartland found, however, that 95 percent of public school eighth graders attend highly departmentalized schools, and that only one in three of these students is taught by teachers working in teams.

5 Culture and Instructional Activity

In Chapters 3 and 4 we emphasized the dynamics of social organization in the community, in schools, and in classrooms. We reviewed evidence that social class—income and education—as well as race, ethnicity, language, and neighborhood tend to replicate themselves in students' affinity patterns and crowds. The Harmony of intersubjectivity between friends acts like a magnetic force to draw friends together. Without some counterforce, the social order and relationship patterns are imported into classrooms. Teachers can either choose to allow exiting affinities to reappear in school or design classroom activities to establish new and more varied affinities, which ultimately promote Excellence, Fairness, Inclusion, and Harmony for all.

In this chapter we consider another force that determines the nature of instructional activity, both in and outside the classroom. Like the community structures of race and social class, culture provides a pattern of habit and unreflective action patterns. And like the affinities discussed previously, cultural patterns tend to replicate themselves in classrooms. While teachers may often effectively use them, these patterns will sometimes need to be countered to produce new learning.

As we described in Chapter 3, sociocultural theory suggests that there will be more Harmony in our interactions with those who are like us because when people are more similar (e.g., in terms of race, nationality, social class, gender, or profession) it is more likely that they have participated in common or similar activity settings, which in turn leads to intersubjectivity.

Conversely, when we find ourselves in activity and conversation with those who are unlike us across a number of dimensions, then (at least initially) we often find that those interactions are less harmonious, until

From Our Files

Xuan and Lily, two first-generation Chinese-American women, met at the university and instantly there was more Harmony between them than either had experienced with other same-age peers who are not Chinese. Although the women grew up in different parts of the country, they were comfortable around one another and discovered they had similar values and social repertoires. These common ways of thinking and acting were likely acquired while interacting with other Chinese-Americans in their homes and communities.

new understandings are co-constructed through interaction and intersubjectivity and Harmony are established.

Thus, Harmony is affected by diversity, and schools are becoming ever more diverse. Recent school reform and policy that emphasizes inclusion of all students, regardless of race, ethnicity, socioeconomic status, disability, or achievement, is contributing to this diversity, but patterns of migration also contribute, as more people migrate to urban and western centers. Each day it is less likely that teachers and their students will all share the same cultural and linguistic communities.

What does this mean for teachers who are concerned about the patterns of instructional activity that create the conditions for Excellence, Fairness, Inclusion, and Harmony in their classrooms? Schools can capitalize on the diversity of their students and faculty if diversity is viewed as a resource, and academic excellence can be enhanced. By drawing on students' rich and diverse backgrounds teachers can connect school to their students' lives. In addition, when students engage in joint productive activity with those who are less like them (including the teacher), they are challenged with different perspectives, different ways of interacting, and other new information. Such a situation is potentially education at its best because it allows for the teaching of complex thinking.

In this chapter we discuss specific ways in which cultural influences may be considered in creating effective patterns of activity. The activity settings in which students have participated in their families and communities, the knowledge and capacities they have developed, and the attendant values and expectations may or may not be congruent with those classrooms of the common tradition. We discuss these phenomena in terms of four crucial dimensions of activity settings along which cultures exhibit sharp differences. These dimensions are (1) individualism/collectivism; (2)

role expectations and their enactment in school activity settings, with special attention to teacher/student roles and gender roles; (3) power distance in activity settings; and (4) the use of different language genres and codes in activity settings, especially those structured for learning. An understanding of these dimensions can assist the classroom teacher in making decisions about who works with whom and in the design of activity settings. It will also help the teacher predict the kinds of disharmonious interactions that may first result when students are sorted into more heterogeneous groups.

Culture and Expectations

Culture refers to the set of ideas, beliefs, assumptions, and norms that are widely shared among a group of people and that serve to guide their behavior (Brislin 1993; Goodenough 1971). Brislin (1993, 1994) points out that people do not often discuss elements of their culture and are thus ill prepared to do so. In sociocultural theory, this difficulty might be explained in terms of cultural knowledge being so internalized or "automatic" that it is relatively resistant to attempts to force it to the surface of consciousness and verbalization (Vygotsky 1978). For the most part, if we spend our time interacting with people who share our culture, we seldom need to think about our cultural values and expectations. It is when these values and expectations clash with someone else's that our culture resurfaces and is most visible (Brislin 1993). Often, we underestimate culture's influence on behavior until we are in situations in which the contrast to another's thinking or behavior becomes apparent.

In a school context, cultural clashes may occur when students do not share the same culture as their teachers or peers, or when their home culture does not reflect the values or norms of the school. A teacher who is quite successful working with students from one cultural community may be surprised and frustrated when the same teaching strategies, interaction patterns, and activities do not work with students from another.

Of course, we must be cautious about stereotyping. Any description of a "culture" can only refer to the central tendencies of its members. In any culture, there are enormous individual variations. There will always be individuals from any culture who no doubt look much more like the members of another group than their own. For example, a number of children in Jody's class were very comfortable looking directly at her when she spoke to them individually. In teaching interactions, there is no higher prescription than being responsive to the specific student. But the design of instructional activity also deals with groups. We offer the evidence for cultural variations as general guidelines, a set of issues any teacher can investigate with profit.

From Our Files

Jody, a teacher new to Hawai'i from New York, was assigned to teach third grade in a rural elementary school on the island of Oa'hu. Early in the school year, Jody was frustrated and confused. Often when she spoke to her students individually, and especially if it involved a reprimand for misbehavior, Jody found that certain children avoided direct eye contact with her. This was different from the students she had taught in New York, and Jody thought the students were rude and inattentive. After a few weeks, Jody asked Michelle, a longtime teacher at the school, why this was happening. Michelle told Jody that in Hawai'i local students might show deference to an authority figure by looking down when that person was talking. Jody's requests to the students to "Please look at me when I am talking to you" was in conflict with a local cultural norm.

Do cultural differences between students, and between teachers and students, make a difference? They need not, as we will see. But unattended, they can create unintended mischief. The real hazard is that cultural differences may preclude effective assistance and guidance. Teaching is assisting performance; assistance occurs in interaction best achieved through joint productive activity; interaction requires mutual understanding; and teaching requires a good measure of intersubjectivity.

Individualism and Collectivism

Classroom activity will be influenced by the expectations, goals, and values that teachers and students bring to it. Rogoff (1990) emphasized the importance of considering the context and nature of the task demanded of students:

> The importance of understanding the variations in what children are expected to learn in different cultures is linked to the assumptions ... that thinking and learning are functional efforts by individuals to solve specific problems of importance in their culture, and that developmental courses vary in their goals rather than having a universal endpoint to which all should aspire. Thus ... it is essential to take into account the particular problems that children are attempting to solve and their importance in the culture (p. 116).

One of the most prominent cultural differences that displays itself in the school setting is the dimension of individualism versus collectivism.

Cultural groups differ in the attributes they consider to be indicators of success. In Western cultures it is often assumed that one succeeds alone, often in competition with others, through hard work and by making use of one's innate abilities. Non-Western cultures, on the other hand, may not equate success with individual achievement. This may be especially true if winning requires competition (so that one's so-called success is another person's loss or failure).

Researchers across a number of disciplines suggest that cultures can be considered relatively more individualist or collectivist (e.g., Bochner 1994; Gudykunst, Yoon, and Nishida 1987; Hofstede 1980; Kim et al. 1996; Kluckhohn and Strodtbeck 1961; Lebra 1976, 1994; Tata and Leong 1994; Triandis et al. 1988). Individualist cultures emphasize the rights and opportunities of the individual: It is assumed that individuals act in ways to protect their own personal interests and to achieve personal goals. By contrast, the personal goals of those from collectivist cultures are often subordinate to the interests of the collective or "in-group" (extended family, school, or work organization). The collective, in turn, is assumed to protect the interests of its members (Hofstede 1980, 1986). Members of individualist cultures may also belong to various in-groups; however, their in-group affiliations are both greater in number and less stable, resulting in relatively less support and security (Triandis et al. 1988).

Whether students come from relatively individualist or collectivist cultures influences the kinds of goals they construct in classroom activity settings. Their goals certainly interact with the goal structures and the systems of reward distribution that teachers create. Students from collectivist cultures will tend to construct goals that are collectivist and will do well when activity settings are structured with such goals in mind, whereas the reverse will be true for students from individualist cultures.

Overall, U.S. society is strongly individualist (Greenfield 1994; Hofstede 1980; Markus and Kitayama 1991; Triandis et al. 1988). In fact, Hofstede (1980) found that of the fifty nations he studied, the United States

From Our Files

A successful and worthwhile life, according to co-author Yamauchi's Japanese grandmother, is one spent helping others. If you succeed by Western standards in getting good grades or a good job, you are lucky; but if you spend your time helping other people, then you are truly a good person.

was considered the most individualist. However, within the United States certain subcultures, for example, Native Americans and immigrant groups from Asia, Mexico, and Latin America, are considered more collectivist because of the influence of a more collective orientation in their "home" cultures. Research indicates that European-American children are more competitive and less cooperative than Mexican-American (Avellar and Kagan 1976; Kagan, Zahn, and Gealy 1977; Knight, Kagan, and Buriel 1982), Cuban-American (Alvarez and Pader 1979), Native American (Brown 1980), Chinese-American (Cook and Chi 1984), and Chinese National children (Domino 1992). African-American students also tend to be more collectivist rather than individualist (Foster 1992; Graybill 1997; Oyserman, Gant, and Ager 1995; Sleeter and Grant 1988).

In addition, there is a consistent pattern among children from more traditional, rural, and communal subcultures to display more cooperative behavior than do children from urban areas. In their review of this literature, Mussen and Eisenberg-Berg (1977) reported that children from Mexican villages are more cooperative than those from urban Mexican areas or Mexican Americans; children from the Israeli kibbutz are more cooperative than those from urban Israel; rural Colombians are more cooperative than urban Colombians; and rural New Zealand Maori children are more cooperative than New Zealand, European, and urban Maori children. Other studies indicate that those who move from collectivist cultures to more individualist ones, as do many U.S. immigrants, begin to adopt the individualist orientations of the dominant society. Immigrants are more likely to show individualist tendencies the longer they remain in that culture and the more they participate in the dominant culture's activities. For example, Canadian Indians who attended an integrated school became more acculturated into the dominant white Canadian culture and were also found to be more competitive than their peers who maintained more traditional Indian ways of life (Miller and Thomas 1972; Thomas 1975).

Students may have difficulty if the goals of classroom activities do not fit with what they are accustomed to in their homes and communities. For example, if individual effort is rewarded, children from more collectivist cultures may modify the rules so that they can still work toward collective goals (Ciofalo 1994; Miller and Thomas 1972; Mussen and Eisenberg-Berg 1977).

Ciofalo (1994) asked a group of Tzotziles Indian preschool children in rural Mexico which of them would want to go first to play a game. Although she had intended to solicit individual volunteers, children who volunteered always named themselves and several others. Similarly, during a pretend game, the children changed the rules by inventing multiple heroines and villains. Characters that were typically portrayed by one individual (Cinderella or the prince) were played by many (Ciofalo 1994).

Ciofalo's study exemplifies that children from collectivist cultures often work together to do what in more individualist cultures is done alone. Hmong students exhibit concern for a fellow student who does not know the answer, and they naturally will tell him the right answer so the group can move forward (Lamb 1998). A collective accommodation to a more individualist system might also result in students "taking turns" to help each other.

Traditional Native Hawai'ian culture is often considered collectivist (Benham and Heck 1998; Pukui, Haertig, and Lee 1972). Native Hawaiian children, in more individualist, teacher-led classrooms, responded with low levels of attention to the teacher and course work and high levels of attention seeking from peers (D'Amato 1988; Gallimore, Boggs, and Jordan 1974; MacDonald and Gallimore 1971). D'Amato's analysis of Hawaiian children's behavior in the classroom and on the playground indicated that the children cooperated with their peers to resist the teacher and the school establishment: Children reinforced each other in attempts to sabotage the teacher's efforts, and this contributed to a developing sense of in-group support. The establishment of in-groups (informal playground gangs) promoted the avoidance of serious conflicts (D'Amato 1988) but was not very functional in terms of academic goals. The Kamehameha Early Elementary Program (KEEP) reorganized classrooms into peer-oriented, small-group activity to be more culturally compatible with the home culture of the Native Hawaiian students it served. Hawaiian students in KEEP classrooms evidenced higher student on-task rates and cooperative behavior with peers directed toward school-related goals (Tharp and Gallimore 1988).

Foster's (1992) review of successful African-American classrooms suggested that one of the common features of these classrooms was the teacher's emphasis on collectivist goals. Student interactions were "marked by social equality, egalitarianism, and mutuality stemming

From Our Files

A group of graduate students from Southeast Asia dealt with the individualism of American graduate school by taking turns helping each other with their "individual" projects. One weekend the group focused on Jang's research project, helping her with the library search and in analyzing the data. The next week the whole group redirected their energies to getting Nong's project organized.

from group, not individual, ethos ... " (Foster 1992, p. 308). In addition, cooperation, rather than competition, was reinforced.

Many studies of Native American Indian children also illustrate a preference for small-group problem-solving structures in school over individual work assignments (Barnhardt 1982; Coburn and Nelson 1989; Leith and Slentz 1984; Philips 1972; Yamauchi 1994). A study of Native Americans who succeeded in graduating from high school indicated that peer support and group activities, such as sports and clubs, were important to these students, and that the students usually achieved more in these domains than in the academic domain (Coburn and Nelson 1989).

Philips (1972) compared the behavior of the Native American students and non–Native American students at the off-reservation secondary schools and found that the Native American (Warm Springs) students participated more in activity settings organized as small peer groups than in the whole-group, teacher-oriented ones. She also noted that in these small-group settings, Native American children, more than their white counterparts, became more competitive between groups:

> It is in such contexts that Indian students become most fully involved in what they are doing, concentrating completely on their work until it is completed, talking a great deal to one another within the group, and competing, with explicit remarks to that effect, with the other groups. Non-Indian students take more time "getting organized," disagree and argue more regarding how to go about a task, rely more heavily on appointed chair for arbitration and decision-making, and show less interest, at least explicitly, in competing with other groups from their class (Philips 1972, p. 379).

Triandis et al. (1988) and Mann, Radford, and Kanagawa (1985) pointed out that individuals from collectivist societies use very different rules when dealing with in- and out-group members: Toward in-group members, they are very cooperative; toward outsiders, they are not. The Indian children in Philips's study who became very competitive toward other groups may have aligned themselves with their own classroom-constructed in-groups.

Perhaps because schools of the common tradition have generally tended to emphasize individual rather than collective goals, most of the research in this area has focused on the experience of collectivist students dealing with individualist classroom activities. We were unable to find research that directly addresses the converse; that is, the experience of individualist students in more collectivist activity settings. Research on cooperative learning, however, does suggest that mainstream U.S. students need assistance in learning to work well in cooperative groups. The research by Cohen and her colleagues (Cohen 1994a; Cohen and Lotan 1997) indicates that without preparation for group work, students often encounter difficulties in small groups. In many cases, a few students tend to dominate the discussion and activity. Cohen (1994a) suggests that the best preparation for group work establishes new norms for participation in small-group activity. Specifically, students need to learn to be responsive to the needs of their group:

> Responsiveness to the needs of the group is a skill required of any kind of cooperative task. If students are oblivious to the problems experienced by peers, the group will not function properly, the group product will be inferior, and the interaction will not provide the necessary assistance for all its members. It is necessary that students learn how to become aware of the needs of other members of the group and to feel responsible for helping them for the sake of the group product (Cohen 1994a, p. 42).

This sounds exactly like the norm of a collectivist society. It is possible that mainstream U.S. students' difficulty working in small groups stems from their tendency to approach activity with a more individualist orientation. That is hardly surprising because schools of the common tradition provide thirteen successive years of individualist training. In preschool and the beginning phases of kindergarten, collectivist repertoires appear in mainstream children largely depending on family size.

The discourse patterns that exist in a classroom activity setting may also characterize it as more individualist or collectivist. Activity settings that can be considered more collectivist encourage co-narrative discourse, build group understanding and consensus, and maintain group Harmony (usually by not expressing negative emotions or argumentative positions). Those activity settings that emphasize sole narration and the individual expression of one's opinions and differences can be considered more individualist. The collectivist "talk story" discourse present in KEEP classroom activity settings was compatible with the collectivist nature of the Native Hawaiian culture. Under these circumstances, Hawaiian children participated readily, finding comfort in the overlapping discourse pattern of their home Creole (Boggs 1985; Tharp and Gallimore 1988).

Students from collectivist cultures may not want to cause conflict by appearing more intelligent than or in other ways superior to others in the group. American Indian students may avoid displaying their academic competence to maintain equality with peers, a display of the humility that is valued among many Native American cultures (Swisher and Deyhle 1987). When Haleck (1996) interviewed Samoan high school students about the "ideal students" in their school, the students noted that those who were considered ideal usually knew the answers to questions that were posed in class but did not "show off" by trying to answer first.

In collectivist cultures group Harmony is also maintained by the guarding of emotional display. Among individuals from collectivist cultures there is less use of direct verbal communication and more emphasis on indirect and nonverbal communication. In an emotional situation, individuals from collectivist cultures tend to respond nonverbally, whereas those from more individualist cultures tend to use verbal responses (Gudykunst and Ting-Toomey 1988). Yamauchi (1993) interviewed two Native American school administrators who oversaw the education of 1,750 (mostly Zuni) Native American children. The two administrators commented on the use of nonverbal means of classroom management, noting that while some teachers (often non-Natives) raised their voices, a more successful and less conflict-ridden approach involved conveying nonverbal cues to the children. One of the administrators illustrated this point by contrasting the way he and a non-Zuni administrator dealt with children at a high school in their community: "I would hear this commotion going on in the hallway, and I would go around the corner to see what was going on. Kids would be arguing with him.... They would agitate him to a point where he would just lose his temper and start yelling at them, and they would yell back at him. They would just stand there doing that. As soon as I would come around the corner and we would make the eye contact, they would stop talking" (Yamauchi 1993, p. 110).

The Zuni children and parents in the study also agreed that a loud and argumentative manner was offensive and that it was culturally inappropriate for adults and children to argue.

Okabe (1983) explained that those from collectivist cultures do not trust direct verbal communication. Although members of collectivist cultures will tend to use nonverbal over verbal forms of communication, even nonverbal displays are used more in individualist cultures than in collectivist ones (LaFrance and Mayo 1978; Ramsey 1979). In classrooms, students from collectivist cultures may not expect to nor in fact be comfortable with speaking up in large or whole-group settings. For example, many local students from Hawai'i often shy away from talking in large groups but interact freely in small-group settings.

From Our Files

Japanese-American college students in Hawai'i reported that the main difference between their experience as students growing up in the Hawai'i public schools (where most of their teachers were Japanese American) and life at the university was that the culture of the university was more mainland "haole" (Caucasian), and this difference was most apparent in that students were supposed to talk in class (Yamauchi and O'Neil 1994). At the new faculty orientations at the University of Hawai'i a major topic is the reluctance of local students to speak out in large-group classes.

Our point is not that students from relatively individualist cultures necessarily participate readily or thrive under whole-group instruction. Recall our discussion of the diminished possibilities of propinquity, joint activity, and dialogue under such a pattern of activity. Rather, our point is that because whole-group instruction relies on individual, verbal contributions, there may be a greater disjuncture for students from relatively collectivist cultures that do not emphasize these means of expression.

Opportunities for success for all U.S. students are predicated on both individual and collective capacities: capacities to work independently, to communicate directly, and to compete with others in academic and employment domains as well as capacities to collaborate, to function as team members, and to work toward the greater good of a collective enterprise, be it a classroom, a research laboratory, or a business. Therefore, teachers need to assist all students to work under both individualist and collectivist conditions, bearing in mind that when the conditions vary from students' cultural patterns, they will need more assistance and may even display some resistance (D'Amato 1988). We cover these issues more fully in Chapter 6.

Finally, the practices of educators from collectivist cultures also reflect the tendency to emphasize equality and group cohesion rather than competition and individual differences. Tracking and ability grouping are very individualist notions. An American researcher studying preschool in Japan observed a Japanese preschooler, Hiroko, constantly misbehaving after he finished his work before others. When the researcher later asked Japanese educators whether Hiroko might be "gifted" and therefore bored with the activities presented, her Japanese colleagues disagreed with this interpretation. They disagreed that Hiroko could be more intelligent than other children; in fact, they worried that he was less so because an intelligent child would not act this way (Tobin, Wu, and Davidson 1989).

The Japanese do, of course, recognize that children are born with unequal abilities and that some children have special gifts, but Japanese society in general and teachers in particular view the goal of education (and perhaps especially of primary and preschool education) as evening out, rather than sorting out or further accentuating, these ability differences. One Japanese preschool teacher responded to a description of programs for gifted children in U.S. preschools by saying, "How sad that by age three or four a child might already be labeled as having less chance for success than some of his classmates" (Tobin, Wu, and Davidson 1989, p. 25).

Role Expectations in the Classroom

Culture influences the patterns of classroom activity also through variations in role expectations. Our cultural experiences provide us with models for how to think and behave while performing the different roles of our lives. We move among these roles, changing costumes and scripts, so that at different times one plays the different roles of parent, child, teacher, student, boss, or lover. Culture also influences what we expect from others playing their roles. So when two or more people come to the same activity setting with different cultural expectations about the roles they are there to perform, "culture clashes" may result (Brislin 1993)— disharmonies laden with misunderstanding and confusion. In this section, we focus on cultural variations surrounding the roles of teacher and student and on variations in gender roles, and we consider how these role expectations affect patterns of instructional activity in classrooms.

An examination of the literature on teacher and student roles leads us to believe that some of the cultural differences in classrooms may be explained by differential experiences with formal education. Formal education refers to teaching and learning as it occurs in schools and related institutions (and here we specifically refer to Western schooling). Informal education refers to teaching and learning that occurs in the home and community. Although the two kinds of instructional activity have much in common, there are striking differences, particularly concerning the formal roles of teachers and students (Rogoff 1990; Scribner and Cole 1973).

The Role of Teacher

In school, the teacher is usually an individual who has expertise in the domain that is being taught, is expected to understand what needs to be learned, and will create activities so that students will gain those skills and knowledge. Although not always as evident, much of the formal aspect of power in classrooms rests with teachers by virtue of the authority given to them by the school system. (A full discussion of power in the classroom follows below.)

In many informal domains, the role of teacher is often diffused across several adults or proficient cultural members (Stairs 1994). For example, a child in a Pueblo Indian village would learn to make pottery by growing up within a family of potters, observing and receiving guidance from many family members, including parents, older siblings, and grandparents (Vallo 1988). In school, children who are not accustomed to one individual as the teacher may be more accustomed to seeking help from many and might often turn to peers, especially if they are used to seeking guidance from siblings. These children may need extra assistance to learn what the role of the teacher is and to be guided in gaining the most from this new person in their lives.

In the KEEP program, young Hawaiian children were taught that the teacher played an adult role that was different from the other adults that they knew. For many of these Hawaiian and part-Hawaiian children, adults were not viewed as the appropriate person to approach if instructions were unclear. At home, especially concerning the day-to-day running of the household, the informal role of teacher was often delegated to older siblings (Boggs 1985; Jordan 1978). With this understanding, KEEP developers worked to communicate this new role expectation—teacher as helpful adult—to the children in school. Similarly, when teachers design variation in the activity settings in their classroom, including small-group discussions or other joint activity with the teacher, they will need to assess students carefully. Are they, like the Hawaiian students in the KEEP studies, not as comfortable working with an individual adult as the authority? Or, like some Asian and Latino students, reluctant to engage authority in dialogue due to respect? In either case, teachers can expect that multicultural classrooms will contain students who will need more assistance in relating to the teacher in joint activity.

Another difference between informal and formal learning settings regarding the role of the teacher concerns the teacher's prior relationship to the student. In urban schools, teachers are usually not related to their students. In cases where parents are teachers at the school where their children are students, care is taken so that parents are not teachers of their own children. When this arrangement is not possible (in the formal protocols of school), the roles of teacher/student take precedence over the role of parent and child.

Informal instructional activity differs sharply. If we are learning to drive, weave, cook, or ride a horse we do not expect our teachers to be strangers, and we do not pretend that we are unrelated. In an informal learning setting, the teacher is most likely someone that the student already knows and has a prior relationship with, such as siblings, grandparents, close neighbors or family friends, or village elder. It is largely because of these prior relationships that the students interact with their teachers in the ways that they do, and it is the roles of these "teachers" in

---

From Our Files

Lynn was the daughter of her high school history teacher. Because Mrs. Anderson taught the only advanced-placement U.S. history class, it was not possible to arrange for Lynn to be in another class that year. In class, Lynn called her mother "Mrs. Anderson" like all her peers did, and Mrs. Anderson treated Lynn like any other student. The other students found it funny that the two used such formality with each other, but they were correctly performing the roles in that context.

the students' ordinary lives (outside this learning situation) that shape their activity as teachers. In many informal settings, a younger member of the family apprentices to an older member, for example a grandmother. The respect and status given to the teacher is related to her role as the child's grandmother. In terms of learning and relationship development, who the teacher is is as important as what she teaches (Scribner and Cole 1973). This situation is very different from the way that we think of schoolteachers.

In some cultures, notably those of Asia, the role of the teacher may lie somewhere between that of relative and stranger. Parents look to the teacher as the authority regarding their child's progress in school and expect teachers to keep them informed regarding problems as well as improvement. Cheon, McClelland, and Plihal (1995) found that Korean immigrant parents were confused at parent-teacher conferences when the teacher only mentioned positive things and did not discuss the child's problems. The Korean parents interpreted this behavior as the U.S. teacher being irresponsible, not providing the assistance needed by the student, and emphasizing self-esteem over academics and ability. One mother commented:

> I feel American teachers are less responsible than Korean teachers in some way. While American teachers didn't want to talk about negative things, Korean teachers told parents what the problem was in order to be corrected. American teachers didn't talk about negative things unless he or she had a really big problem. So I have to bring up my children's problems when I feel those problems. Otherwise, teachers always said, "good, good, no problem" (Cheon, McClelland, and Plihal 1995, p. 9).

Cultural differences regarding the teacher's role affect instructional activity patterns in classrooms because they determine much of what students and teachers expect from each other in school. These expectations determine how teachers place themselves in the various activity settings of their classrooms, how much responsibility and authority they give themselves, and the ways in which they develop their "presence." In addition, cultural variation requires that teachers create activity settings that develop the role expectations, for both teacher and students, that a quality education requires. That is, when designing activity settings—both to capitalize on the cultural tendencies of students and to teach them new ways of relating—teachers will need to be explicit about the role performances that are required. In Chapter 6 we describe explicit activities for developing shared expectations for activity in the classroom community. But in addition to these class-wide patterns, teachers must be ready to provide individual assistance to students in settings where the roles of teacher or student are less familiar. Increasing students' social repertoires in these ways promotes educational excellence by expanding students' knowledge about and familiarity with relating to others in a variety of settings.

The Role of the Student

Parallel to teacher role expectations are cultural variations in the role expectations for student or learner. In school, students are usually found in same-age groups, are junior to the teacher in age or experience, and are usually expected to defer to the teacher's expectations and wishes. Blumenfeld and her colleagues describe the role of the student in school as twofold: becoming a scholar and becoming a citizen. They point out that in addition to learning the "stuff of school" or academic content, students are required to understand and follow procedural expectations (Blumenfeld et al. 1983). Among other things, students need to know when and how to talk; what and how to read; how and what to write; how to accomplish tasks alone and with other children; how and when to sit quietly and listen without bothering their neighbors; and how and when to speak up, ask questions, and/or express themselves in a large group (Blumenfeld et al. 1983; Dyson and Genishi 1991).

How do children come to learn these role performances and expectations? Teacher interactions with students concerning their role as students in school are largely reactive rather than prescriptive; they consist for the most part of reacting to violations rather than proactively establishing role expectations:

> The teacher is a manager who mainly reacts, and reacts to things she does not like. Those things are mostly violations of the procedures that probably must be maintained if the show is to go on. Relatively rarely, and primarily when spurred by a negative event, is the teacher prompted to provide further socializing information involving her expectations. . . . The student is essentially a socializee who absorbs on-the-job experience geared to passive citizenship in an ongoing institution (Blumenfeld et al. 1983, p. 186).

Students somehow must learn the role of school learner and school citizen, which may be difficult if the expectations are different in their accustomed informal learning settings. In school, part of the student role is to ask questions of the teacher when something is unclear. Questioning is also considered a part of the inquiry process in which students are expected to engage. Whether a student comes from a more individualist or a collectivist culture may influence whether asking questions of the teacher is comfortable and expected. As we discussed earlier, collectivist cultures do not emphasize open expression or otherwise drawing attention to oneself. In many cultures and informal learning settings, it is more appropriate to observe in silence rather than to ask questions of the teacher. Appropriate and expected student behavior in these cases is to not ask questions but to learn through observation and demonstration (Rhodes 1989; Suina and Smolkin 1991; Tharp, Dalton, and Yamauchi 1994). While individualist-oriented students may be quite comfortable—even aggressive—in questioning teachers, this is not appropriate in every activity setting. In Chapter 6 we discuss in detail the needs of the entire community of the classroom for clarity, assistance, and preparation in the performance of the various roles required in the different activities of effective education.

In school, part of the student's role is to function as a member of a fairly large group of same-age mates. This means that once in school propinquity is based on birth date rather than on family membership or family acquaintance. Grouping by age also implies a general attempt to group by developmental or skill level. Typically, sorting proceeds next by ability either within or across classrooms. At the start of each new school year, most experienced seventh-grade teachers have certain expectations about what their students will be like. Although they will expect variations within the group, in general these teachers have a sense of the average, above-average, and below-average seventh grader and design their classroom activity settings accordingly.

The point is that teachers expect their students to be somewhat homogenous when it comes to age-related skills and experiences. This kind of sorting is unlike many instructional activity settings outside of school. In most informal learning settings, participants are not grouped by age or skill level. Rather, participants represent a wider range of ages and skills grouped together by kinship, interest, or other wider community ties. When Native Hawaiian children work together to clean the house, they work together as siblings and cousins (Jordan 1978), so it would be unlikely that they would be working within (and learning from) a group of only same-age peers. Susan Philips (1972) observed that upper-elementary Warms Springs Indian children tended to play and maintain friendships with large groups of children from different classes and grade levels. This contrasted with non-Native students of the same age who tended to have just one or two friends from the same class. A Zuni administrator once opined that it would be better to use the already existing and multi-age clan system that exists in Zuni to group students for instruction rather than grouping students by grade level and then calling those grades "clans" as they did at the reservation school. There is a national movement toward multi-age grouping of students in schools to reap potential academic and social benefits (Nye 1993; Pratt 1986; Stone 1995).

Gender Roles

Cultures differ in the extent to which male and female role expectations are rigid and differentiated or more flexible and overlapping (Hofstede

1980). Hofstede called this dimension masculinity-femininity and explained that his focus on men's roles, rather than women's, was due to the universality of women bearing and caring for children, which leads to less potential variability of their role. We argue, however, that gender role flexibility for both men and women can be used as a marker for gender role differentiation among different cultures. The cultures Hofstede considered "masculine" were those in which the distinction between men's and women's roles were the most rigid: "They expect men to be assertive, ambitious and competitive, to strive for material success, and to respect whatever is big, strong, and fast. They expect women to serve and to care for the non-material quality of life, for children and for the weak" (Hofstede 1986, p. 308). By contrast, feminine cultures were those in which men were not expected to focus on achievement and strength, and it was acceptable for men to engage in activities considered more traditionally female, such as caring for others. In Hofstede's (1980) analysis, the countries that indicated the most rigid gender roles were Japan, Austria, Venezuela, Mexico, and Switzerland. The United States was also considered somewhat rigid in this respect, but to a lesser extent. Sweden, Norway, Denmark, and the Netherlands were considered flexible regarding gender roles.

From this perspective, boys would be more competitive than girls in cultures where gender roles are more rigid and traditional. Strube (1981) conducted a meta-analysis of ninety-five studies comparing differences in competitiveness between boys and girls in fifteen different cultures. His analysis indicated that the gender differences favoring male competitiveness were not found in all cultures. In three cultures that were classified in Hofstede's analysis as highly rigid, boys were consistently found to be more competitive than girls (European American; Indian subcontinent; Mexican, including Mexican American). Strube's meta-analysis also indicated that in studies of Israeli children, a country classified as more flexible regarding gender roles, girls were consistently more competitive than boys.

More rigid gender roles may affect the harmony of interactions across gender lines. One example of why gender role expectations should be considered in the design of instructional activity comes from the attempt by KEEP researchers to transplant the organization of their reading classes designed for Native Hawaiian children to classrooms for Navajo children in Arizona. The "Hawaiian" KEEP organization involved children working independently in small gender-mixed groups. Navajo children refused to work in gender-mixed groupings. When forced to, they divided the work themselves between boys and girls and worked separately. This is consistent with the gender-divided activity structure of Navajo adult life, an arrangement that is typical of hunting-gathering and pastoral societies, in which assortive mating is ritualized into more ceremonial contact periods (Jordan, Tharp, and Vogt 1985).

The inflexibility of gender roles reported in the United States may help to account for the inequities in school experiences of American males and females (e.g., Gabriel and Smithson 1990; Sadker and Sadker 1986, 1994). Studies in the United States have demonstrated what has been called "female inhibition" or the tendency for adolescent girls to alter their behavior in competitive situations when moving from female to male opponents. When girls change their behavior to compete against boys, they tend to be less successful than when they compete against other girls (Weisfeld et al. 1983). Highly skilled girls tend to exhibit this phenomenon, especially when they compete against less skilled males (Morgan and Mausner 1973; Weisfeld et al. 1983), as do girls with more traditional attitudes about gender roles (Peplau 1976). Female inhibition was also more evident when the task involved athletic competition (Weisfeld, Weisfeld, and Callahan 1982), perhaps because this is considered a more masculine domain. The recent emphasis on female athletics, due to Title IX policy initiatives, may well alter these patterns, as indicated by the explosive popularity among girls of the new women's professional basketball leagues.

We emphasized earlier that individual differences in personality, tastes, and motives exist among those from any cultural background. It is thus important to consider how individual differences interact with larger group (cultural) tendencies. With regard to individual differences and gender roles, one study found that although some U.S. women do exhibit traits more traditionally considered masculine (in this case, dominance), the culturally prescribed roles still appeared. Megargee (1969) measured the personality trait of dominance among college students and arranged her subjects in pairs so that one person was always more dominant than the other. Half of such teams were same-gender pairs and the others were gender mixed. Interaction patterns were studied during the teams' joint problem solving. In same-gender pairs, the more dominant person always took the lead; however, in the mixed-gender groups, the male became the leader even if he was considered the less dominant at the individual level. This study indicates that gender roles (in this case, males as leaders over females) may take precedence over individual behavioral tendencies or traits.

Gender role expectations affect teachers' behavior. Many studies have documented U.S. teachers' (often unconscious) tendencies to promote independence among male students and dependence among females. Teachers praise boys more than girls and give them more attention, encouragement, and criticism (Brody and Evertson 1981; Sadker and Sadker 1986, 1994). If teachers are not talking as often with girls, then they are probably not engaging them as often in Instructional Conversations, talk that challenges their thinking to promote educational excellence. If girls are not participating as fully as their male counterparts, they may not be developing the same intersubjectivities about school and academics as do boys. From elementary to graduate school, female students talk less in class than their male counterparts and report feeling more uncomfortable during classroom interactions (Sadker and Sadker 1986; Treichler and Kramarae 1983).

Sadker and Sadker (1986), who have done extensive research on differential treatment of male and female students in U.S. schools, suggest two possible reasons why males received more attention from teachers than did their female counterparts. First, they point out that the majority of the classrooms they studied were sex segregated and that teachers tended to "gravitate" to the boys' sections and spend more time and attention there. Second, the Sadkers note that boys tended to demand more attention: Boys in both elementary and secondary classrooms were eight times more likely than girls to call out and demand attention. And teachers reacted differently to these demands: "When boys call out, teachers tend to accept their answers. When girls call out, teachers remediate their behavior and advise them to raise their hands. Boys are being trained to be assertive; girls are being trained to be passive—spectators relegated to the sidelines of classroom discussion" (Sadker and Sadker 1986, p. 513). Although their research was conducted in the United States, the Sadkers noted that their experience with British classrooms indicated similar differential treatment of boys and girls.

We return again to the major themes of this book and remind the reader that educational Excellence is promoted by introducing students to a diversity of peers and expanding their school-relevant repertoires. Effective classroom design requires that a teacher be well informed regarding cultural (and individual) tendencies to promote Inclusion, Excellence, and Harmony. In cultures where gender roles are more rigid and differentiated, children will need assistance to develop the necessary capacities and to achieve Harmony while working in gender-mixed groupings. In rare contexts, such as with Navajo children, educators may decide to design activities so that expectations regarding joint productive activity among peers are almost always gender segregated. More often, to expand students' gender role repertoires, teachers will want to work against both their own and students' tendencies by systematically mixing males and females for a substantial portion of instructional activities, just as is required for success in today's workplace.

Effective variety in instructional activity will include tasks that allow girls to display competencies in the presence of and in competition with boys. Similarly, some tasks should allow boys to work more collaboratively with females and males. When children from cultures with traditional rigid gender role expectations work in gender-mixed groupings, collectivist goal and reward structures might be especially productive. Female students from these cultures might be more comfortable displaying expertise and skill in the presence of males if this results in rewards shared by the group, rather than putting girls in direct competition with boys. The latter condition appears to result in girls doing less well, regardless of previous performance within gender-segregated settings. Nonetheless, even in these settings, teachers may need to take action to ensure that all members contribute to the collective product.

Power

Cultures differ with regard to who has power or control in different situations and how this power is acquired and maintained. Cultural differences also exist regarding the acceptance of power differentials (Hofstede 1980; Shackleton and Ali 1990). The existence and acceptance of power distribution both within and outside activity settings must be considered in designing instructional activity. Within the context of activity settings that involve a small group of peers working on a task, there may be power differentials between the students and the teacher, between students in the group (recall the discussion in Chapter 4 related to peer status), and between participants and others outside the activity setting.

Power Distance

Hofstede (1980) coined the term "power distance" to refer to the extent to which members of various cultures accept inequity. He pointed out that although there are power differentials in all societies, cultures vary regarding the extent to which members are accepting of those differences (high power distance) or are less tolerant of inequity and seek to equalize power (low power distance). In Hofstede's (1980) study of cultural differences across fifty countries, people in Austria, Israel, and Denmark scored the lowest on power distance, while those in Malaysia, Panama, Guatemala, and the Philippines scored highest. All Asian and Latin-American countries were considered high power distance. Among countries that Hofstede classified as low power distance, the United States and Canada scored highest on this dimension.

When considering how to create classroom activity settings to promote Harmony and Excellence, power distance should be considered because it shapes students' expectations regarding their relationships and interactions with teachers. In all cultures, teachers possess power and control over their students. In cultures that do not accept inequity, students expect more choice and autonomy for the management of their activities. "Student-centered" educational movements and those in which students are given more freedom to choose their own educational paths are consistent with low power distance (Hofstede 1986). It also follows that low power distance leads to the belief that students should be allowed to express themselves spontaneously and that teacher-student communication should involve two-way interactions (Jamieson and Thomas 1974). Conversely, students from high power distance cultures would tend to expect more deference to teachers. In her study of Chinese and British graduate students and their tutors, Spencer-Oately (1997) found that although British students and tutors expected some subordination of students, the Chinese students and tutors held stronger beliefs that (1) teachers should correct students but students should not correct teachers, (2) teachers should advise students but students should not advise teachers, and (3) teachers should express any dissatisfaction with students' performance but students should not reciprocate.

Autonomy and Control

In this section we highlight Native American students' experience in school as an example of cultural influences on power relationships in the classroom. Although we are not aware of any explicit research on power distance and Native American cultures, the literature on Native American attitudes about children's status and responsibility indicates that these children are afforded more autonomy than their non-Native peers. A study of the informal activity settings of Navajo and Hopi Indian children suggests that in these societies adults assign children their chores but leave the children to perform these chores alone without adult supervision. Rhodes (1989) notes that the types of chores that are assigned to children in these cultures might be considered inappropriate from a European American's point of view. (For example, seven- or eight-year-olds are often assigned to herd sheep alone or to care for an infant sibling.) When children require assistance in fulfilling these responsibilities, they often turn to peers or siblings. Adults also expect children in these cultures to entertain themselves. Thus, most out-of-school learning for these children takes place in small peer-oriented groups (Rhodes 1989).

Descriptions of Native American children learning a cultural skill, such as being able to perform a certain traditional dance or ride broncos for a rodeo, involve children practicing alone for some time before it is appropriate to perform in front of an adult. An adult model is first observed, then children practice alone until some level of proficiency is reached, at which time assistance from peers is sought. This is followed by more practice in front of peers. When a higher level of proficiency is reached, performance in front of adults is at last appropriate (Rhodes 1989; Suina and Smolkin 1991).

Deyhle and Le Compte (1994) describe the "noninterference" of Navajo parents regarding their nine- to fifteen-year-old children. They contrast this attitude toward youth with that of white "Anglo" educators, who often teach in the schools.

> Authority relations between parent and child are egalitarian among Navajos, in contrast to the hierarchical relationships found among Anglos. Anglos expect, at some level, to "rule" their children: Navajos do not believe such a degree of control is possible or appropriate. This means that many Navajo parents ... are unwilling to make decisions for their children, even if it means poor school attendance. By contrast, school personnel, who view this culturally specific behavior as "permissive," are critical of Navajo parents' "lack of control" over their children" (p. 159).

Consequently, children from Native American cultures come to expect and prefer classroom activity settings in which they are granted more power: increased freedom to choose the topics of study, how they will proceed in the learning process, and when and where they will do the work (Lipka 1990; Yamauchi 1994). When Yamauchi (1993) interviewed Zuni Pueblo Indian children about what they liked and didn't like about their school and classes, many of them said that they often felt rushed to complete assignments when they would prefer to proceed at their own pace. As one girl explained, in contrast to school, at home she learned things by choice and not because someone was forcing her.

There are some descriptions of Native American teachers providing more student control in their classrooms by allowing students to choose whether and when they wish to participate in activities (Lipka 1990) and by allowing them to set the pace and rhythm of their activities (Esmailka and Barnhardt 1981). This contrasts with the more common practice of teachers setting the pace of the activity and then expecting students to adjust to it. In the latter, more common case, correct answers given out of synch are often misinterpreted as wrong (Erickson 1980). In one example, Native Athabaskan teachers adjusted the rhythm and tempo of their interactions to that of their students (Esmailka and Barnhardt 1981). Teachers allowed students to provide answers to questions in their own "time slots." That is, children were given opportunities to set their own pace and were not penalized for calling out answers to questions that were out of synch with the teachers' own rhythm. The Athabaskan teachers spent relatively less time talking and more time listening. Like jazz band conductors who provide direction and information to students only when necessary, these teachers served a more supportive or resource role and did not appear to feel obliged to constantly perform. "Like the jazz conductors, they often melted right into their group" (Esmailka and Barnhardt 1981, p. 15).

Culture, Power, and Social Organization

In high power distance cultures, those in a higher position (teachers) are expected to have more control and power over those at the lower position (students). In these cultures, there is a great deal of respect for teachers and their authority, and classrooms are expected to be teacher centered (Gudykunst and Ting-Toomey 1988; Hofstede 1986). Students from such cultures also expect more directive teachers who tell them exactly what they need to do and how they should proceed. Asian students are often perplexed by the amount of autonomy they are given as students at U.S. universities. Coming from cultures that are relatively accepting of power differential, they expect a more authoritarian relationship with their teachers.

In considering power relationships in the planning of classroom instructional activities, teachers must once again decide when to work with and when against existing cultural tendencies. Often teachers would like to shift power to their students by encouraging them to act

---

From Our Files

Yati, who came from Indonesia to Hawai'i as a graduate student, said that she was shocked when she came to the United States and for the first time was assigned to write a paper on "a topic of her choice." It further surprised her that the U.S. professor would not even tell her how long the paper should be. Yati explained that in her culture, people believe that the teacher knows what is appropriate and should tell the students what that is. To deal with "a topic of her choice" Yati did not approach her teacher. Because she assumed that teachers (not students) should initiate communication, Yati asked a fellow Indonesian student for assistance in dealing with this difficulty.

In the meantime, Yati's children were attending public school in Hawai'i and becoming accustomed to a model of more equal teacher-student relationships. When the family was ready to return to their home country, Yati exclaimed that she was afraid her son had become "too American" in his attitudes, especially toward teachers. To her dismay, her son Choki had actually challenged his third-grade teacher about the grade he received in math (the teacher had included her judgment about Choki's behavior in her assessment of his math skills, thus lowering his grade). Although Yati was horrified by Choki's behavior, her U.S. friends were both pleased and amused by Choki's confidence and independence.

more autonomously, to ask more questions of their teachers, and to participate in decision making. For example, while engaging students in Instructional Conversation, teachers must relinquish some of the power they once held in directing exactly how the discussion proceeds. In this case, it may be necessary to create classroom activity settings in which teachers assist students to learn new patterns of interaction that require more initiative and responsibility. For other students, there may be an adjustment to develop more acceptance of teachers' authority. In either case, activity settings specifically designed to afford these opportunities will need to be created and students assisted.

Educational sociologists Cohen and Lotan (1997) advocate shifting power and control in classrooms by having teachers delegate their authority to students through the organization of peer-directed work groups that do not involve direct teacher supervision. They argue that direct supervision diminishes the amount of student-to-student interaction that they feel leads to the most learning. This presumes that the teacher, whenever present, remains in a traditional dominant role that can only be reduced by withdrawing. In fact, teachers are also flexible and can learn new patterns of interactions, just as students can. While student-to-student interaction is a necessary component of any successful classroom, educational Excellence is best promoted by having a portion of instructional activity include teachers' direct involvement in joint

From Our Files

One strategy for building these new repertoires involves simulating settings in which the desired repertoire is now performed. Continuing the University of Hawai'i example, researchers there at the Center for the Study of Multicultural Higher Education (CSOMHE) discovered that many professors who complained of low student engagement during classes and office hours had independently discovered that their best teaching occurred in the hallway, before or after class. CSOMHE staff were able to demonstrate the small step of intentionally lengthening the time when the professor stood casually outside the classroom door, engaging in lively discussion with the "reticent" students. The next step was to design an activity setting in the classroom in which the hallway pattern was emulated. During one class session per week, small-group discussion circles were arranged, and when the professor rotated to each for an Instructional Conversation, that group stood against the wall for some "hallway teaching." The standing up did not continue to be necessary, but the lively classroom discussion persisted—so long as there were small groups.

productive activity with students. The Instructional Conversation balances teacher and student input but is also cognitively challenging, leading to the most intellectual development, while maximizing positive student relationship and identification with the teacher. In Chapter 6 we discuss how this activity setting can be incorporated regularly into classrooms that are also rich in student-to-student activity and discourse.

Language Genres and Codes in the Classroom

The final cultural dimension that we discuss involves the variety of language genres and codes found in all classrooms, and especially those with students from diverse backgrounds. To some extent, culture is "situational" (Okamura 1981). That is, most individuals participate in multiple cultural communities, and their expectations and values may vary according to the situation.

From Our Files

David is a school counselor in a high school in a large urban city. David is Latino and grew up in a working-class neighborhood near the middle school where he now works. In fact, some of the middle school parents were David's peers from his childhood. One of these parents, Maria, commented that she thought David acted very different in his role as counselor. "No offense," she told him, "but you don't seem like a Latino when you're at school. When you're at the grocery store or at a party you seem like your old self, but in school you're really different."

Maria's comment underscores the flexibility of cultural tendencies and the ability we have to switch between the cultures and subcultures to which we belong. From our perspective, David is a good example of a well-educated person. David's capacity to function in both the formal work and informal community contexts is predicated on his expanded repertoire.

Throughout this chapter we emphasize the importance of creating activity settings that increase students' skills and repertoires in ways that may be different from their home cultural tendencies. The overarching goal is for all students to be able to participate fully in many and varied activity settings, some that they were initially comfortable with and others that became familiar in school. It is important to emphasize that this is an additive process, not one of replacement. Students need to develop a varied set of repertoires for relating to others in school because they will need it in the workplace and elsewhere. New repertoires are not designed to replace those of the home and other community settings, which students will also continue to need and value. Rather, students must learn to vary their behaviors according to the contexts of home, school, and other situations. Like David, successful students will be prepared to function effectively in multiple contexts as adults and will be able to switch among the capacities, expectations, values, goals, and languages of home, school, work, and community.

When students switch between their cultural repertoires for home and school, their switch in behavior is often accompanied by a switch in language genres and codes. Sociolinguistic researchers note that alternating between language genres or languages (codes) themselves occurs in many contexts and is a universal phenomenon (Valdés-Fallis 1978). The term genre comes from literary analysis and is used here to describe the organization of spoken and written language (content, style, and structure) (Bakhtin 1981). A genre includes the language code (Japanese, English, Russian) as well as the style and social expectations associated with that particular function of speech or writing. An example of genre switching occurs when a speaker shifts from the more formal genre of a prepared speech to a less formal genre when making a spontaneous comment to someone sitting in the front row. Code switching occurs between languages and often is observed among two or more bilingual speakers (Gumperz 1982). For example, many of the students David counseled at the high school were bilingual Spanish and English speakers. When speaking to each other, the students sometimes switched between English and Spanish, depending on the context and content.

Culture and Switching

Genre and code switching are not random acts (Gumperz 1982; Valdés-Fallis 1978); switching reflects the intersection of cultures and the negotiation of meaning between them (Aguirre 1988; St. Clair and Valdés 1980; Gumperz 1982):

> Code switching is not random linguistic production, in the sense that it is only speech mixture, but rather is the product of ordered linguistic selection. It ... is not an indication that a bilingual speaker is linguistically incongruent with ongoing social interaction: it is instead an active process of negotiation that ensures a high degree of linguistic and social congruence within a given context (Aguirre 1988, pp. 30–31).

Cultural variation thus affects when, why, and to what extent switching occurs (Gumperz 1982; Gumperz and Hernandez-Chavez 1971). When creating instructional activities teachers need to consider the language genres that are required in school and which genres learners already possess.

Switching reflects one's understanding of the social context and often implies changes in role expectations and power relationships. For each speaker, certain codes and genres come to be associated with particular activity settings and the roles that are required:

> A specific language becomes identified with certain roles (for example, English for teachers, employers, and policemen, and Spanish for grandparents, the aged); with certain topics (family chitchat, neighborhood gossip, and religion as opposed to the work domain, academic subjects, politics); and with certain settings (private vs. public). Code switching, then, can signal the fact that two bilinguals are shifting their role relationship with regard to one another, are shifting topics, or are responding to the particular characteristics of the setting (Valdés-Fallis 1978, p. 8).

Recall our earlier example of high school student Lynn switching to a more formal genre when talking to her mother, who is the teacher of her history class. Addressing her mother as "Mrs. Anderson" rather than "Mom" indicates that in this setting Lynn acknowledges a switch in their roles to one that is more formal and requires more social distance and power differential.

St. Clair and Valdés (1980) use the game metaphor of linguistic interaction to emphasize the importance of participants' intentions and awareness of verbal interactions. In the "game" of linguistic interaction, participants use verbal and nonverbal strategies to manipulate the situation toward their own goals and needs. Switching is one strategy that participants employ toward this end. For example, if participants believe that social distance needs to be increased or decreased, they could shift up or down to achieve the desired effect (St. Clair and Valdés 1980).

Participants might also use genre or code switching to indicate to their communication partner that they are "on the same side." Switching in this sense is a marker of in- and out-groups (Gumperz 1982). Gumperz and Hernandez-Chavez (1971) studied code switching among bilingual Spanish-English speakers and found that switching was related to social and ethnic identification. Switching to Spanish from English appeared to be an indication of solidarity among participants as members of the same community:

> Codes alternate only as long as all participants are [C]hicanos and while their conversation revolves around personal experiences. Towards the end of the recording session, when a new participant enters, talk goes on. The newcomer is an American of English-speaking background who, having lived in Latin America, speaks Spanish fluently. Yet in this context she was addressed only in English and did not use her Spanish.... It is evident ... that it is social identity and not language per se which is determinant in code selection (p. 118).

The researchers also found that teen-aged members of this Latino/Latina community tended to prefer English even in informal conversations, indicating, perhaps, their desired identification with the more dominant Western culture. Later, if they married within the community, the former teens' language usage tended to reflect a change back to Spanish (Gumperz and Hernandez-Chavez 1971).

Genres and Classrooms

Many genres appear in classrooms, but regardless of the language involved, the ones that are more common to classroom settings often favor middle-class students and those with more school-like experiences (Dyson and Genishi 1991; Heath 1983; Toole 1990). These genres are part of the "student role" in classrooms and are integral to appropriate behavior in school. The kind of talking and writing that goes on in school will be relatively more or less familiar to students from different cultural backgrounds. For example, working-class African-American parents tend to ask their children for analogic comparison about "what things are like" (Heath 1983). This differs from the genre of test-like school talk that asks children for answers that are already "known" (Dyson and Genishi 1991; Mehan 1979). Known-answer questions are those for which there are specific responses the questioner is expecting:

> This test-like situation, the "school talk" genre is one that many middle-class children are familiar with because their parents have asked such questions during countless comfortable interactions at home, for example, games like peek-a-boo or book-reading (Cazden 1983; Ninio and Bruner 1978). Although working-class parents may talk about topics that appeal to their children in engaging ways (Tizard and Hughes 1984), they may not include "test-like" questions to which adults already know the answers (Dyson and Genishi 1991, p. 9).

Dyson and Genishi (1991) suggest that adults make judgments about genres that do not meet their cultural expectations, and caution educators against forming quick judgments about what children are able and not able to do.

Foster (1992) reviewed the differences in narrative styles of African-American and European-American students during sharing time. The "sharing time genre" of European-American students is similar to a short, well-organized lecture presentation of facts about an object or event. These narratives focus on a topic and usually include one temporal marker (yesterday, last night). In contrast, the sharing by African-American students tends to be longer, more elaborate, and marked by several temporal markers that express a series of events. In addition, African-American students' narrative style is more like a dramatic performance; it often includes gestures, dialogue, and sound effects. Foster (1992) suggests that these different narrative styles evoke different responses from teachers:

The African-American students in these classrooms were invariably frustrated because the teachers, all of whom were Anglo, failed to comprehend or appreciate the stories being narrated. Frequently interrupting students with inappropriate questions or attempting to redirect the narrative to focus on a particular but often insignificant aspect of the story, one more familiar to themselves, the teachers questioned the African-American students' intellectual competence and emotional stability. In contrast, in the single classroom where the teacher, an African-American, did not participate in the activity but, instead, let the children direct sharing time themselves, the African-American students were consistently among those named as the best sharers by their classmates (p. 305).

In this example, the African-American teacher legitimized students' preferred narrative style by allowing its use in the classroom. Other examples of successful African-American classrooms include teachers' own incorporation of stylistically more "African-American" ways of speaking. For example, Foster's review (1992) suggested that some successful African-American teachers use a style of speaking that is similar to oral genres from the African-American community. Those genres include the style of talking used by African-American preachers, the "verbal art" used by males and adolescents, and African-American children's play songs (Foster 1992). Making classroom talk more familiar to students can affect their participation in school. In one study, a teacher's deliberate use of language that mirrored genres from the African-American community increased students' participation to the point that students spoke as frequently as did the teacher (Foster 1989).

By understanding the genres students bring from their homes and communities, teachers can also assist students in adopting new classroom repertoires. Lee (1995) studied a teacher's use of "signifying" to assist African-American high school students' literary interpretation. Signifying is a form of talk in African-American communities that includes figurative language and sometimes ritual insult. Lee noted that because signifying almost always involves double entendres and a play on meaning, it is very similar to literary interpretation. She found that African-American students could be assisted in understanding this similarity and using these strategies in an academic context. Lee (1995) called signifying "a bridge over which the students traversed" to acquire the classroom genre of text interpretation (p. 625).

There is a lively debate now about whether high levels of literacy and numeracy can be fostered by using call-and-response, a set of discourse features well studied in African-American English (Cazden 1998; Meier 1996, 1998; Foster 1989, 1992, 1995). There is good evidence in these studies for some beneficial effects. The essence of the debate (by no means confined to African-American English, but one requiring study in all genres) is whether genres evolved for social discourse can be used with profit in subject areas whose technical language features have been developed specifically for analysis of academic subject matter. Discovering the most effective balance between the requirements for contextualization and the requirements for subject matter precision is a fascinating and important area in current research (Foster and Peele in press).

Educational Excellence and Harmony for all students requires that students learn the genres expected in school and be able to switch among them appropriately. Students whose families do not engage in these school talk genres, regardless of language of origin, need to be assisted to learn these new genres and in ways that do not assume prior experience. Educators need to rethink what it means to speak the school genre and to create activity settings that allow students to learn the lexicon and expressive conventions required in all of the content areas: the kind of language that is appropriate during a literature lesson, a science discussion, or for asking questions of a social studies guest speaker. As described in Chapter 1, this is important to develop the meta-goals of developing language and literacy across the curriculum and to engage students in Instructional Conversation.

Genre and code switching mark activity boundaries, imply norms, and accompany role expectations. Students who do not respond to these cues may not be prepared to meet the expectations that are intended. Educators can help students to understand the implications of code and genre switching (Jorgensen 1992). During the 1990s "language awareness" programs in Denmark attempted to teach the implications of switching and other verbal strategies to children. One study indicated that over time and with increased second language proficiency, immigrant Turkish students were better able to use code switching as a strategy to gain power in a conversation with peers (Jorgensen 1992).

Conclusion

In this chapter we have reviewed four dimensions along which cultures vary (1) individualism/collectivism, (2) role expectations, (3) power, and (4) language genres and codes. Each of these dimensions influences the expectations, values, and behavioral repertoires that students and teachers bring to classrooms. When students share the same expectations and values as their teachers and peers, there will be more Harmony in these interactions. "Cultural" clashes and misinterpretations can result when participants come from more varied communities. Some of this may occur simply due to variations within the same community. As a general rule, the greater the classroom diversity, the greater the necessity for building the community of the classroom in such a way that common values and expectations, through the use of a shared classroom language, build classroom intersubjectivity.

Equity, Inclusion, Harmony, and Excellence can be created in the instructional activity pattern of the classroom, and designing for those goals can be guided by an awareness of the four cultural dimensions. In all classrooms, teachers will want to use their knowledge of students' cultural tendencies to create activity settings that are familiar and comfortable to students so as to promote maximum engagement and involvement that is harmonious with students' cultural backgrounds. However, educational Excellence is also promoted by creating opportunities for students to interact with those who are unlike them and by developing capacities that are not as familiar. In either case, teaching involves providing assistance and guidance in learning these new roles and repertoires. In all classrooms teachers should also create activity settings that challenge and expand students' present repertoires and capacities. Effective assistance involves creating new and varied activity settings while at the same time incorporating knowledge of students' cultural tendencies and existing affinities.

In Chapter 6 we provide systematic guidance for any teacher to develop a classroom that is designed to provide that assistance most effectively. On the surface, Chapter 6 appears to be a step-by-step guide. On a deeper level, it is a developmental analysis. Like all developmental analyses, it reveals dynamics not available to any other method.

6 Designing the Organization of Instructional Activity

I N THE NATION'S CLASSROOMS, we have little experience setting and sustaining high expectations for any but the most privileged students. Schools and classrooms have not been organized from a shared value system to assist widespread accomplishment of all participants. Classrooms of the common tradition certainly have long held a uniform value system, enforced by a variety of classroom management systems and a set of building-level sanctions, but that system requires that students listen, obey, convey deference and respect, follow teachers' instructions, and remain silent. There is no particular guideline for student relationships among themselves unless it is mediated by teacher direction. After all, classrooms of the common tradition were built from a bureaucratic model that viewed personal relationships among participants as interfering with efficient production, even of teaching and learning. This chapter describes classroom design for the organization of instructional activity that builds communities of learners. These classrooms are characterized by a shared value system that promotes interaction and relationship for the purpose of achieving teaching and learning Excellence, Fairness, Inclusion, and Harmony for all students.

Can a teacher in a diverse classroom generate an alternate shared value system supporting pedagogy and curriculum that achieves academic Excellence, as it is understood today? Studies of student achievement in high school mathematics and science show increases where teaching is conducted with less hierarchy, more cooperation, and high levels of teacher and student collaboration (Lee, Smith, and Croninger 1995). Others report necessary common values that include both teachers and students believing in the possibility of positive outcomes for all while using highly productive pedagogy, organization, and instructional task designs (Rowan

1995). Quality teachers who are effective with all students in their diverse classrooms are reflective practitioners who apply observational and analytical skills to monitor, evaluate, and refine their own teaching practice. Quality teachers are also culturally competent, interacting comfortably and harmoniously with others whose languages and backgrounds differ from their own. In other words, they respect others' differences and are aware of their own cultural perspective, particularly the assumptions that support their own expectations, beliefs, attitudes, and behavior that influence instructional activity and affect student learning (Chisholm 1994).

Classrooms such as those described in the Phase 5 section of this chapter have physical, pedagogical, and curricular arrangements that support students and teachers interacting and producing together on academic topics. Simple repetitive activity patterns of the common tradition are replaced by more complex organizations of variety and vitality encouraging modeling, observation, relationship, physical movement, mutual exchange of ideas, and academic success. This organization of instructional activity is accomplished without reducing class size. In fact, the more students, the more diversity is available to enrich classroom interaction and activity. Classrooms such as those described in this chapter ideally function with twenty-five to thirty-five students.

Organizing classrooms for these effects means designing the organization of instructional activity as a functioning community. Because today's diverse students come to the classroom with disparate talents, values, and attitudes toward learning, the first and foremost purpose of the teacher and students must be building the values for forming a community that supports its members' learning. The most elaborate arrangements of furniture or compelling groupings of students will have little effect unless they are based on jointly held values and expectations for how the group will work together for all to succeed.

This chapter describes a developmental approach to creating such a classroom in any school. Teachers can use the process, which is described in terms of five phases, to build classrooms as communities of learners who can achieve Fairness, Equity, Inclusion, and academic Excellence. When applied systematically, the five-phase sequence produces a classroom in which joint productive activity, language development, meaningful and complex instructional activity, and academic dialogue are constant features of the instructional setting. In Phase 5, academic teaching and learning is a value-added function characterized by cooperative working relationships among students and teacher, quality work that occurs independently and jointly with peers and teacher, and high expectations for everyone's potential to participate and learn. Figure 6.1 is a schematic view of the final achievement, the Phase 5 classroom. This example is intended as a generic model, which would of course differ in the specific content and number of the activity settings depending on grade level and subject matter.

FIGURE 6.1   Classroom Organization for Multiple, Simultaneous Activity Settings

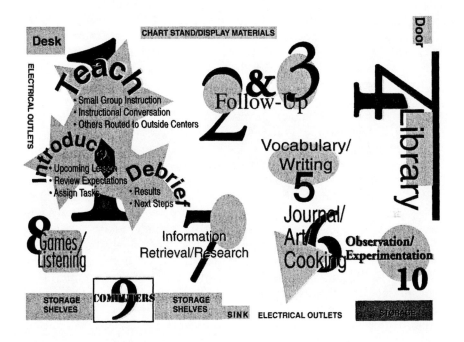

Grade Level, Diversity, and Content Area

Teachers at every grade level must increase the rate and quality of all students' participation in complex tasks, such as real-world problem solving and extended discourse about content concepts, using today's technology tools to achieve significant academic gain. Unlike classrooms of the common tradition, teachers in reformed classrooms are capable of providing activities at higher levels of frequency and wider-ranging modalities that increase rates of student participation to yield academic learning gains for all students, including language minorities, the disabled, and at-risk students.

Any classroom can be organized as a functional equivalent to Ms. Young's Phase 5 classroom (pp. 15–16), where simultaneous and differentiated activities and interaction occur frequently. But it is important to recognize that the surface features will look very different in every Phase 5 classroom. Kindergarten classrooms differ greatly from high school science laboratories, not only in their size, furniture, and equipment, but also in the nature of the activities that are appropriate for students of different capacities and academic goals. However, the principles guiding classroom functions are similar across grade levels for activity, interaction, and academic discourse.

Applications of the phases discussed in this chapter will produce different social organizations and role relationships, depending not only on student age but also on the nature of the communities and cultures of the school's locale. Classrooms designed for specific cultural groups such as those described in Chapter 5 or for specific combinations of those populations would and should exhibit different patterns of activities than those for other communities or combinations. Examples of these variations can be found in many sources (e.g., Vogt, Jordan, and Tharp 1992; Tharp 1997; Dalton and Youpa 1998; Dalton 1998a; Foster 1992, 1995). The Five Standards for Effective Pedagogy themselves were discovered by abstracting agreements from programs across numerous ethnic and cultural groups.

Subject matter also affects the design of instructional activity. The nature, sequence, and structure of knowledge are different in mathematics than in history, and tasks in one content area lend themselves to some kinds of products more than others. Because of subject matter differences, surface appearances of reformed classrooms in social studies will be quite different from those involving the same students in science. Nevertheless, at the level of organization and of pedagogy, there are fundamental similarities across subject matters. The first four developmental phases described below (Phases 1, 2, 3, and 4) are organized around subject matter relating to an Early Content Theme (ECT) appropriate to grade and intended curricular emphases. Whether the ECT is Neighborhood, Patterns, Global Networking, or Privacy Since Deoxyribonucleic Acid (DNA) Testing, it is the generator of tasks, materials, and activities useful for review, practice, format familiarization, reteaching, success experiences, and community building. ECT is the curricular context of the Phase-in period, which may continue from six to ten weeks depending on the experience of the teacher and the students.

From the first phase, design of activity, tasks, and products requires considering diversity of persons and variety of roles/interaction patterns in structuring activities. Achieving a variety of roles, participants, and tasks is a universal prescription, which must be enacted with effective pedagogy across a multiplicity of subject matters, locales, and grades. To clarify these considerations, we discuss each phase of the developmental model in terms of three design facets: roles and relating, grouping and routing, and tasks and products. Balancing these elements across activity settings is necessary to nurture an emerging community of learners and for accomplishing the highest-quality instruction and student learning.

A Developmental Model

We present a developmental model of classroom organization in five phases. Often teachers use an Early Content Theme (ECT) as the source of content and activities for the early phases and a thematic link, or bridge, to the formal subject matter of the grade level or course. ECT activities are heavily contextualized in the experiences of the students, offering familiar content laced with new information and concepts. Through the ECT, the teacher applies the Standards for Effective Pedagogy as the basis for instruction; during the first three phases Standard I: Teacher and Students Producing Together; Standard II: Developing Language and Literacy Across the Curriculum; and Standard III: Making Meaning: Connecting School to Students' Lives are particularly emphasized. The ECT is a vehicle for teachers to increase cooperation and participation in joint activity with students on familiar topics while reducing hierarchical relations and whole-group, same-task activity. Simultaneously, teachers review and assess students' baseline knowledge and language, reteaching and previewing concepts, content lexicon, and skills where needed in preparation for the formal curriculum. Even though beginning at the beginning may not be necessary for every reader, a full model is useful even to the master teacher because every group of new students is a new beginning. Thus the presentation of this model can be read in two ways: as a sequential process for beginning every new class or as a transformation of Ms. Lee's teaching into that of Ms. Young.

In the design process, Phase 1 is a beginning and Phase 5 is a fully achieved, complex design that implements the Five Standards to facilitate academic learning for all students. An overview of the phases is presented in the Appendix in Figure A.1. Our account of Phase 1 is the longest because it presents the basic vocabulary and ideas of design, including discussion of the development of classroom values that build communities of learners and classroom management. In Phase 1, the dynamics of the elements of classroom activity will be discussed fully, so that their function in Phases 2, 3, 4, and 5 is clear.

We prepare for the developmental model by first considering the two basic organizational structures, activity settings (the basic units of instructional organization) and the next higher level of structure, the Frame (which contains its activity settings). In this sense, the Frame is the design element for lessons or units, which are successions of Frames. For example, a reading lesson that requires five days of reading, discussing, and complex follow-up activities might constitute an Instructional Frame. In the beginning of the year, a single, large-group, teacher-directed event and its follow-up, completed in a single day, also make up a Frame.

Activity Settings

In Chapter 3 we discussed in detail the basic unit of analysis in sociocultural theory, the activity setting. Activities in which students engage, and the language and problem solving that accompany them, form their developing cognitions, perceptions, motives, and values. Instruction is designed in terms of its activity settings and how these activity settings are interrelated within a Frame.

Activity settings can be designed for small groups; the entire class; and triads, dyads, or single students. Activities may occur at an identifiable setting in the classroom or in a location outside of it, but each requires provision of materials and resources related to the academic tasks. Activity settings may operate independently of the teacher or each other or they may interrelate where useful, but each activity is crafted by the teacher as a part of an instructional plan to be enacted within a community of learners. The patterned collection of activity settings constitutes the life of the classroom community and its purposes, actions, and productions.

The who, what, when, where, and why questions used to describe activity settings in Chapter 3 are also useful in designing activity settings. Who refers to which students and teachers are included. What refers to the participants' actions and the scripts or routines that guide them. When and where refer to the times and the places where the activity occurs. Finally, why refers to the motivations of the members, the meanings of the activities to them, and the activities' objectives or products. In designing activity settings, the teacher can use this "5 Ws" checklist as an easy structure for assuring that each activity of the classroom is thoughtfully and practically planned.

Design: Roles and Relationships, Grouping and Routing, and Tasks and Products

As mentioned above, there are three other major dimensions of activity settings: (1) roles and relating, (2) grouping and routing, and (3) tasks and products.

Consider a teacher whose instructional goal is to introduce his students to visual representations of data such as graphs, maps, drawings, or architectural blueprints. He has designed an activity setting that will include five students; take place at the Drawing Station furnished with drawing and writing supplies in the back, right-side corner of the classroom; and have as its product a map based on descriptive information students collected on a field trip. The teacher has decided to have the activity last twenty minutes and begin next Tuesday at 9:00. Even with this clarity, he still has numerous decisions and choices within the three facets of roles and relating, grouping and routing, and tasks and products.

Roles and Relating. What will the teacher be doing during the activity? Will the teacher interact with students? If so, how? Will the teacher work alongside them as a collaborator? Ignore them? Observe them at a distance and assist if a need arises? How will the students relate to each other? As collaborators? As competitors?

Grouping and Routing. Which five students will participate? There are thirty-three in the class. If the teacher decides that four groups will rotate through the activity, which students will work with whom? Shall the teacher assign those groups or let them choose their partners? If they are assigned, on what basis will it be? Should he group students to distribute skills? Let friends work with friends? Take this opportunity to develop new propinquities? How will the students know who is to go where? Is access to the task accommodating for all students, including those with disabilities?

Tasks and Products. What do the students need to know to complete the task successfully? Should there be one map or five? Should issues of scale be introduced now or held for an instructional conversation after a version of the map is drawn? (The specifications for the map might vary greatly depending on the basic subject matter of the class. Is it geography? Or mathematics?) Whatever the subject matter, should the map be created for use in subsequent activity settings? How will all the students know how to meet the production standards? Will the products be informative as visual displays for easy viewing by each student in the class?

Combinations of these decisions may result in effective activity settings, depending on context issues such as how well the teacher and students know each other, the pattern of diversity in the students, the phase of development of the classroom community, the subject matter, and especially the context of the other activities planned for the same Instructional Frame. Does this mean that there are no clear quality criteria for designing activity settings? On the contrary, very clear criteria have been articulated throughout this book; we demonstrate here that they can be applied not only to individual activities but also to sets.

Quality Criteria for the Design of Instructional Activities

The quality criteria for the design of instructional activity are those that will foster Fairness, Excellence, Inclusion, and Harmony. Such classrooms are characterized by high levels of student interaction with one another and the teacher and the provision of performance assistance when needed. In classrooms designed to meet these criteria, high activity and interaction levels will offer all students choice and opportunity to contribute as experts. The highest criterion for instructional activities is that they be organized to support enactment of the Five Standards through the Three Necessary Conditions of (1) simultaneous activities involving (2) a variety of roles, abilities, and interactions, all imbued with (3) a consistent set of values.

Certainly the Standards and Necessary Conditions cannot all be enacted within any single activity setting. The teacher with the map activity is not even attempting to teach this activity through dialogue (Standard V); rather, he uses the map as the stimulus and preparation for a later dialogic activity setting. And, the prescription for variety of persons and roles can be achieved only across several activities, several Frames of instruction, and even several weeks or months.

Nevertheless, the quality criteria are borne in mind as each activity is designed so that the overall pattern is productive for academic learning. For example, meeting the criterion for Inclusion can be facilitated through arranging groupings over time so that all students have opportunities for joint activity with the teacher, with male and female peers, with peers of affinity and those of lesser acquaintance, with those in the same and in other crowds or cultures, with those of the same talents and abilities, with high- and low-status peers, with disabled peers, and with students who speak the same language as well as those who are now learning it. In the panoply of activities, all students should experience leading, following, assisting, and collaborating; occupying many different roles, some in patterns that reflect their own cultures and some that expand their skills and perceptions.

Likewise, tasks and products are diversified so that each student is involved productively in individual (tailored to specific needs), routine (familiar formats, regularly occurring activities), independent (experience-based, hands-on, real-world problems that students can solve on their own), collaborative (tasks with joint products), and conceptual (abstract, text-based, research) activities. Such a complex mix of experiences, involving diversity of individual/collective, power, role, and language code use, alternates comfort and challenge.

Before discussing in detail how task variety and quality criteria are achieved within a Frame of activity settings, it is first necessary to consider the nature of the Frame itself. The Instructional Frame provides for a specific, structured approach in which academic work is done, but also in which shared values are created and maintained through Standard I (Teacher and Students Producing Together, such as working together to build community) and Standard II (Developing Language and Literacy Across the Curriculum, such as developing the language of the community of learners).

The Instructional Frame

Teachers who use the Instructional Frame from their first encounter with students provide them with a predictable pattern, a comfortable rhythm, and a regular opportunity for communication with the entire class. Whether students sit on the rug at the elementary level or in their homeroom seats or other seating arrangements typical to later grades, the Frame is used from the teacher's first contact with the class. The Frame includes two activity settings as its "handles." The two handles are the introduction or Briefing activity (beginning a Frame) and the summarizing or Debriefing activity (following it). The handles of the Frame introduce the activity settings inside it; in the common tradition, these are typically a whole-class instruction activity and a follow-up task of worksheets or problems. The Frame itself is a systematic pattern for classroom activity that has become familiar and predictable for generations of classrooms. But just adding the Briefing and Debriefing handles, as shown as Figure 6.2, introduces a crucial element for transformative development.

Using the Basic Unit: Briefing Handle, Instructional Frame, Debriefing Handle

Inside each Frame are several activity settings. In Figure 6.2 we see a familiar and very simple Frame of two: first the teacher instructing and second a follow-up activity in which the teacher floats around the room assessing or assisting student performance on follow-up or practice tasks. For the moment, let us concentrate on the two activity settings at the beginning and ending of the Frame, labeled Briefing and Debriefing. These activities consist of discussions about the activity settings inside the Frame and any topic of the classes' experience with the Frame. Typical topics—from the first day of school—include announcements, daily business, class planning, problem solving, celebrations, directions, community building, and generating or reviewing community rules. These two handles are opportunity activities, opportunities for modeling expectations, courtesy conventions, and discussing values arising from the teacher's instructions and the students' examples. Here are opportunities for values to be made explicit in language, spoken and written, repeated and reminded, and exemplified in real and explicit classroom behaviors.

FIGURE 6.2   Instructional Frame with Handles

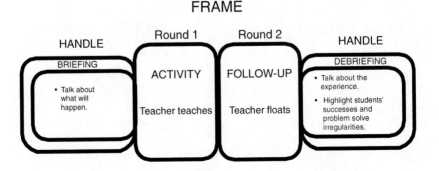

How can this come about? To meet the quality criteria for a community of learners, the community must be built on values and behaviors that support student self-control. Only when students are self-guided by shared values can classrooms become academically productive. It is the function of the Briefing and Debriefing activities to build and maintain those values. Each instance of Briefing and Debriefing signals the community as a whole to convene, talk about what will happen and what did happen, and build community values. To succeed as a community, these activity settings must both precede and follow every Instructional Frame.

In Figure 6.2 these values discussions appear as handles attached to the basic unit. Handles are an informative metaphor in other ways as well. These handles are values-focused activities providing the secure grip that will keep the complex activities within the unit balanced, secure, and under control. No matter how complex the activity patterns inside the unit become, the handles remain—simple, predictable, and necessary, from the first day of school straight through to the last. Handles are best when brief. Even though they are about logistics, directions, and common understandings about what is next, they are most useful when not longer than, and often shorter than, ten minutes.

Briefing.   The Briefing activity setting is designed to provide information from the teacher and students about what is necessary for successful participation in the Frame of activities to follow. It is a place to model and practice the cooperation and collaboration that will characterize the community. From this Briefing, the classroom community understands the expectations for a work product as well as the ways students will interact with one another and with the teacher.

This handle is vital. It guards against jump-starting activities before teachers and their students are ready. For example, at the very beginning of a high school math class in California, a teacher said, "Get out your individual evaluation sheet." The students were sputtering and mumbling, "I don't have mine. Where are they? What is one?" In this situation, the teacher has two choices: Drive on with those who managed to locate their sheet while ignoring the others and inviting a management breakdown, or stop and deal with the problem of materials and the loss of instructional time. If this classroom had a handle for Briefing, students would have known what was needed and could assist in locating the materials, in the case that they were not readily available, before precious instructional time began.

Briefing handle brevity is assured when it draws on students' expertise. What the students already know from years of experience performing instructional tasks, the teacher does not need to elaborate. Because students beyond the first grade have enormous experience of classroom task activity, they know or can anticipate the type and formats of most tasks teachers assign. When students are expected to explain or give clarifying directions, it provides them with an opportunity to enact the role of expert for the teacher and peers. By eliciting such contributions the teacher encourages joint participation, Inclusion, role validation, and student responsibility. Student participation is key to building values for cooperation and responsibility in the classroom community.

So the Frame includes a Briefing that introduces the activity settings to follow, including its tasks and roles. The Briefing function is critical, whether the Instructional Frame includes reading period, going to the library, setting up or performing experiments, boarding the bus for a field trip, or the writing of individual journals. In the following example, the teacher, Cynthia, conducts a Briefing about the first activity setting in the upcoming Frame. Note that she elicits the sixth-grade students' experience with the task to explain the performance expectations:

A Briefing Conversation

TEACHER: Okay, today what we're going to do is, we're gonna make journals.

KIDS [groan]: Oh, no, boring!

TEACHER: Have you ever done it before?

MANY KIDS IN CHORUS: Yeah ...

TEACHER: Where have you done it?

[Students mention two other teachers who have had them write journals.]

TEACHER: Okay, so you've made journals before. What did you use them for?

STUDENT: For what you have done in your class?

TEACHER [nods her head and repeats]: You write about what you did. What other things can journals be used for? Or what have you used them for?

STUDENT: Put important things in.

TEACHER [nods]: Yes, put important things in. Okay, why do you think we're using journals in here? Why do you think we're going to do that?

STUDENT: 'Cuz every class does.

TEACHER: Because every class does it? Okay, why else will we be doing journals in here?

[Student responds.]

TEACHER [nods and repeats]: To tell what we do in here. What else can we use our journals for?

[Various students answer.]

TEACHER [nods and repeats]: Put important things in the journal, yeah. Like taking notes, right. Write what we think. Okay, we're going to make our very own journals and decorate them.

Activity.   The Instructional Frame depicted in Figure 6.2 represents the most basic pattern of activity settings in schools of the common tradition, consisting of two basic activity settings. The first is a large-group event, often lecture or question and answer, in which a few articulate students participate. The second is follow-up, in which the students complete worksheets, answer problems or questions from the textbook, or practice, while the teacher floats around the classroom observing the student work and offering assistance or comment or withdraws to her own desk.

Although this common Frame, reminiscent of Ms. Lee's classroom, has little resemblance to the sorts of activity settings suggested by the quality criteria, it is from here that most classrooms begin. In the early stages of the school year, in the early stages of Phase I, it is an appropriate design. Students and the teacher must learn to understand one another's communications, and student habits of responsibility and task completion are likely to need development. In the boxed example below, a teacher mentor describes the development work she observed her novice teacher perform. Note how she affirms the teacher's efforts while offering guidance.

Debriefing.   When all the activity settings inside the Frame have been completed, in a Debriefing of no more than ten minutes the teacher asks for feedback from students about the activity they have just completed. The discussion encourages student problem solving. For accomplishment and cooperation, for creating the community that will work for all, the teacher gives praise and rewards. Like the Briefing, Debriefing needs to involve students as much as possible. The teacher in the example in the last box would have the students discuss their listening skills. Do they

From Our Files

You set the time ... twenty-five minutes with an incentive to get out early. You state how each person must have their own paper although they work together. You have them write down volume and surface area. You state this ten times at least. You walk around to make sure they are all writing it down. You walk them through the first problem. It is amazing how many times it takes to repeat the directions. What you did was perfect—stopping and having them listen for clarification. It's okay if there is not enough time left to complete the assignment, if clarification takes more time than expected. They are almost there with you. They still need practice on following directions. You did great examples of surface area with the eraser!

want to hear the teacher restate the directions ten times or can they help each other get the information the first time? The teacher would also consider the clarity of her own directions and how she can involve the students more in direction giving.

This handle is important for clarifying the values of the community for joint problem solving and decision making. Discussions may occur about appropriate noise level, interaction, peer assistance, materials availability, clean-up, quality of the activity from the students' point of view and ways to improve it, rewards, and ideas for next activities. The first Debriefings are often directed to management topics. Because it occurs at the end of the Frame, scheduling time for this handle is important—after clean-up and before bells ring. Initially, teachers may keep the Debriefing handle very brief and motivating, as the following exchange demonstrates. Here, a middle school teacher is guiding her students through a debriefing. She has asked the students to consider their accomplishments, and she is noting them against their class self-reward system:

From Our Files

Debriefing Conversation

HENRY: We put it away ourself.

TEACHER: You put everything away yourselves.

HENRY: We're responsible.

ARTHUR: We didn't throw that stuff around.

TEACHER: So were you responsible?

CLASS: [chorus] Yeah!

TEACHER: That's three ... [referring to the classes' point system for rewards]

WILLIE: We were calm.

TEACHER: Example ...

HENRY: We didn't throw this in our eye!

TEACHER: You didn't throw it in your eye! Right, five-dollar day, go ahead and go.

From Our Files

"How did it go? What about the experience was good? What about it was successful? What about it made everyone feel comfortable? What about it showed that we were considerate of each other?... I'll even look for very mundane accomplishments—whether they got their name on the paper, and the date, or whether they accomplished something much more complicated. But this is the place to let everybody know the ways that it went right. And while letting everybody know, I'm writing the rules on the chart. We are making it explicit—if we do this every day, everybody knows the rules in the context of the actual behaviors that occur. And I'm sharing feelings about what that meant, what it meant for the students and what it meant for me, and about the whole thing. That's the way we build community."

In another classroom, an experienced high school teacher described her dialogues with students during the Debriefing activity (see box above).

In summary, the Instructional Frame includes the "handles" of Briefing and Debriefing, and inside the Frame are all the activity settings that interrelate in achieving the instructional goals. The handles provide regular occasions for communicating about the experience all participants are having in the community, thus facilitating student and teacher interaction by focusing on expanding student expression. The handles support the development of supportive relationships between students and the teacher and support productive task completion by modeling and inviting everyone to participate in the Briefings and Debriefings. The product of the handles activity settings is clear communication about expectations and new understandings about academic topics.

Inside the Frame are the interrelated activity settings. The basic two-activity Frame in Figure 6.2 can be expanded once the community values of mutual respect, self-control, and productive work have a sound base. In Phase 1, the basic Frame is used to establish the foundation for developing a complex classroom organization for increased student interaction and activity. Task construction for independent and joint productive student work is also the focus of Phase 1. Phase 2 involves group formats and the formation of as many student groupings as possible. Phase 3 introduces activity settings in which students perform various tasks in a variety of groupings. Phase 4 is a full implementation of the organization, with stable groups and standard rotations through activity settings, or routing. Phase 5 builds on the conditions for academic learning put in place through previous phases by introducing the premier pedagogy for academic learning, the Instructional Conversation. But before proceeding to further complexity in the Frame, we should pause and consider the other aspect of uniform community values. How does the teacher manage this classroom that encourages high levels of student interaction, activity, choice, and independence?

Classroom Management

Using the Frame with Handles for Classroom Management

As all who have taught know, it is sometimes necessary to deal with student disruptions. In classrooms with well-developed handles of Briefing and Debriefing, disruptions are minimized because students experience success (DiGiulio 1995). Inclusive teaching requires sustaining everyone's successful participation in all activities to develop not only community but a community of learners. Briefing that precedes activity provides simple and clear instructions for tasks and procedures and brainstorming to anticipate problems. For example, what does a student do if she finishes before the time allotted to the activity is up? Having a clear plan will prevent her from wandering and being disruptive.

From the first day, Briefing and Debriefing involve dialogue, before each activity or set of activities, about what works for everyone, including the teacher. Discussions in the handles are always brisk and brief, with high student participation whenever possible. These activity settings have an explicit joint product, the classroom rules and procedures. Experienced teachers post those rules in bright, visually appealing displays for easy reference and modification. Most rules will have a first version within two weeks, a written record that can be used as a reference point for discussing specific instances. Another entry in our file of "Mentoring Remarks" says:

From Our Files

A Mentor to a Beginning Teacher

"It's important to establish your rules and procedures now, in the second week, so (the students) become accustomed to them, and then all will go quickly in the future." She then added, kindly, to her apprentice, "But don't be hard on yourself. It takes time to establish procedures and get them used to routines."

When disruptions do occur, teachers can ignore small violations, delaying a response for the Debriefing handle, when the infraction can be discussed by the classroom community. That discussion will be in the context of invoking the relevant rule, praising the student for whatever portion of the activity was handled appropriately, and having other students comment about how to help their peer. This is an opportunity to review consequences for continuing to disrupt. When a disruption is more severe, merely making eye contact or writing the student's name on the board may be sufficient to quell inappropriate activity. If that is ignored, calling the student's name, thus inferring later consequences, may persuade the student to participate appropriately. If the behavior persists, time-out, parental contact, and other interventions can be used.

The teacher can also, at any time, stop the entire Frame. "Stop the music," one of our favorite teachers used to say with her hand in the air. She meant that the class was to stop all activity and talk about whatever she perceived was causing a problem. It might have been an event that occurred during recess, the car wreck over the weekend that has everyone too upset to concentrate, or the fight on the sidewalk before first bell. During Phase 1, it is wise to stop whenever there is a clear instance of a lack of understanding or lack of self-control. During Phase 1, community building should happen on an "as-needed" basis as well as regularly in Briefing and Debriefing sessions. Later, during full implementation in Phases 4 and 5, students participate as a community of learners, and it is rarely necessary to interrupt the flow of activity.

From Our Files

From an Experienced Teacher of the
Kamehameha Early Elementary Program (KEEP)

"I always think of going to see the dolphin show at Sea Life Park, in Hawai'i.... They would start off doing a dolphin trick, but if the trainer saw that they were off, she'd shut it down right away. The trainers said that is one of the very important principles of this kind of work. If it doesn't start out right, stop it, shut it down, and start over, because it's so hard to try and correct it when it's in motion. You can't ever get complete control again. For me, that was directly applicable to my classroom, and I carried it back. When it wasn't going right, we stopped and tried something else, or just started again, because it wasn't going to get any better, but only more complicated and worse."

From Our Files

An Elementary Teacher Describes an Activity

"In a cooking activity, I expected students to perform independently of me, but I found out they didn't follow the directions on the quick-and-easy pudding box or the task card I set out for them. All of the materials and utensils were available, and the instructions were reviewed during our Briefing. The students said they understood. But, they didn't do it by the instructions at all, they played with the food and there was a terrible mess, all over the tables and the floor and their clothes. So, all the Jell-O pudding went into the trash can. They spent their recess cleaning up every bit of the mess. After that, they were very careful to follow instructions."

Certainly for the first month or so, a teacher should freely stop and restart whenever the community performance feels "off." In addition to talking about events, the class rules and consequences need review and application.

Following a stop-restart, particularly if there has been some contingency imposed, it is important that the event be discussed in Debriefing. The students should participate in the analysis because it is important that both students and teacher understand the dynamics that led to the disruption. Error analysis is valuable in community building just as it is in content learning. What was that pudding mess all about? What do we need to do in the future to enjoy eating together? What conditions are they leaving for the classmates who are coming next to perform the task? It is equally important to include praise for success in a Debriefing session so that the Frame ends on a positive note for all.

From Our Files

"They were policing themselves so I didn't have to say much. However, I stopped the role-playing game when they had tallied four hatch marks on the board. I talked about the good things they did and where we had trouble. I told them I wasn't willing to go on with the "acting" activity any more that day, but I might give them a chance another day. They understand that I need to change the activities they do to help them stay in control."

Using a Rubric for Classroom
Management and Maintenance of Values

There are many systems that address management issues (DiGiulio 1995; Zabel and Zabel 1996). One classroom management rubric, SCIPP, is a tool that well supports performance of the classroom community values. SCIPP—Simplify, Cooperate, Ignore, Praise, and Promote—supports a classroom climate in which a quality Instructional Frame can function. Teachers report that when used systematically and sensitively, SCIPP guidelines help them manage their own and students' participation in positive ways. Students vary in their reactions to attention from authorities like teachers, especially when it is observed by their peers. It is essential that teachers be attuned to their own and their students' behavior by communicating simply and clearly and by learning quickly from students about their homes, communities, and non-school experiences (Zabel and Zabel 1996).

"SCIPP" to Learning Community Management

S=Simplify.

Simplify early tasks to ensure all students succeed.
Use familiar and everyday language that students understand to talk about classroom activities.
Invite students to provide and prepare task directions, instructions, relevant examples, rationales, etc.

C=Cooperate.

Ask students what to do: How can we build a community for teaching and learning together?
Listen to students.
Respond to students' views authentically.
Put students' suggestions and advice to immediate use.
Give important community responsibilities to students.

I=Ignore or Consequences.

Ignore minor irregularities.
Attend (look, speak, act) to what is going right.
Expect inappropriate participation to disappear if it is given no teacher or student attention.

When inappropriate participation continues, enforce consequences the community has previously agreed are suitable interventions.

PP=Praise and Promote.

Showcase what is going well by sharing examples of quality work.
Seize every opportunity to praise and promote appropriate student participation.
Applaud students for participating as responsible community members.
Praise academic effort and products by describing how they meet standards.

An approach like SCIPP supports the activities in the Frame, providing a rubric that can be systematically applied in difficult moments between the handles. It assists students to know what to expect and provides guidance when irregularities arise in the classroom community. During the handles, students' responses inform the teacher about how to communicate sensitively about student achievements. While one student may experience a teacher's smile and praise as reward for his or her effort, another student may view this as an intrusion into personal space or an embarrassment in front of peers (Zabel and Zabel 1996). As the community develops common understandings about how it operates for everyone's preferences and best interests, students learn more about managing themselves. Applications of the Frame and handles, plus SCIPP, help teachers maintain positive management while they also promote students' capacity for self-governance.

From Our Files

A Mentor Teacher Comments to Her Beginning Colleague

"You walk them through how to proceed very clearly. You state what needs to be out on their desks. You ignore negative comments from your "favorite student" and you move on efficiently. You are extremely clear and positive. Students seem very safe and clear.... You're doing a fantastic job of organizing your classroom. They were all on task during that first part of class—in many others it's very hectic. Most students seemed to have their stamp sheet ready. Even Charles was on task."

Phase 1: One to Four Weeks: Building an Academic Learning Community Using Activity Settings and Instructional Frame

The Instructional Frame, handles, activity settings, classroom management, and SCIPP are the conceptual tools that, once in hand, allow the teacher-designer to begin not only the designing but also the actual practice of developing a community of learners. No community, even of stable membership, is ever completely static. Development is a state of being. Phase 1, the beginning of the developmental process, is an experience that every teacher passes through with each new class of students. It may require three weeks, and even up to four weeks for inexperienced teachers and/or students. Experienced teachers and students will pass through this initial experience with ease in a week. There is no necessity to race through this phase or any of the others, but it is critical that the teacher and students feel comfortable about their capacity to function effectively for the goals of each phase before they move to the next.

During Phase 1, ECT is the source of materials, lessons, and tasks that drive classroom activity and support the development of the community. In Phase 1, as in all the other phases, teachers implement the Five Standards to provide effective assistance to all students from the beginning of instruction. The first three standards (I: Teacher and Students Producing Together; II: Developing Language and Literacy Across the Curriculum; and III: Making Meaning) form the basis for tasks and activities in Phases 1, 2, and 3, and their implementation supports the evolving community of learners described in this chapter. The use of an ECT helps bridge students to the Subject Area Content (SAC) by making connections with students' prior and non-school experience that add real-world meaning to the curriculum.

General Design Considerations

For an overview of the Phase-In process, it may be helpful to refer to Figure A.1 in the Appendix . It offers a road map of sorts that briefly describes the major emphases of the five phases and their cumulative outcome. With this overview, the purposes of the developmental sequence described in this chapter will be clearer. For example, the focus of Phase 1 is not on new content teaching because in this system students, at entry level, are neither socialized into community nor attitudinally or cognitively prepared to participate in the quality and quantity of activity and interaction that results in every student's academic learning. But students are ready to relate to peers and the teacher for community building, and they can experience satisfying success through review and reteaching that lays the foundation for the shift into challenging academic teaching in later phases.

Students' experience of success in the early stages of community formation is critical for the formation of positive attitudes about performing instructional tasks and activities at high levels of quality. Equally important is the teacher's demonstration to students that he or she has the skill to provide them with tasks they can complete successfully. Assuring high rates of student success in tasks and activities from the beginning requires teachers to be skillful informal assessors, observing and talking to students to infer their language, social, and academic skill levels. Phase 1 also focuses on clarifying what students need to relearn or review, can do, know, and know well. Tasks that are too difficult, particularly at this phase, destroy students' confidence in their ability to learn and in the teacher's capacity to assist them. Building a high-powered learning community depends on students' ability to trust the teacher and his or her instructional expertise on their behalf, a prerequisite for the harmonious activity of teaching and learning to come.

The community's capacity to engage eventually in a high-achievement mode depends on the foundational work of Phase 1, building positive values for learning and discovering students' language, social, and academic capacities and needs. All Phase 1 tasks, whether individual, dyad, or small or large group, are designed at an independent level, that is, assuring a high rate (90 percent or better) of correct completion to motivate students to perform tasks that reveal their knowledge bases and the gaps in their skills. Teachers are not the only ones who can design independent activities, and students are invited to contribute their own, in consultation with the teacher, for the class to use.

Phase 1 Goals

- Build a classroom community.
- Apply the Instructional Frame with handles as a daily routine.
- Use a positive management approach such as SCIPP.
- Observe and assess student affinities, talents, academic skills, and role capacities.
- Set up the classroom for students to work in a variety of instructional arrangements.
- Assure student success in all Phase 1 tasks.
- Introduce joint productive activities enabling teachers and students to work together.

Practical Design Considerations

During Phase 1, the Frame is applied routinely and briskly. Briefing and Debriefing are no more than ten minutes each. When needed, extended class discussions for community building—the generation of rules, charters, compacts, or other guidance—occur within the activity settings inside the Frame. If conversation remains vigorous and useful at the end of a Briefing or Debriefing, the topic should be shifted into subsequent activities in the Frame, or whenever there is more time available for conversation. Early in the year, activities are typically kept to twenty or twenty-five minutes in length. This sets expectations that work schedules are concentrated, brisk, and have high priority over other activity. A timer bell or other indicator to signal the end of a work period is very helpful for emphasizing and staying on schedule. The following generic example of a Phase 1 Frame shows the process and its usefulness for ECT material.

Phase 1: Frame 1 (60 Minutes)

Frame 1 is based on Figure 6.2, which is the routine of the common tradition. That is, the interior of the Frame consists of two activities: (1) The teacher instructs, sometimes inviting dialogue for clarification and (2) a follow-up activity takes place in which students practice and demonstrate their ability to apply the content. In this Frame, however, the Briefing and Debriefing handles give this traditional format a developmental potential. The process of the basic Frame is: (1) a ten-minute conversation about what is going to happen (Briefing), (2) content instruction and dialogue to assist student understanding (about twenty minutes), (3) a follow-up activity (about twenty minutes), and (4) a ten-minute conversation about what happened (Debriefing).

This first Frame uses an ECT, and it can be recommended as the first instructional unit of the first day of any class. This first lesson is about building community itself. The goal is to develop a community charter of rules and consequences using a joint productive activity.

Sample Contents for Figure 6.2 Frame (60 Minutes)
Goal: Community Building

Briefing (Ten Minutes).   The teacher introduces the Frame. The activities involve writing the rules for the first community charter. The teacher asks students what will help them cooperate as a community. The teacher writes a few student statements on the chart; this provides several minutes of demonstration to the students of their upcoming tasks in the activity settings to follow. Then the teacher explains the next activity: Teacher and students will assemble their ideas about a community charter.

Activity Settings in the Frame
(Two Simultaneous Activities in a Twenty-Minute Round).

Activity #1: The teacher instructs (twenty minutes). In the first activity setting, the teacher leads the whole group of students in a brainstorming discussion about what community means to the class. The teacher elicits as much student participation as possible on as many topics relating to community as they can offer. They agree about how a community functions, for example, in terms of practicalities such as noise levels, talking, bathroom breaks, getting the teacher's attention, speaking out or raising hands, giving or getting help from other students, finishing early and proper free time use, signals (timer bell or clock), and other issues that every participant, after grade one, can anticipate in classroom life. Older students may choose to discuss grading, judgments about work quality, attendance, and other classroom policy issues. Before the end of the activity, the teacher summarizes, pointing out multiple perspectives and asking how the community can reconcile these. Then the teacher explains what students are to do in the follow-up activity in greater detail. They are to prepare a community charter from the ideas they have just brainstormed. They will work with a partner to produce, in drawn and/or written form, their version of three of the community's rules for getting along and getting quality work done.

Activity #2: Follow-up (twenty minutes). While the students and their partners work on the task, the teacher floats, conversing, assisting, and observing students' participation. The teacher is alert to opportunities to praise students for individual contributions and community participation. At the end of the time period, the teacher collects the charters, which are the joint products of the partners.

Debriefing (Ten Minutes). During the Debriefing, the teacher and students express their feelings and experiences about the Frame of activity, particularly about the process of giving and getting help from their partners and from the teacher. A value for individual accountability for work must be carried over from Phase 1. Did all students perform well together? Probably not everyone, so talking about better procedures and better rules is the problem-solving activity of Debriefing. A review of logistical details is also useful; in this case, a review and reconsideration of finding, completing, storing, and turning in materials and completed tasks.

Throughout this Debriefing dialogue, the teacher finds opportunities to praise and promote what went well in the activity, explaining why student interaction and work products met the goals of the class community for learning. This models the standards for classroom work formats and substance and builds value for talk about tasks among peers. For planning, the teacher uses the charters for the next Frame, when the partners will explain their work together. The class decides how they will compile their work so that every student will contribute to the final product. The teacher provides a large scrapbook, computer, or other format for the purpose.

In an urban magnet school in the Southwest serving low- and middle-income students (60 percent language minority), a teacher and her twenty-five first-, second-, and third-grade students managed effective and equitable joint productive computer activity. According to the teacher, two classroom rules about computer use, Share and Produce, helped the students understand how working together could help them be independent, creative, and self-assessors:

RULE 1 required students to share and help each other with the computer. The teacher frequently modeled and pointed out student models to show how students could produce something together.
RULE 2 required a product from their activity at the computer. "Creative people are producers," said the teacher. Products and partners were often self-selected; regular requirements, such as writing class news, were rotated (Chisholm 1995–1996, p. 167).

Designing Phase 1

Overall quality of instruction is achieved by balancing, across the activities within a Frame, the three design facets of roles and relationships, grouping, and tasks and products. Each activity setting will differ, perhaps in each of these facets, but the overall goals of Inclusion, Fairness, Excellence, and Harmony will be achieved through the interaction of the three facets within the Frame.

Roles and Relating.

- Build a classroom community.
- Apply the Instructional Frame with handles as a daily routine.
- Give students positive feedback about their individual and community participation.
- Assess students' affinities, talents, academic skills, and role capacities.

Students' experience of Phase I develops values for individual and community achievement. Teachers promote values development by expressing interest in students' school history and lives outside of school through individual conversation opportunities, large-group discussions, and follow-up tasks. These events occur as ordinary social exchange and during the application of the Frame as a daily routine for all of the day, a portion of the day at the elementary level, or for class periods at high school. Teachers learn about students during community-building activities that are included in the Frame. Discussions about how the community will perform its work together for individual and community achievement are rich opportunities to observe students' strengths and problem-solving abilities while enacting Standard I and Standard II.

If teachers do not live in or know their students' community, they can quickly learn about students' out-of-school experiences from conversations with students and parents. The value of students' non-school sources of experience, knowledge, and accomplishment is communicated when teachers contextualize it in the curriculum of Phase 1, the ECT. By designing instructional tasks that draw on students' knowledge from non-school sources, teachers focus on Standard III.

The overall role of the teacher, in every phase, is to assess and to assist. In each phase that role is played out somewhat differently, but as we have discussed earlier in this book, teaching itself consists of assisting student performance, and accurately leveled assistance requires careful assessment of student capacities. To accurately assess, careful observation is required, as is some formal structured assessment device. But assessment also requires interaction and dialogue. Here, a little archaeology of the concepts, by examining word origins, can be informative. Etymologically, to assess derives from the Latin *adsidere*, meaning "to sit beside." To assist is from the Latin *assister*, "to stand beside." Sitting beside and standing beside are marvelously expressive of the teacher roles in high-quality instruction. How close should this sitting and standing beside be? Within observation distance, certainly, and often shoulder-to-shoulder, in joint activity. In Phase 1, the teacher is always available for student assistance and always assessing—sitting and standing beside.

Grouping and Routing.

- Set up the classroom for students to work in a variety of instructional arrangements.

Classrooms organized to promote student interaction with peers and with the teacher in compelling academic activities require a supportive classroom arrangement of furniture and materials. The appendix contains a checklist for teachers to plan the arrangements of their classrooms.

Some set up a complex classroom arrangement for the first day, while others move furniture and resources on an as-needed basis. In any event, classroom furniture must provide for large-group, small-group, dyad, and singles' work spaces, with ready access to materials, technology, and resources. In one example, a teacher organized space for students' computer use and joint productive activity as follows:

> The classroom contained an Apple IIe and a Mac LCII computer, which were placed on two tables set in a reversed-L configuration near an exit door. These computers were primarily for student use, rather than teacher productivity. A dot matrix printer also rested on the table nearest the door. The first computer sat beside a wall and behind a third table. This computer's color monitor was clearly visible to those students who stood or sat directly before the computer and to the teacher as she walked behind the computer. The monitor was essentially unobservable from other areas of the room. The second computer located at the bottom of the L-configuration was in a high traffic area, and its monitor was visible to anyone passing by or standing nearby. The teacher said she chose these locations for two reasons. One, there was less dust in the area. Second, this put the equipment close to other students so children could readily seek computer help from classmates (Chisholm 1995–1996).

In Phase 1, each lesson activity is in a large group, but in the follow-up segment of the Frame, teachers can arrange students in two smaller groups or as pairs and individual arrangements. Most teachers use large groups for follow-up in the beginning but soon wish to combine students in different arrangements that encourage interaction and peer assistance on particular tasks and activities. Throughout Phase 1, the teacher is floating and available for assistance and intervention during the follow-up segment of the Frame. In Figure 6.3, activity setting #1 is in whole group; activity setting #2 (follow-up) displays a large-group follow-up for beginning but suggests arranging students to sit in clusters that break up the large group.

FIGURE 6.3   Instructional Framework with Handles

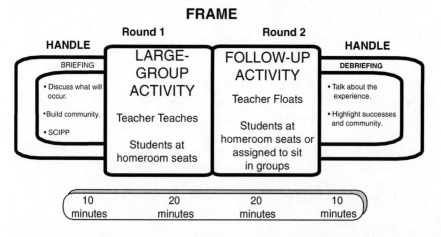

When the class is ready to proceed to Phase 2, the teacher will become more active in arranging groups to ensure that all students have experiences working with one another in a variety of combinations. From follow-up observations in Phase 1, teachers quickly gain knowledge of their students' role capacities and social and academic skills. This information is vital for predicting students' interaction potentials and problems. Early group work builds community as students learn more about how collaboration can facilitate their work. Our emphasis on assuring student success from the first classroom experience both builds student confidence to perform the role of student and contributes to positive teacher-student relationships. For student-student relationships, Phase 1 introduces them to joint productive activity—in the first activity of this Frame, through working in pairs on a joint charter display.

Tasks and Products.

- Assure student success in all Phase 1 tasks.
- Introduce joint productive activities.
- Engage students in joint productive tasks.

Because community building is the major task of Phase 1, teachers often select local community, global politics, or some other aspect of human relations at home or elsewhere as an ECT for the period of Phase-In. These topics may have a high presence in the media, encouraging the use of technology to access the Internet and print resources related to the topic. ECTs, contextualized in what students know and have experienced, lend themselves to tasks and products students can accomplish with high levels of success. They are available from publishers, but teachers often create their own around topics such as patterns, family, neighborhood, community, global and environmental issues, current events, popular media stories, and characters from programs or stories (such as Star Trek for math and science). Whatever the content theme, it organizes reviewing and reteaching, practicing, and beginning instruction.

We have emphasized the need for Phase 1 tasks to produce high rates of student success. Frustration or failure should be prevented for everyone, students and the teacher. Task design that errs on the easy side is more desirable than setting students up for a disastrous stall before their peers and, most important, for themselves. To ensure students' initial success, Phase 1 tasks and activities emphasize routine, familiar tasks, especially while students work in large-group settings.

For the teacher, the routine application of the Frame requires that Briefing and tasks match the time allotted for them. For example, during the ten minutes allotted to Briefing, discussion must cover directions, task and materials logistics, use of reference materials and technology, task collection, storage, and task review. Students also need to know what options they have if they finish tasks early (free reading, computer-based work, helping others, and puzzles or games, for example). Importantly, students must be able to actually finish the task assigned during the Frame. Again, erring on the side of task brevity, with students having to decide how to spend their extra time, is preferable to subjecting students to unnecessary failure to finish because a task requires more time than allotted. Teachers report that accurate task timing and leveling is a challenge at the beginning of the year, but it is critical for building students' confidence in their ability to complete learning tasks in the time allotted and for assessing students' skills and knowledge.

Teachers must be sensitive to student performance levels to set tasks at the appropriate level of difficulty. Accurate task leveling will improve as teachers observe and assess students' language, academic, and social skill levels in their work together. Assessment (or measurement or testing) refers to the measurement of what students know and can do in relation to a criterion (McLaughlin and Shepard 1995). The higher-order goals of innovative pedagogy and curriculum require a variety of forms of assessment. This variety is reflected in the terminology used; such words as "authentic," "direct," and "performance-based assessments" emphasize the need to closely align measurement of students' knowledge and learning goals. For example, students' lack of English-language proficiency must never be mistaken for limited subject matter knowledge. When necessary, students should be allowed to express themselves in their primary language, and all efforts must be made to ensure that students understand what they are being asked to perform during instruction and assessment. Even in Phase I of the classroom developing here, such assistance would be available from peers as well as the teacher. The large-group activities of Phase 1 are designed as compelling activities, but they are also the means of gathering baseline evidence of students' knowledge and skill levels. The assessment information will inform the teacher about students' skill and knowledge levels while guiding task design that ensures students' success at the rate of 90 percent correct responses. This level of success needs to be in place as soon as possible for all tasks that students are to perform without teacher assistance.

Phase 1 whole-group activity should often require a joint product that draws on many students' knowledge and skills. Joint productive tasks are very common in families, communities, and the workplace, but are not so common in kindergarten through twelfth-grade classrooms. They require students to exchange resources with others before the task can be completed, which contrasts with typical grouping activities in which achievement can be produced through a single student's effort. In joint tasks, one student's performance is dependent on every other's because all must participate to accomplish the product. Joint productive tasks are best when they require multiple abilities for solution (Cohen and Lotan 1997). This fosters maximum Inclusion, builds mutual respect, and provides a press for collaboration. Mapmaking is an excellent example of a multi-ability task, requiring abilities of observation, memory, drawing, coordination, group discussion, scaling, leadership, listening, and negotiation. Students jointly develop a product that captures and integrates the variety of their impressions of their shared experience.

Phase 1 also includes the building of systems and capacities for accessing assigned tasks and storing student work. Depending on grade level and content area, these systems might be as simple as providing students with a folder for storing their work or as complex as art portfolios or lab manuals and demonstration kits. Access and storage can involve heavy student responsibility and design participation. Likewise, the teacher will be preparing record books, portfolio formats, or other storage and display systems for collecting and commenting on students' products.

Ready to go to Phase 2? Here are the checkpoints:

1. Teacher and students use the Frame routinely and comfortably.
2. Tasks emphasize skill review, reteaching, format and material introduction, and everyday problem solving.
3. The teacher enacts Standards I: Teachers and Students Producing Together, II: Developing Language and Literacy Across the Curriculum, and III: Making Meaning: Connecting School to Students' Lives.
4. The teacher assesses students' language, social, and academic skill levels.
5. The teacher praises students often for individual and community participation.
6. Students interact over tasks to give and receive help.
7. Students perform tasks with high rates of success.
8. Students complete tasks within the allotted time.
9. Students know how to use extra time.
10. The teacher collects baseline samples of students' work products for portfolio assessment.

Phase 2: Two to Three Weeks: Grouping for Independent and Simultaneous Activity

In Phase 2, teachers continue to draw on the ECT for compelling tasks students accomplish with peers and without teacher supervision in a more complex Frame of activities. In addition to independent work habits and tasks with joint products, Phase 2 students experience a classroom of simultaneous activities. When they are not working with the teacher they see other students who are and also see others working on tasks that are different from their own. Most students have little experience of Standard I: Teachers and Students Producing Together, which produces such differentiation in the working patterns of their classrooms.

General Design Considerations

The role of peer interaction in student learning receives greater focus in Phase 2, which emphasizes Standard II: Developing Language. Teachers plan more group work in Phase 2, designed to maximize diverse peer contact across several dimensions. In Phase 2, the teacher continues to decide where the activity settings will be—perhaps at homeroom seats, perhaps moving about the classroom to work with others of their group. Student input into classroom arrangements is actively sought. Briefing and Debriefing time is spent discussing the kinds of activity and talk that occur in preparation for the academic emphasis soon to come to the classroom. Students brainstorm about talk that relates to task accomplishment and peer assistance and the value of social talk for their learning goals. In transitioning from Phase 1's focus on community building, student success, and joint productive activities to Phase 2, SCIPP or another systematic, positive management approach continues to be vital. Briefing and Debriefing are daily opportunities for dialogue, problem solving, and community building. These handles will remain strong if they remain brief. Experienced teachers and students spend at least two weeks in this phase; more may be required to provide the grouping experiences all students must have with each other.

Phase 2 Goals

- Use the Instructional Frame routinely.
- Provide experiences for students to accomplish tasks independently, without direct teacher assistance.
- Encourage student interaction to accomplish tasks.
- Group students in activity settings in a variety of ways, both heterogeneously and homogeneously, by affinity, language, diversity, ability, gender, and common interests.
- Rotate groups of students to accomplish different tasks simultaneously.
- Provide tasks that students can accomplish without teacher assistance in the allotted time frame.
- Collect samples of student work for students' portfolios.

Practical Design Considerations

For Phase 2, classroom furniture, materials, and resources need to be arranged to accommodate regular small-group activities. Many teachers like to have identified places, or stations, where tools, resources, space, and furniture support certain types of activities. So do students. When secondary students come to history class, things go better if they know which table/area has the material for working on their video storyboard. Of course, for the next Frame of activities, that place may be used for other activities. As the classroom and the Frame itself become more complex, students should take a role in community maintenance; setting up and cleaning up the classroom; and replenishing materials for back-up activities such as puzzles, games, and library books.

In Phase 2, teachers can route students to the independent task by dividing the class in half and explaining the task in the Briefing. The goal of this phase is to move every student through varied experiences of assisting and relying on one another. Here, the norms for independent work are forming, and the teacher assists students to build this capacity by resisting requests for help that can be provided by peers or reference to a task card. Of course the teacher responds to emergencies. But most student requests of teachers under these circumstances can be handled by peers; if not, the teacher needs to focus on this during the Briefing, both in the form of clearer explanations and by building the value of students' listening. The plight of students who seek teacher assistance when they are expected to accomplish tasks independently can be reviewed by the class at Debriefing.

Figure 6.4 illustrates a Frame for independent work using halves of the class (or other proportions if preferred). This Frame design has some stu-

FIGURE 6.4   Frame for Simultaneous and Independent Activity Settings

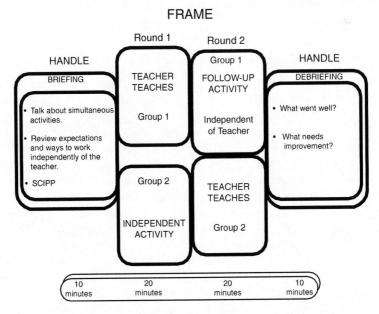

dents working independently of teacher assistance while the teacher works directly with a second group. The goal is for the independent group to accomplish its tasks and solve its problems for the entire round without calling on the teacher in the "teaching" group. Those problems will include equipment breakdowns, resource sharing, bathroom visits, and whatever routine issues arise. Perfection is not expected at the beginning, and the teacher will have to monitor and encourage the independent groups. The Briefing and Debriefing handles are lively during this transition.

This Frame is used repetitively until everyone, especially the teacher, is satisfied that the community can handle independence and travel to activities. However, it is characteristic of Phase 2 that the class will continue to require monitoring and management maintenance using SCIPP or another positive management system.

Although Briefing, Debriefing, and SCIPP support the development of students' working independently, the teacher needs to check and praise appropriate participation as it occurs. This reassures students that they are not really out of the teacher's mind and builds their self-maintenance into gradually lengthening periods. If the teacher positions herself strategically as she works with a small group, she can frequently scan the room and praise students who are working independently. Students also develop the understanding that working apart from the teacher is as important for the learning community as working closely together. Phase 2 is the period when teachers still need to reassure students that they and the teacher are working together even when she is not interacting with them continuously. When the class is successful, everyone needs to celebrate this major step toward becoming a community of learners.

Increasing Phase 2:
Independent, Simultaneous, and Teacher Independent Activity

When the students' and teacher's comfort level is high enough for that pattern, the Frame can be expanded. The Frame illustrated in Figure 6.5 displays an increase to three student-only simultaneous activities. In this display, the groups attending the activity settings are thirds of the class, which means they are still relatively large. Adequate seating and materials must be available for the groups, which teachers will monitor closely to inform students about how well they are working together. The Briefing activity explains group membership and tasks but focuses on routing or how and when to travel between activity settings. After Briefing, the students progress in their groups through the rotations for the twenty-minute tasks, as displayed in Figure 6.5.

Figure 6.5 presents an eighty-minute Frame for three groups of students working simultaneously, two independent of teacher supervision and one where the teacher is present to actively assist. Note that the stu-

FIGURE 6.5   Frame of Three Groups, Three Tasks

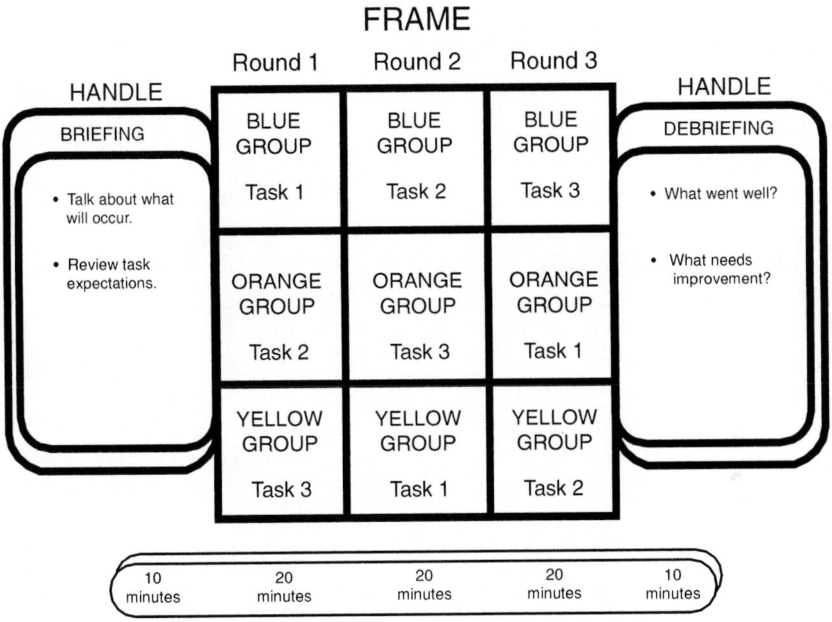

FRAME

	Round 1	Round 2	Round 3	
HANDLE				**HANDLE**
BRIEFING	BLUE GROUP	BLUE GROUP	BLUE GROUP	DEBRIEFING
• Talk about what will occur.	Task 1	Task 2	Task 3	• What went well?
• Review task expectations.	ORANGE GROUP	ORANGE GROUP	ORANGE GROUP	• What needs improvement?
	Task 2	Task 3	Task 1	
	YELLOW GROUP	YELLOW GROUP	YELLOW GROUP	
	Task 3	Task 1	Task 2	

10 minutes	20 minutes	20 minutes	20 minutes	10 minutes

dent groups have color labels and the tasks are numbered. Each group rotates through the tasks in round-robin sequence. The materials and instructions for the tasks may be picked up from a staging area or placed in three different areas of the classroom. Teachers whose students are ready to move about the classroom as groups can arrange for the three activity settings to occur in different areas. If movement around the room is chosen, travel pathways for students with disabilities and wheelchairs must be unobstructed. One minute is sufficient for travel.

During Briefing the teacher introduces the tasks in the activities of the Frame, routing and peer assistance. Then the students commence the activity. When the timer signals clean-up at the end of the round, students prepare to travel to the next task area. Difficulties or irregularities in the rotations are discussed in Debriefing. Figure 6.5 displays the grouping, the routing, and the timing.

This Frame for three groups and three tasks can be completed in less than an hour and a half. It may be interrupted for class schedules that run in an hourly fashion and resumed at the next meeting time. For example, after Briefing and one or two rounds, the class can break and resume at round two or three on the next day. Breaking between the third round and Debriefing is less desirable. The linkage of the Briefing with the first round and the Debriefing with the last round grounds the Debriefing discussion in the concrete experience of the activity settings. It must be fitted to the community's time constraints, but this expanded Frame is adapt-

able for most schedules. For example, it can be implemented in the following two different circumstances.

If the class has a block time schedule with ample time:
DAY ONE   eighty minutes (Briefing and three rounds and Debriefing)

If the class has limited time for implementation (only thirty minutes
available per day):
DAY ONE   thirty minutes (Briefing and one round)
DAY TWO   twenty minutes (Round two alone)
DAY THREE   thirty minutes (Round three and Debriefing)

This Frame is useful as a second step in Phase 2 because it provides
variety in formats and accustoms students to multiple simultaneous activities and all the attendant courtesies, self-control, and routines required. The grouping can continue to be random or systematic, but
across all the frames of Phase 2, each student should be observed working with every other.

The contents of the Frame and the three activities vary of course by
ECT and the review and reteaching needs of every class, but a sample is
provided in the next section. The teacher has chosen to work with one
group at a time on listening and language development for this Frame.
The other groups will work independently on related tasks as described.
Each task area must have an easy-to-see task card with clear directions
about how to accomplish the task.

Sample Contents for Figure 6.5 Frame
Goal: Listening and Language Development

Briefing (Ten Minutes).   Students learn during the Briefing handle about
their group assignments; they may have noticed colored paper lists of
names on the bulletin board or some other postings of groupings. Some
teachers tell students why they have grouped students in a particular
way during Briefing. Students are reminded about the task cards with directions. Travel is also discussed: where they will sit, how to carry work,
and what to do with their work products. The teacher has planned to
have the three groups move in round-robin fashion to an area of the
classroom for each activity. The students labeled Blue will start in area #1
with the teacher; the Orange Group will start at the area for task #2; and
the Yellow Group will travel to the area assigned for task #3. When the
bell rings to change, Blue Group will go to task area #2, Orange Group
will go to task area #3, and Yellow Group will meet with the teacher at
#1. After twenty minutes, the groups will shift again to the task areas
they haven't attended.

Activity Settings in the Frame
(Three Simultaneous Activities in a Twenty-Minute Round).

> Activity #1: The teacher and students work together. The teacher reads a
> compelling story or plays a recording appropriate to the stu-
> dents' level, asking them to listen carefully so they can retell the
> story events. The teacher asks the students to talk about the story
> idea, sequence of events, or details of setting and writes their
> comments on a chart or has the students write them. They dis-
> cuss how well they recalled the story material and rate their own
> performance. Then they are given copies of the story or they lis-
> ten again to the recording to check their accuracy.
> Activity #2: In a joint productive activity, students write a story together
> that relates to the ECT. Each person is responsible for producing
> three sentences that develop the story. If there are students who
> cannot yet read, they will draw a sequence that tells a story.
> (What happened first? What happened next?) Everyone produces
> his or her own copy of the story.
> Activity #3: Students make a list of information about the individuals in the
> group. The list includes the names, addresses, telephone numbers,
> birthplaces, siblings' names, courses, and teachers' names of all
> the students in the group. All the groups edit and compile their
> lists and produce a Classroom Directory.

Debriefing (Ten Minutes). Students convene to discuss the experience of
their groups and routing. Did everyone participate? Complete the work?
Feel included? Did everyone operate independently or was the teacher
interrupted? If so, what was the problem? How can the community solve
such as problem independently next time? Can the teacher or the class
improve the experience of this Frame?

Figure 6.6 displays a four-group, four-task rotation that functions in
the same manner as the three-group, three-task rotation of Figure 6.5.
Increasing the number of task sites is an opportunity to experiment
with new groupings using what has been learned about students' role
capacities and affinities to improve mixed and matched groups' productivity. Considerations for group seating and working space in the
classroom must be reviewed with each change so that every student is
accommodated comfortably for travel, seating, and work. The teacher
may continue to experiment, but the expectation that groups work independently of teacher supervision remains a priority. As usual, challenges and problems are discussed in Debriefing. Or, one round of a
Frame may become a class community meeting for planning and problem solving.

FIGURE 6.6   100-Minute Frame of Four Groups, Four Tasks

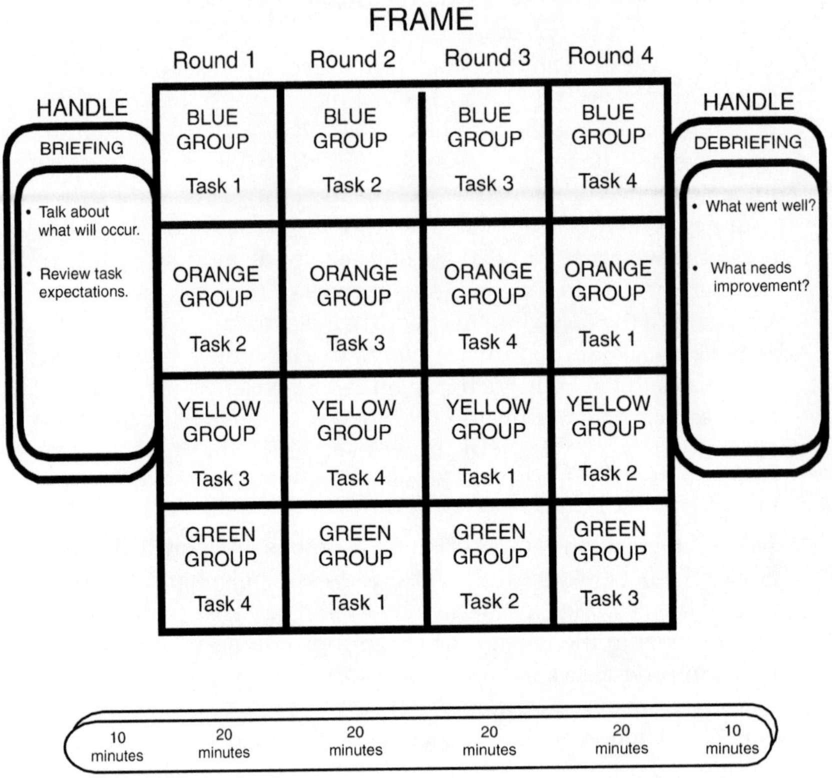

Designing Phase 2

Roles and Relationships.

- Use the Frame routinely.
- Provide experiences for students to accomplish tasks independently, without direct teacher assistance.
- Encourage student interaction to accomplish tasks.

The teacher's basic roles continue to be assessment and assistance of students' skills levels, content knowledge, language, and experience. But, instead of the teacher floating from one student group to another to talk and listen to students, the teacher will work with one section of the class while the other works without teacher assistance. The teacher's role is beginning to differentiate from that of a constantly available resource to one that performs in a variety of expert roles. In Phase 2, and in all subsequent phases, the teacher will no longer be continuously available to provide on-call student assistance. Thus the community will activate its own resources for assistance. This is one of the values that a learning community must adopt: Everyone participates to perform his or her tasks and assists others to perform theirs. Phase 2 establishes the teacher's role, which is to teach, that is, to provide assistance to student performance.

Student-to-student roles take on greater importance in Phase 2 as students come to rely more on each other in joint activity. Students are encouraged to exchange information, solve problems, and perform tasks without direct teacher assistance. Student talk about tasks and related topics is essential, in content language, in English, and in home languages—whatever is useful to them. This is especially important for students working without teacher assistance. Whatever needs arise, students are to assist one another. During Briefing and Debriefing, the students who are resources for class are identified and praised. Even very young students can have skills on the computer or the calculator, or fix a tape recorder, or help with the myriad of problems that arise in rooms with twenty to thirty or more people working closely with each other and equipment. Students' skills and talents are highly valuable resources for facilitating classroom management, organization, and instruction.

Grouping and Routing.

- Group students by affinity, language, diversity, ability, heterogeneity, gender, compatibilities, and common interests to perform a task.
- Rotate groups of students to accomplish different tasks simultaneously.

In Phase 2, students are first grouped for independent work that they can accomplish without teacher assistance. When the class has experience with this, teachers group students in a variety of homogeneous and heterogeneous combinations by affinities, compatibilities, language, interests, and skills. Phase 2 is the time to experiment with grouping students to work with members of other crowds, other cultures, and other language groups. For some purposes and tasks, teachers will group bilingual students by home language, while for others they will group students of different cultures and language groups together. It is useful to have a record of the group memberships formed to reflect on how students cooperated and assisted one another. That record also provides assurance that every student has had task experience with every other student in the developing community.

Grouping serves several purposes, but a primary one is to combine students who can support one another to complete tasks without teacher assistance. Phase 2 prepares the community of students to exercise self-control and cooperation so that the teacher can eventually focus on intense teaching of small groups (in Instructional Conversations) while the rest of the class manages itself. To do so, the teacher depends on students' cooperation and the community's high value for academic instruction. Cooperation in the community of learners will arise from common understanding and valuing of the different ways individuals work. Only as relationships are formed to become a cooperative community can teachers advance classroom capacity from its ordinary limitations into a system of highly organized, simultaneous, and diverse activity settings. Within such a community, there is room for a range of perspectives, drawn from the local community and families, individual teacher's preferences, task demands, subject matter activities, and developmental stages.

Tasks and Products.

- Provide tasks designed so students can accomplish them in the allotted time without teacher assistance.
- Collect examples of student work for students' portfolios.

Phase 2 emphasizes the use of the variety of formats students will encounter throughout the year. If reports on a laboratory experiment, financial forms, newspapers, maps, equipment (tape recorders, calculators, computers), observation formats, animal care protocols, recipes, or other formats will be used, begin to familiarize students with them. As an additional development of community responsibility and of cognitive growth, students can be encouraged, or even assigned, to design tasks for review, reteaching, and basic skills application. Some of their activity settings can include the task of constructing worksheets, review problems, or simple teaching games for their classmates.

Phase 2 tasks continue to draw from the ECT, increasing the number of joint productive activities that emphasize community building and self-management of work. As teachers come to know their students' strengths, skills, and experience, their design of tasks at students' independent levels is more accurate.

The task requirements for Phasing-In the Frames of multiple simultaneous activities are high. In fact, students' rapid and successful consumption of tasks and activities indicates that the classroom community is developing well. But teachers can share task production with students by actively involving them in producing and designing activities for their peers. All students can design tasks such as puzzles, word games, and problems for use during activity settings for practice and review. As previously suggested, designing these tasks can be scheduled as a finishing activity when students complete their work early, as an assigned task in a specific activity setting, or as homework. Student participation in task preparation builds their sense of being stakeholders in the community. Of course, the product is actually a joint one by teacher and students, because the teacher must assure quality and that task levels meet students' needs. Student-generated tasks must meet the same high standards as expected for those prepared commercially or by the teacher. Remember that these tasks in Phase 2 are to be accomplished by students at 90 percent accuracy.

Success in joint productive tasks is just as important as in individual tasks. Such cooperative tasks can be hands-on, real-world problem-solving activities that students find compelling, especially in collaboration with peers. When the information needed to complete a task must come from every member of the group, students are moved to cooperate and to assist one another. Examples of joint products include graphs and charts displaying information about funds of family knowledge or expertise, siblings and grandparents, sports, meal planning, the class's height and weight, eye and hair color, and so forth. Other joint tasks have very traditional academic products: a facsimile of a coral reef or volcano that erupts, scientific experiments, research and writing projects, murals, maps, newspapers, books. Joint productive tasks, like any other, are those the teacher is sure the group can accomplish. If not, management concerns will soon emerge that could damage the fragile community norms that are emerging in Phase 2.

Ready to go to Phase 3? Here is your checklist:

1. The teacher uses an expanded Frame routinely.
2. Teaching focuses on review, reteaching, and instruction related to ECT.
3. The teacher enacts Standards I: Teacher and Students Producing Together, II: Developing Language and Literacy Across the Curriculum, and III: Making Meaning: Connecting School to Students' Lives.
4. Students work without teacher assistance on independent tasks.
5. Students work in a variety of groupings with every other student.
6. Students interact over tasks to give and receive help.
7. Students perform joint work for a product.
8. Students perform tasks with high rates of success in the time allotted.
9. Students use extra time appropriately.
10. The teacher monitors students frequently.
11. The teacher praises students often for individual and community participation.
12. The teacher observes and notes students' social and academic skills.

13. The teacher collects baseline samples of students' work products for portfolio assessment.

Phase 3: One to Two Weeks: Teaching and Learning in Activity Settings

Now students have experienced a variety of groupings and have had success with different tasks in a classroom of simultaneous activities. Great advances have been made since Phase 1: The teacher and students routinely participate in joint productive activity, students accomplish tasks appropriately in groups without teacher assistance, and students rotate round-robin fashion through a sequence of tasks focused on review and reteaching within an ECT. Both the teacher and students prepare tasks for class use, leveled and timed so that students experience success. During Phase 2, every student has worked with every other student in the class, or soon will. In Phase 3, students are introduced to at least one activity station. Activity stations are venues where similar types of activities predictably occur; many contain tools and resources. For the rest of this chapter, almost all activity settings take place at such stations. They learn how to travel to an activity setting where they work individually and collaboratively with their peers on the independent, joint productive, and academic tasks.

General Design Considerations

Phase 3 has two foci. First, as in Phase 2, the teacher continues grouping students so that every student has experience working with every other student. Second, the teacher introduces at least one activity setting, preferably more. These activity settings have academic foci as well as others, but all must include compelling and student-generated tasks to motivate students to perform productively. We have seen first activity settings wrapped as a huge gift to be opened and enjoyed by the emerging community of learners. Success at the first activity setting is a benchmark of the progress of the group as a learning community. Teachers often choose to celebrate the event. In this phase, the tasks of activity settings in the Frames continue as independent and joint productive activities that complete review and relearning of basic skills. Also in this phase, the ECT may culminate in tasks and activities that bridge to the main content topic of the class. Phase 3 establishes activity settings as stable structures in the classroom that will make up the majority of students' learning experience. The accomplishment of activity settings for teacher and students establishes the critical infrastructure that promotes academic teaching and learning through activity and collaboration.

All activity settings occur in identifiable places, and they require appropriate tasks, materials, and resources. Most activity settings will operate independently of direct teacher supervision, will interrelate with other activities where useful, and are a collective responsibility of the classroom community.

Phase 3 Goals

- Introduce and operate one or more activity settings.
- Recognize students for taking responsibility for finishing activities, designing tasks for class use, community administration, and housekeeping.
- Track and route student groupings to ensure that all students have the opportunity to work with every other student.
- Observe students for skills, affinities, and compatibilities that increase individuals' academic learning in groups.
- Provide tasks and activities relating to ECT that accomplish review and reteach in preparation for academic instruction.
- Monitor and assess students' basic skill levels, content knowledge, and language competence.
- Collect representative student work samples for portfolio assessment.

Practical Design Considerations

Even in Phase 1, it is often economical and functional to have specific stations (tables, areas) that contain resources useful for certain types of activities. Establishing these places for a particular type of activity should not be confused with designing the activity. The activity matters, not the place. So even when activities are designed to use resources (or furniture) of a particular type, the design of activity settings should not be restricted to those that must occur in a specific small location. Many activities will have multiple settings: library, mailroom, computer, or math lab. Wherever it is, the location(s) of the activity must be made clear to students in the Briefing.

In discussing this Frame we depart from the previous descriptive format. Instead, we provide transcripts of actual classroom events, again enacted by Cynthia. Her two goals are exactly right for Phase 3: building community capacity by introducing a mapmaking activity setting and assigning students to work in small groups.

Now a word about Cynthia: At the time of the events reported here, she was a first-year teacher of sixth-grade language arts, working in an apprentice-like role with one of the authors (Dalton), principally through telephone and e-mail interaction, with occasional personal visits. Cynthia's placement was a tribally managed school on a Native American reservation in the southwestern United States. Clearly an at-risk group (limited English proficient and living largely in poverty), the students—like most other American children—were accustomed to classrooms of the common tradition, using a recitation script. Cynthia had moved through Phases 1 and 2 in about seven weeks. She and her class had produced a set of rules that helped them get along and work together productively. The students were able to apply several of their already familiar rules to this new situation.

Cynthia assigns journal writing and journal construction in addition to mapmaking. She will "float" around the tables where the students are seated, observing and offering assistance as needed. We have already presented the transcript of the portion of the Briefing in which she introduced journal writing (see p. 147).

FIGURE 6.7   Frame for Introducing an Activity Setting (AS)

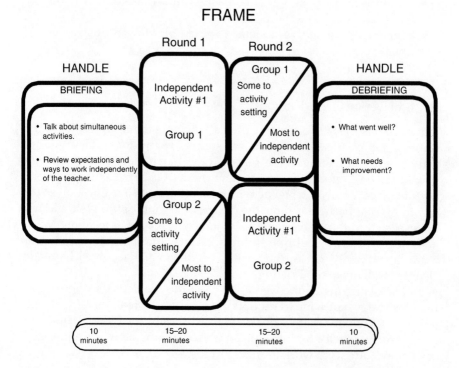

As we re-enter the Briefing scene, Cynthia has moved on to introduce the first activity setting. This small group of five students is to collaborate on drawing a large map of Eustice Lake, the site of a recent class field trip. Not only is this a new activity for the class, but organizing the class for three concurrent activities, one of them completely independent of direct teacher supervision, is also a new development. Figure 6.7 shows the Frame that was designed.

In this Briefing meeting the students are seated in their usual arrangement, around small tables, in groups of three to five, with Cynthia standing in front, referring to chart paper tacked on the chalkboard. On the chart paper is a list of the activities and expectations for the upcoming Frame of activity.

Briefing (Ten Minutes).

TEACHER: All right. What is this?

MALE STUDENT [reading aloud from poster]: Making a map.

OTHER MALE STUDENT: Use a huge piece of paper to write it, draw a map, use colored pencils.

GROUP OF STUDENTS IN CHORUS: Show where you went to Eustice Lake.

TEACHER: Right. Now who's gonna go? Here's what we'll do: I'll tell you how it's gonna work. Put your hands down 'cuz I'm gonna tell you how it works. [Boy in the back continues to wave his hand, which Cynthia ignores.] While we do this activity with the journal I'm gonna walk around and I'll pick five people to go there. Okay? So what do we do there?

MALE STUDENT: Make a map.

TEACHER: Make a map of what?

SEVERAL STUDENTS [chorus]: Eustice Lake!

TEACHER: Right, Eustice Lake and its surroundings. Okay now, um … let's see, here I'm gonna show you this, this is called a task card. This is your first task card, you'll be learning how to use these more. Okay, this is what a task card looks like and it's gonna be clipped onto this [demonstrates attaching it to a small wooden stand]. Clip it on like this, and then it'll go over in your activity center. So the five people who go over there, they get to read this and do what it says.

[She walks over and places it on the table].

TEACHER [continues]: Now, um, what do you think you're gonna do there? How are you gonna get there?

MALE STUDENT: By working your self-control!

TEACHER [approvingly]: Working your self-control! Okay, now, for us to get this rolling I need to have a student model for us how to get up out of their seat and walk over to the center.

[Two boys in the back of the class immediately wave their hands in the air.]

TEACHER: We need to have this right if this is going to work. Okay Bryant, why don't you go ahead.

BRYANT: Okay. Where?

TEACHER: [Nods toward his destination station.]

[Bryant begins the journey, smiling self-consciously.]

TEACHER [commenting as Bryant progresses]: Yeah, okay. How we get up out of our chair ... excellent, he pushed it in ... is he, is he bothering people as he walks? [Pauses, shaking her head.] Nooooo, he's doing really great. He's doing it softly and calmly. [Bryant sits in a chair at the "map station" and looks at the teacher with a suppressed, pleased smile.] All right, good job! Okay come on back. All right very good. Okay now, now, let's have two students model how they can go over to the center. Okay? Okay, let's have ... Okay, Joshua [laughs, covers her face] I mean Alexander! and Alonzo [who is raising his hand excitedly].

[Alexander and Alonzo rise and walk toward the map station.]

TEACHER: They remember to push their chairs in, and they're walking calmly and quietly, and they sat, very good!

[About half of the students are following the boys with their eyes.]

TEACHER: Good, you guys did it perfect. [Walking to the map station.] Now when you're over here at the center, are they gonna talk real loud?

CLASS [chorus]: Noooooooooooo.

TEACHER: Why not?

TWO MALE STUDENTS: Cuz!

ANOTHER STUDENT: ... bother ... [indistinct].

TEACHER: Yeah. What happens, how about when they're here, can they get up and walk over and sharpen their pencil any time they want?

MALE STUDENT: No!

TEACHER: Can they do that at all? [Pause] No. No. When they're over here, are they to ask me for help? [Pause] No. Are they to ask any of you for help? No. Are they to get up at all? No. They stay. If they need help what are they gonna do?

ALEXANDER: Ask them [pointing to Alonzo].

TEACHER: Right. Alex said they're going to ask their table partner, their activity partner.

MALE STUDENT: What if they don't know?

TEACHER: What if their activity center partner doesn't know?

ANOTHER MALE STUDENT: Ask their teacher.
TEACHER: No. They can't ask me.
A STUDENT: They read the card.
TEACHER: They read the card. They can ask each other or read the card.

Following this interaction, Cynthia selected five students (from those who volunteered by hand waving), closed the Briefing, and the next activities began.

Activity Settings in the Frame
(Three Simultaneous Activities in a Twenty-Minute Segment).

   Activity #1: Journal construction. Half the students construct their journals using colored paper for covers and notebook paper for the writing area, punching holes for brad insertion to hold them all together. For this activity, students work at their homeroom seats while sharing equipment and assisting one another to decorate the journal covers in preparation for making an entry.
   Activity #2: Large group journal writing. During this activity, half the students in the class are writing entries. Cynthia is walking slowly around the class, observing the students who are largely on task, exchanging occasional comments. She answers some student questions. Occasionally, Cynthia uses her public voice to praise someone who is writing diligently or offering help to a peer. Her eye is cocked toward the new activity setting, which she is covertly monitoring with great care. But it never becomes necessary to intervene, as the transcript below illustrates.
   Activity #3: Mapmaking (twenty minutes). In the mapmaking activity setting, the five students are immediately absorbed in the task. Eustice Lake is a major and familiar feature of their community, and in previous weeks the sixth grade has been working on an integrated thematic unit that has had them surveying the lake site, cleaning it up, writing essays about it, and other activities. With this deep contextualization, the students move with energy and purpose. Cynthia has butcher paper covering the table at the station, and there are several colors of marking pens, enough for all five students. Following is a portion of the transcript of their interaction:

ALEX: See, this is divided into a "Y" like ... [strokes a line with felt pen] this.

HAYES [standing at far end]: Yeah. Make it like that ... and then
  make that stream come down right there. [Pointing.] Somewhere
  around there.
JOCELYN: There? [Points with pencil.]
BILLIE: Make that stream coming down right here [drawing in the
  air above the chart paper] ... and then [swirling motion with
  hand] there's a pond.
[Alex begins to draw.]
HAYES: Just a little bit ... oh yeah, make that big, make a little bit
  ... right there, stop! Right there, stop! Make that big one, make
  that big one. Remember? That big old pond, that's right there?
  And it ...
JOHNNIE: Oh ... and it's going down here and that big old pond?
[Jocelyn is drawing.]
HAYES: Yeah. Make that big old pond ...
JOHNNIE: Right here?
HAYES: Yeah, like that. Just make it like that.
JOCELYN: [unintelligible].
HAYES: And then that little stream that comes ...
BILLIE: This one?
JOHNNIE: No, it went like this. It goes around like this and ... here's
  a pond and it breaks down like that.

The activity proceeded very well indeed, with students purposefully
and thoughtfully interacting over the mapping task.

Debriefing (Ten Minutes).   When the timer bell sounded, Cynthia began
the second handle, Debriefing, whose general script is "Talk about what
happened and build community values." She walked toward the map-
drawing table, where the two girls and three boys were still intent on
their map, one girl still busily drawing.

TEACHER [in her "announcement" voice]: Papers down, and look up
  here.
ALEX [disappointed at the interruption to their mapmaking]: Aw,
  man ...
TEACHER [calling names of individual students to draw their eyes
  toward her]: Cora ... Shannon ... [Now addressing the entire
  class.] Okay, let's do a Debriefing. Okay, let's talk about what they
  did right, let's be positive, what did they do right?
FEMALE STUDENT: Nothing.
TEACHER: Nothing? Did they do their map activity like they were
  supposed to?
STUDENTS [variously]: No. Yes.

TEACHER: Yes, they did that. Were they quiet for most of the time?
STUDENTS: No.
TEACHER: Were they supposed to be silent?
STUDENTS: Yes.
TEACHER: No. They were supposed to talk to each other.
STUDENT: But not that loud.
TEACHER: But not that loud. Okay, but for the most part they did okay. And they have a beautiful drawing ...

Although this interaction is brief, it contains all the essential elements of an effective Debriefing activity. Cynthia's goals were to provide students with success, to build relationships with them, to help them learn the rules and consequences, and for students and herself to learn how to get this new system to work. Clarifications were necessary; apparently some of the students thought that the mapmakers were to work in silence. As frequently happens, students were harsher in their judgments of each other than was Cynthia, who consistently emphasized positive achievements. In this transcript, one can see the actual process of values development through discussion and negotiation over the interpretation of shared events.

Designing Phase 3

Roles and Relationships.

- Introduce and operate one or more activity settings.
- Recognize students for taking responsibility for finishing activities, designing tasks for class use, community administration, and housekeeping.

In Phase 3, the teacher carefully introduces the first activity setting and hints at others to come. At this point, teachers and students have learned about working in groups and traveling to new workstations in the classroom. Through a variety of tasks, such as routine review and joint productive activity, students have learned to take responsibility for their own productivity and for helping and showing one another how to accomplish a task. Phase 3 applies all the foundational work of Phases 1 and 2 to establish multiple activity settings in the classroom. Students are usually enthusiastic about the process and are reluctant to return to traditional classroom organization.

If classroom management continues to need attention, selecting those students who can provide models of working appropriately is wise and provides an implicit incentive to others.

From Our Files

The Bus Trip for a Field Trip

The students insisted that they continue working in their scheduled groups while riding in the bus to and from the zoo.

Grouping and Routing.

- Track and route student groupings to ensure that all students have the opportunity to work with every other student.
- Observe students for skills, affinities, and compatibilities that increase individuals' academic learning in groups.

In early Phase 3 Frames, most teachers (as did Cynthia) choose to work in two groups, one teacher assisted and the other teacher independent. Then a small group of students is selected to attend the new activity setting. This establishes working at the independent activity as of value, as a privilege. Teachers may pre-select students for the independent activity, or they may choose them spontaneously (as did Cynthia). During the Briefing activity, the teacher provides directions for moving to and from the independent activity. Figure 6.7 diagrams this Frame.

After the initial rotation, Cynthia continued to send students to the map-making activity setting in small groups until every member of the class had attended. This Frame provides full rotations within a period of fifty to sixty minutes. Cynthia designed this expanded Frame to fit the schedule of the middle school, where she had each class for one hour. It is important to note that Cynthia is focused on the students traveling appropriately and briskly to activity settings. Experienced students can transition between activities in no more than one minute.

From this point on, Cynthia developed her classroom community rapidly and soon introduced other activity settings. For each new Frame, or when any new activity setting was introduced, she used the Briefing time to introduce the new format, but as her students gained experience with the system the time required for introduction rapidly decreased. Soon she had established five activities in her classroom, a regular schedule of varied groups, heterogeneous or mixed and homogeneous or matched for some feature like language, interest, ability, or need. She routed intact groups from one activity to another in round-robin fashion. Cynthia's workday consisted of five classes of students each day. Each hour was organized into multiple, diversified, and simultaneous activity settings, in which the Five Standards were employed as an integral part of instructional activity.

In Frames as simple as Cynthia's introductory pattern (Figure 6.7), the students and teacher can talk and can post grouping information. Routing to this point has been mainly round-robin, with students moving from one activity to another in intact groups. As Frames become more complex, students will need schedules to route them to their multiple activities. The preferred number of students for small-group work is from three to seven. For most classrooms, it is possible to enact Frames of activities for matched and mixed groupings with as few as five activities.

In Figure 6.8, student groups are matched for a particular feature to attend activity settings (ASs) 1 and 2/3, but mixed to work at the remaining activity settings. A sample grouping and routing worksheet for planning how students are grouped, randomly or strategically, to attend five activity settings over five rotations in a 120-minute Frame is presented in Table 6.1.

In Table 6.1, all students attending AS 1 and 2/3 as a matched group will be mixed when they attend the other ASs. Students who attend ASs 1 and 2/3 together are designated by a color that identifies their start point. Usually students have much more creative ideas for naming their groups, but the colors will serve the explanatory purpose here. Students are routed to the five activity settings on the set schedule provided in Figure 6.8 (or some variation of it). The schedule is usually pasted into the folders students use to carry their work from station to station.

Cynthia's judgment that her students were ready for Phase 3 was correct. The independent academic activity setting could hardly have gone better; the students could hardly have been more task focused or more cooperative. However, it should be noted that these Native American children were of a culture deeply imbued with collectivist values and behavior patterns. Native American children much younger than these sixth graders are accustomed to highly cooperative community behavior. Cynthia's group worked together this first time smoothly and without the necessity for her to specify specific roles or responsibilities, which might have been necessary for children from more individualistic cultures. Making the decision about whether the students need specific teaching or role assignments to work together productively is achieved by the systematic observation of students' work in Phases 1 and 2. When there is a range of cooperation among the students, the more able may be grouped together to provide models and resources. However, a goal of Phase 3 is to give all students opportunities and assistance (from teachers and peers) to perform appropriately as students at independent activities.

186

FIGURE 6.8   Five ASs with a Variety of Student Groupings

	Round 1	Round 2	Round 3	Round 4	Round 5
	Teacher works with Blue Group at AS1	Blue Group to AS2&3 follow-up	Blue Group dispersed to ASs	Blue Group dispersed to ASs	Blue Group dispersed to ASs
	Orange Group dispersed to ASs	Teacher works with Orange Group at AS1	Orange Group to AS2&3 follow-up	Orange Group dispersed to ASs	Orange Group dispersed to ASs
	Yellow Group dispersed to ASs	Yellow Group dispersed to ASs	Teacher works with Yellow Group at AS1	Yellow Group to AS2&3 follow-up	Yellow Group dispersed to ASs
	Green Group dispersed to ASs	Green Group dispersed to ASs	Green Group dispersed to ASs	Teacher works with Green Group at AS1	Green Group to AS2&3 follow-up
	Red Group meets first at AS2&3 follow-up	Red Group dispersed to ASs	Red Group dispersed to ASs	Red Group dispersed to ASs	Teacher works with Red Group at AS1
	20 minutes	20 minutes	20 minutes	20 minutes	20 minutes

HANDLE

BRIEFING
- Talk about what will occur.
- Review task expectations.

10 minutes

HANDLE

DEBRIEFING
- What went well?
- What needs improvement?

10 minutes

TABLE 6.1   Routing Students to Five Activity Settings (ASs)

Student Names	Rounds	A	B	C	D	E
TWO MATCHED ASs (#1, 2/3) AND THREE MIXED ASs (#4, 5, 6) GROUPS						
Blue Group						
1.S		1	2/3	4	5	6
2.S		1	2/3	6	5	4
3.S		1	2/3	6	4	5
4.S		1	2/3	5	6	4
5.S		1	2/3	4	6	5
6.S		1	2/3	5	6	4
Orange Group						
7.S		4	1	2/3	6	5
8.S		6	1	2/3	4	5
9.S		5	1	2/3	6	4
10.S		5	1	2/3	4	6
11.S		6	1	2/3	5	4
12.S		6	1	2/3	4	5
Yellow Group						
13.S		5	4	1	2/3	6
14.S		4	5	1	2/3	6
15.S		5	6	1	2/3	4
16.S		4	5	1	2/3	6
17.S		4	6	1	2/3	5
18.S		6	4	1	2/3	5
19.S		5	6	1	2/3	4
Green Group						
20.S		6	4	5	2/3	2/3
21.S		4	6	5	2/3	2/3
22.S		6	5	4	2/3	2/3
23.S		5	4	6	2/3	2/3
24.S		4	5	6	2/3	2/3
Red Group						
25.S		2/3	5	6	1	1
26.S		2/3	6	4	1	1
27.S		2/3	6	5	1	1
28.S		2/3	6	4	1	1
29.S		2/3	6	4	1	1
30.S		2/3	4	5	1	1
Total Students						
at AS 4		5	6	6	6	7
at AS 5		6	5	6	6	7
at AS 6		6	6	5	6	5

In Phase 3, it is crucial that students experience the diversity of their classmates across the Frame of activities. Increased experience with joint productive activity has the power to increase the shared understandings of intersubjectivity. Here begins the opportunity for a creative disturbance of the status quo of affinities. Working together draws students together, creates intersubjectivity; a broadening web of affinities creates community Harmony. That ideal is attainable; in fact, this form of organization of instruction will reliably create it.

Tasks and Products.

- Provide tasks and activities relating to ECT that accomplish review and reteach in preparation for academic instruction.
- Monitor and assess students' basic skill levels, content knowledge, and language competence.
- Collect representative student work samples for portfolio assessment.

The tasks and products of activity settings in this phase continue to relate to the ECT, but previewing Subject Area Content (SAC) should begin. Review is completed in this phase, although reteaching can occur anytime. Activity design is guided by the same principles used in Phases 1 and 2; tasks must be designed to guarantee student success even when students are working away from the teacher or other expert assistance. If students cannot complete a task alone or with available peer assistance, they quickly lose motivation and become frustrated, and management problems ensue. In Cynthia's map-drawing activity, the task was leveled to ensure every student's success. The students found it cognitively challenging, motivating, and so pleasurable that they were reluctant to stop.

In Phase 3, the large-group activity can also be used to review and reteach, as needed, and other small-group activity settings can be designed for practice and exercise of the students' developing skills. Whatever the tasks and products, it is important to prepare precise directions for the activity setting, presented first at the Briefing handle, then through task cards placed at the activity station, or prominently displayed on the wall, or on instruction sheets prepared for each student. Activity settings can feature any topic integral to ongoing academic activity. These might include writing, keeping journals, computing, library work, research and information retrieval, or cooperative art or theater projects. Operating activity settings involves a number of logistics and supply issues, such as securing and storing supplies, accessibility, and replenishment. Table 6.2 lists the major duties of teachers and students for maintaining installed activity settings.

TABLE 6.2 Activity Setting Support and Logistics

- Students carry folders to hold contract, schedule, and work in progress.
- Students need to know paperwork cycling system and personal, center, and school materials storage routines.

WEEK PLANNING

No.	Name	Weekly	Preparation	Product	Materials
1	Teaching	5 visits	Each lesson	Joint product indicating progress in IC	Poster paper, board, supplies available, texts stored nearby
2&3	Follow-up	5 visits	Each lesson	Application and/or extension	Workbooks, texts, materials stored nearby
4	Library	1 visit	Community consensus	Reading log	Borrow from library; bring from home
5	Vocabulary/ Process writing	1 visit	Each lesson	Written, creative, and collaborative	Supplies for vocabulary system, texts, workbooks, dictionaries
6	Journal	1 visit	Community consensus	Written entry	Journals, storage room, easy retrieval
7	Information Retrieval/ Research	1 visit	Project guidelines	Written product	From classroom, home
8	Games/ Listening	1 visit	Community consensus	Scores on game listening log	Find, make, borrow school supplies
9	Computers	2 visits	Community consensus	New file on disk printout	School supplies
10	Observation/ Experiment	1 visit	Community consensus	Written findings	Equipment, recording paper, references

Peer interaction, mutual assistance, and universal success at activity settings are continuing topics for discussion in Briefing and Debriefing. Students can assist others in certain tasks, but it takes experience and careful observation to know which students are resources for which needs. An advantage of mixing and matching of students is that student strengths are varied; so too are their resource potentials for academics in various subject matters and also in technology, leadership, management, conversation, arts, emotional support, and the full range of the classroom community's concerns. A part of the development of the learning community is to allow students to recognize their various talents and to cooperate and assist according to their talents.

Teachers must judge when to begin the instruction of new material in the curriculum of their content area. It is unlikely that a community of learners has developed sufficiently in Phase 3 to begin new academic activity. However, Phase 3 is the time to think about how to shift to academic instruction in Subject Area Content (SAC) in Phases 4 and 5. The main question is: How ready are the students to engage complex content through problem-solving activities and conversation about it?

During Phase 3, as always, the teacher continues to collect representative student work samples (group and individual) for portfolio assessment. (That first map remains in Cynthia's personal teacher's portfolio to this day.)

Problems with tasks, materials, or students' motivation for a task can be shared in Debriefing. This feedback can be useful for the teacher and can inform subsequent decisions about adjusting or individualizing the task. Teachers and students can work cooperatively to level tasks appropriately for the independent activities.

Ready to go to Phase 4? Here is your checklist:

1. The teacher uses an expanded Frame routinely.
2. The teacher installs one or more activity settings.
3. The teacher enacts Standards I: Teacher and Students Producing Together, II: Developing Language and Literacy Across the Curriculum, and III: Making Meaning: Connecting School to Students' Lives in the first three phases.
4. Students function appropriately in mixed groups at activity settings.
5. Students move to and from activity settings in less than a minute.
6. Students have worked with every other student in the class or soon will.
7. Students accomplish review and reteach activities of the ECT.
8. The teacher informs the students often and specifically about their progress.
9. Students complete tasks in the allotted time and use extra time appropriately.
10. Students use and maintain classroom systems for storing, retrieving, and circulating work products.
11. The teacher collects samples of students' Phase 3 work products for portfolio assessment.

Phase 4: Two to Three Weeks: Teaching Through Activity Settings

An activities-based classroom, designed to meet the highest criteria for learning through interaction and activity, only happens with considerable planning. Classrooms of Phases 3 and 4, with simultaneous, differentiated activity and interaction (often noisy and vigorous), do not resemble classrooms of the common tradition and may not match the norms of the teacher's kindergarten through twelfth-grade school. In Phase 4, students begin to exercise choice in planning routing patterns for the week. The teacher will need to communicate about these new learning conditions to administrators, and often to parents. Administrators, colleagues, and parents who support and visit developing classroom communities through Phase 4 come to understand, admire, and enjoy the reformation.

General Design Considerations

The five main tasks of Phase 4 are to (1) complete installation of all independent activity settings, (2) stabilize student groupings and routing for a period of time, (3) routinize a schedule of fully developed Frames, (4) experiment with student choice contracts, and (5) implement Standard IV: Teaching Complex Thinking. When all classroom activity settings have been installed, they reflect a variety of forms but are uniform in supplying work space, resources, paperwork flow systems, storage, and other needs. At the primary level, activity settings are usually labeled to fit the ECT and children's developmental needs. For example, a kindergarten classroom would have activity settings labeled and suitably furnished for developmental activities: Building Blocks, Housekeeping, Discovery, Water Table, Art Area, Puppetry, and the like. In contrast, first grade may appropriately offer additional academic activities, such as Reading, Keeping a Journal, Writing, Games, Puzzles, Cooking, and Arts and Crafts. The focus of work is reflected in the station labels, but students become accustomed to performing tasks and activities wherever necessary. A Phase 4 classroom has installed activity settings that are clearly marked, with lively displays and decorations.

Direct, personal teacher assistance will be provided in the small-group activity settings in which the teacher is a member. Standard I emphasizes that learning is most likely when teacher and students work together to create a meaningful product. In one sense, freeing the teacher to work together with students is the most compelling purpose for organizing a classroom of multiple, simultaneous activities. During the rotations in a Frame, each student will often have the opportunity for close, shoulder-to-shoulder, sitting-beside and standing-beside interaction with the teacher over an academic task. Talking together over common tasks is the central process by which intersubjectivity is built, in which teacher-student affinities are born, and in which community is created. Whether these teacher-student joint productive activities are science experiments, turning out a school newspaper in the journalism class, close critical reading of a text together, or working on a class play, the Five Standards are emphasized.

Although all the Standards are present and operable at some level, this phase focuses on implementing Standard IV: Teaching Complex Thinking.

The ECT is replaced in this phase with Subject Area Content (SAC), which generates tasks and lesson activity in the Frame. Planning for this phase means thinking about how this Standard is enacted in the tasks and activities of Phase 4 Instructional Frames for group and individual needs.

Phase 4 Goals

- Apply Standard IV: Teaching Complex Thinking.
- Teach the SAC.
- Teach through interaction and conversation with students in groups.
- Install all activity settings (eight or more).
- Routinize the use of the Frame to route students through multiple, simultaneous activity settings.
- Make grouping decisions for academic instruction.
- Route students in groups matched for instruction through Teaching (activity setting 1) and Follow-up (activity settings 2/3).
- Route students in mixed groups through other activity settings.
- Experiment with student choice contracts.
- Plan/prepare appropriately leveled academic tasks for activities.
- Acquire representative student work samples for portfolio assessment.

Practical Design Considerations

Phase 4 implements the full design of multiple and simultaneous activities, grouping, routing students through activity settings, and providing all necessary logistics to support the system. (See Table 6.2 and Appendix A.2.) The design and groups are stable for a predetermined period of time, such as a quarter, six weeks, or another unit of time that aligns with grading periods or other schedules. A sample routing schedule for eight activity settings is presented in Table A.2. At the end of the time period, groupings are reviewed and changes made. At that time, adjustments to ASs can also be made. A worksheet for arranging students' schedules of activities, grouping, and re-grouping can be created to meet local needs. (A model is provided in Table A.3.) Phase 4 classrooms routinize the system so that those mechanics require a minimum of time and attention and cause no disruptions. After this phase the physical environment and logistics are no longer a central concern, so that the teacher, as well as the students, can attend to academic learning through activity and, especially, conversation.

Introducing Multiple,
Simultaneous Activity Settings

In the Briefing example that follows, Cynthia develops a Phase 4 classroom using multiple, simultaneous activity settings. The class has previously been organized into two groups, Blue and Red. Cynthia is experimenting with student contracts, which use a format like that of Figure 6.9. Contracts allow students to choose a week's routing pattern. When students rotate to AS 1 Cynthia reviews their contracts, negotiating AS attendance where needed. She will also check the groupings formed by students' choice contracts at the ASs. She uses Table A.3 (see Appendix) to track students' grouping and routing. During the first round, Blue Group will be with Cynthia in Center One, and Red Group students will distribute themselves among the other activity settings according to the students' contracts.

In this Briefing session Cynthia introduces six multiple, simultaneous activities and six stations where specific activity settings will be located: (1) Student Generated Activity (SGA), where each rotation of students designs activities that will be used later by their classmates; (2) journal writing; (3) vocabulary; (4) library; (5) games; and (6) a joint productive activity, where Cynthia will work together with a small group of students.

Some of these activities are already familiar to the students; others are new. However, this large number of simultaneous activities is a leap forward, and Cynthia takes care that everyone clearly understands the more complex traveling and routing.

Briefing (Ten Minutes).   Cynthia reminds the class of the activities at each activity setting; has the students reiterate the rules (especially for the library); describes the rotation pattern; and reviews finish-up and clean-up procedures, if needed. Then she hands out students' folders, which hold schedules and will be used to house today's work. When the students are ready to move into ASs, she reinforces rule observance by praising good models of travel and AS start-up. This is an opportune time to set a timer for the twenty minutes this round is scheduled to take. With ASs in progress, the teacher takes her place with her instructional group.

[Students seated around tables, Teacher at front of class]
TEACHER: Okay, intro to centers. Um, SGA [Student Generated Activities], you have this [carries materials to the SGA Center].
   [Now walks to Games Center.]
What do you think you're gonna be doing [here]?
MALE STUDENT: Games.

194

FIGURE 6.9   Student Contract for AS Attendance

TWO-HOUR FRAME

HANDLE

BRIEFING

- Talk about choice and taking responsibility for learning.
- Students contract for activity settings.

HANDLE

DEBRIEFING

- What went well?
- What needs improvement?
- Renegotiate contracts.

	Round 1	Round 2	Round 3	Round 4	Round 5
	Teacher teaches Blue Group	Blue Group to AS2&3 follow-up	Blue Group chooses remaining ASs		
	Orange Group chooses AS	Teacher teaches Orange Group	Orange Group to AS2&3 follow-up	Orange Group chooses remaining ASs	
	Yellow Group chooses remaining ASs		Teacher teaches Yellow Group	Yellow Group to AS2&3 follow-up	Yellow Group chooses AS
	Green Group chooses remaining ASs			Teacher teaches Green Group	Green Group to AS2&3 follow-up
	Red Group to AS2&3 follow-up	Red Group chooses remaining ASs			Teacher teaches Red Group
10 minutes	20 minutes	20 minutes	20 minutes	20 minutes	20 minutes	10 minutes

CONTRACT: Teacher and students decided on required and choice activity settings visits. Contract allows students to plan work on projects or research by combining rounds where needed.

TEACHER: Games. What game is this, do you remember?

MALE STUDENT: Trivial Pursuit.

TEACHER: Trivial Pursuit. Okay ... at writing center, you'll be doing a follow-up to this activity, I'll explain it. Who goes to writing center first today? What color?

MALE STUDENT: Blue Group.

TEACHER: Blue Group. Do you all know who's in Blue Group, do you all know who you are?

STUDENTS [chorus]: Yeah!

TEACHER: Okay. Who goes there next?

MALE STUDENT: Um, Red Group.

TEACHER: Yeah, Red Group. Blue and then Red, good. For journal [writing activity], same as always, write a full page on a topic of your choice and I'll write back to you. Um, vocab [vocabulary development activity], same as usual, library [free reading activity], same as usual. Let's review real quick what are our library rules?

STUDENT: No talking?

TEACHER: Yeah, what else, what about from here?

TEACHER: Did he miss anything?

MALE STUDENT: No.

TEACHER: Okay, then that's it. I want the Blue Group here, no one at the writing station, the rest of you pick your vocab and fill it or your choice, so let's get started.

[Students begin moving to the various ASs. Teacher monitors students' travel to activity settings.]

TEACHER: Okay, the Blue Group is moving to where they're gonna be, very good. Good, Veronica's chosen vocab, so has Alysia. [Aside, to herself]: What did I need, I know I needed something, what did I need? [Selects papers from her desk.] You two are gonna do journals? Okay, very good. Okay. Good, Chris is remembering to fill out his contract, good, contracts are being filled out, excellent. Good, John is looking at his contract to fill it out, good, Michelle, good Shyla. Good. Monica's filling out her contract, very good.

ERIC: Where's the paper?

TEACHER: Use your own. [Eric continues to look at Cynthia without moving.] You use your own ... or there's scrap paper up there. [Eric retrieves scrap paper from the top of the file cabinet.]

TEACHER: All right, okay. [Goes over to join the Blue Group and sits down with them.] You all have your contracts filled out? Okay, stick 'em underneath the table. [Scans the classroom once more.] All right, here we go.

As Cynthia says "here we go," she could mean that the class is moving right at that moment into Phase 5, because the joint productive activity that she plans with her group is an Instructional Conversation (IC), which is like a seminar whose facilitator has an instructional goal and a plan for assisting students through thoughtful dialogue about content topics. Cynthia can employ IC because she has implemented Phases 1, 2, 3, and 4 organization successfully. Through earlier phases, Cynthia's students regularly accomplished two types of tasks: (1) routine, independent tasks where stronger students helped and demonstrated for needier students and (2) joint productive tasks, where every student was required to participate for a joint product. Joint productive activity guaranteed that every student participated but did not regulate the duration or quality of that participation. While these experiences promote interaction and activity, discourse that leads to academic learning demands more sustained conceptual exchanges among teacher and students than is available in the activities of the first four phases. A Phase 5 classroom enacts the pedagogy that will achieve academic learning through dialogue, known as Instructional Conversation.

Activity Settings of 20 Minutes in a 140-Minute Frame.

> Activity #1: Student Generated Activity (SGA), where each rotation of students designs activities that will be used later by their classmates.
> Activity #2: Keeping a Journal.
> Activity #3: Vocabulary.
> Activity #4: Library.
> Activity #5: Games.
> Activity #6: Teacher works with a small group of students in joint productive activity.

Debriefing (Ten Minutes).   During the debriefing, the entire Frame is reviewed—not only the experiences in each activity, but also the movement among them and the performance of the community in each of the independent activities. The Frame supports the community's activities no matter what their complexity.

Designing Phase 4

Roles and Relationships.

- Apply Standard IV: Teaching Complex Thinking.
- Teach the SAC.
- Teach through interaction with students in groups.
- Install all activity settings to total approximately eight or more.

- Routinize the use of the Frame to route students through every activity setting.

In Phase 4, the teacher and students support one another to maintain and develop the community's common values, such as the importance of peer assistance for accomplishing tasks in a classroom that is designed to enhance every student's learning. Standards for work that encourage students' more complex thinking about everyday topics are reiterated in Briefing and Debriefing handles. Student work that reflects the standard is often shared and samples made public, on bulletin boards, in displays, or in publications. The teacher continues to recognize students for taking responsibility for helping others, finishing tasks, using extra time appropriately, designing tasks for class use, setting up stations, and housekeeping.

In Phase 4's more complex classroom organization, the teacher interacts with students over tasks to encourage their thinking about content area concepts. In this phase the teacher may work at a station with students rotating to her, or she may rotate through student groups working at activity settings. The distinguishing feature of teaching in Phase 4 is its conversational approach, which engages students in sustained talk about content material. There is an ease to this interaction so that students are comfortable expressing their thoughts and feelings, knowing the teacher will be an active and responsive listener.

During this phase the teacher continues to collect student work samples for portfolio assessment. This assessment information continues to inform teacher decision making about designing and assigning tasks and activities, grouping, and the initiation of academic instruction. For students who continue to underperform, the teacher needs to check that assigned tasks are accurately leveled and make adjustments where necessary, including tailoring assignments, and the community needs to provide additional support for the student. The culmination of this developmental phase is seen in students' growing independence, capacity to take responsibility for their own and others' learning, and successful accomplishment of content-related tasks and assessments.

Grouping and Routing.

- Make grouping decisions for academic instruction.
- Route students in groups matched for instruction through Teaching (activity setting 1) and Follow-up (activity settings 2/3).
- Route students in mixed groups through other activity settings.
- Experiment with student choice contracts.

In Phase 4, students are assigned into groups for a set period of time. Teachers use all they have learned about their students from Phase 1's random and strategic grouping, Phase 2's complete matrix of matches, and Phase 3's emphasis on mixing students by all important variables. All of these grouping combinations created new propinquities, some new interactions and negotiations, and opportunities for assessment of student strengths and needs. Through inclusive, diverse, and equitable grouping, the teacher-designer will have seized the opportunity to create a cohesive classroom community approaching Harmony. In the propinquity and joint activity of the groups, students relate to students they may not otherwise meet. Here is the opportunity to experience cooperation and mutual understanding of the work products beyond the confines of the students' crowds, ethnicities, race, cultures, gender, or language. The work of the groups also provides students with experiences of human differences; they learn about the variety of speaking, thinking, and performing abilities of their peers.

In Phase 4, students are assigned to five or six groups of no more than seven students and no less than three. If teachers group students in the matched groups for instructional purposes, those students will be together at two activity settings for one rotation or round, but in following rotations they will join other students in new groupings for other activity settings. In the grouping worksheet in Figure A.3 in the Appendix, students are assigned to home groups named (arbitrarily) by color. Across the top of the worksheet are the rotations or rounds. The activity settings are identified by a number. So, all matched students go to activity settings 1 and 2/3. But, for 3, 4, 5, etc., the groups disassemble and students join others from other groups at each of the activity settings. This worksheet is useful for planning every student's groupmates throughout any instructional Frame.

Once the grouping decisions have been made, the following illustrations can assist in planning the routing of groups through the activity settings:

Table 6.1: Routing Students to Five Activity Settings
Table A.2 (in the Appendix): Sample Grouping and Routing to Eight
    Activity Settings
Table A.3 (in the Appendix): Grouping, Rotation, and Routing Work-
    sheet

On the worksheets, each column represents a rotation to an activity setting where students gather who have the same number on the schedule. Teachers assign students to an activity setting at the same time based on affinities, compatibilities, and other factors.

Tasks and Products.

- Plan/prepare appropriately leveled academic tasks for activities.
- Acquire representative student work samples for portfolio assessment.

The appropriately leveled academic tasks of this phase engage students in analysis, problem solving, and other complex thinking activity. Phase 4 tasks include some that are relatively routine, in which stronger students can assist or model for the weaker, some that are complex, and some that require joint products. More cognitively challenging tasks are generated by the transition from teaching the ECT to beginning instruction in the Subject Area Content (SAC). Joint productive tasks are a greater guarantee of Inclusion, especially when their topic and problem are compelling for students. In addition, the developing community provides incentives for individuals and groups to produce. But that motivation continues to require bolstering from Debriefing self-assessment, problem-solving options, and community support. The wise teacher also has many rewards and pleasures to energize students.

A Phase 4 classroom consumes many tasks and activities. Teachers inexperienced in complex classroom organization must enlist their students as task and activity designers as early as Phase 1. This collaboration is a joint productive activity because the teacher and student must work together to ensure a quality product for classroom use. A high school history teacher, Jack Mallory, uses the same principle to motivate his students of different talents and interests to experiment with a variety of activities in his Civil War unit. Their joint productive activity is student generated from materials relating to their topic of study, and students self-select their membership in a group.

From Our Files

A Student Teacher's Journal Entries, Fall 1998

(Monday). Wow, what Jack did today! He came in, threw down these stacks of readings for everybody, and told them, "You all read these, and then get into small groups, and by Friday you make a report to the whole class about them." He said they could make any kind of report they wanted to, he didn't care if it was a play or a poster or whatever. They could hardly believe it. Jack and I didn't have to help them very much; they were really into it!

(Friday). What a day. The first group did hand puppets, and wrote a little script between Lincoln and Grant. The collage the other group did was fantastic. The video the other group did was really good, but they didn't have time to finish it. They're going to work on it some more after school this week. The game show we get to play tomorrow! I really liked the way Jack let them switch groups if they liked another project better.

We have seen other teachers devote one activity setting in the first Frame of a unit to designing future tasks and activity settings. Of course the teacher has the responsibility for quality and adjusting activities to meet the curriculum and class progress, but even this responsibility can be delegated to a rotating committee. Some teachers have set up an activity setting devoted to student task generation. Students quickly understand the quality criteria for substance and legibility when they realize that feedback about the appropriateness of the task will be coming from their peers. Like the teacher, they must balance the challenge in a task with the need to guarantee a high rate of student success using peer assistance and other resources in the classroom. Most students find this challenge extremely engaging, providing opportunities to apply their skills, languages, interests, and potential for leadership. It is also a self-affirming enactment of a functioning community of learners.

Ready to go to Phase 5? Here is your checklist:

1. The teacher has installed all activity settings.
2. The teacher uses the Frame as a daily routine.
3. The teacher enacts Standards I: Teacher and Students Producing Together, II: Developing Language and Literacy Across the Curriculum, III: Making Meaning: Connecting School to Students' Lives, and IV: Teaching Complex Thinking.
4. The teacher relates tasks at activity settings to subject area's instructional goals as well as group and individual students' needs.
5. The teacher routinely routes matched and mixed groups of students to activity settings.
6. The teacher and students properly use classroom systems for paper flow, materials access, and storage functions.
7. Students contribute to activity setting logistics, tasks, and community functions.
8. The teacher builds portfolios for assessment of students' progress.

Phase 5: Routine for the Rest of the Year: Teaching Through Instructional Conversation with Multiple, Simultaneous Activity Settings

In the nation's premier educational institutions, seminar settings for academic discourse are a regular activity setting, but teaching through dialogue rarely occurs in kindergarten through twelfth-grade classrooms. This is not surprising because classrooms of the common tradition actually have been organized to discourage discourse. Complex activity-based classrooms like those in Phase 4 are instructional settings that can support the highest-quality teaching-and-learning interactions, characteristic of the graduate seminar or science laboratory. But quality teaching in such venues means teachers must develop pedagogical as well as organizational skills. Success in Phase 4 means a teacher and the classroom community have achieved the conditions necessary for academic learning. In Phase 5, the teacher implements Standard V: Teaching Through Instructional Conversation.

In Phase 5, the teacher claims a regular, scheduled activity setting slot for the IC. This does not mean that there is no "telling time" or time to lecture to students; rather, there is a predominance of teacher and student interaction patterns weighted toward dialogic instruction among teacher and students. We have previously discussed the telling times available through the handles of Briefing and Debriefing. In fact, any round of activity settings can become telling and lecturing sessions when needed. The Phase 5 classroom is flexible but has the superordinate goal to teach more through sustained dialogue using academic language to talk and think about complex topics and less through lecturing and telling. Elementary teachers choose to work in a Phase 5 design all day using a multidisciplinary approach to content or in a large-block subject area such as language arts. In any case, the class is a learning community that continues to develop common values and new understanding through mutual exchange and instructional assistance of the kind available through IC.

Phase 5 transforms the classroom into a dialogic-centered learning environment with IC as premier learning strategy. Because every student in Phase 4 has been assigned to a matched group that stays intact for two rotations, this provides a ready opportunity for the teacher to establish an IC activity setting. The teacher employs IC in the first round and provides application and follow-up in the second round. Once this AS sequence is in place, the teacher is more than a management specialist for tasks, group work, and proper behavior; his or her teaching assumes a conversational form to link students and their experiences to new ideas. Now, the teacher uses dialogue to advance the conceptual and application experiences of the students as far as they can be led. During each rotation, the teacher assesses and assists students through conversation in groups of from three to seven. In IC, teaching is strategic. Questions that promote dialogue and thoughtfulness are prepared before lesson time. Informal assessment in small-group discussion is also preplanned by teachers.

In IC, teaching and learning mean close communications between the teacher and students. IC has clear goals for students' learning and understanding, and its frequent interaction opportunities make students' thoughts and beliefs visible. Teachers build on this strength by using visual displays of the progress of conversations, particularly as categories, cause and effect, and other complex relationships are examined. Visual displays developed during IC reflect the goals of the conversation to encourage elaboration, negotiation, and collaboration about ideas and beliefs. Such clarification of both process and content of conversation aids students' metacognitive understanding about their learning, which is advantageous for all students, but especially for those most at risk.

As an IC develops, students are encouraged to express themselves in a variety of roles: as advocates for their own and other's interpretations of text or other learning material, as negotiators, and as validators. But IC is also a gateway for connecting students to the larger community beyond the classroom through follow-up tasks using the Internet and media. Connecting to the Internet, for example, has potential to extend students' thinking and expressing on academic topics. This form of teaching, in addition to and beyond tasks, is an exchange, a conversation in the broadest sense, that stimulates thought and reflection on conceptual topics using the language of the content area that belongs at the center of our classrooms.

Goals of Phase 5

- Apply all Five Standards, particularly Standard V: Teaching Through Instructional Conversation.
- Teach the Subject Area Content.
- Assess students' knowledge, experience, and preferences through academic conversation about activity.
- Activate the power of the community of learners.
- Offer students choice of activity settings.
- Collect representative samples of student work for inclusion in students' portfolios.

General Design Considerations

The Instructional Conversation takes place in small groups. Although a teacher may have some effective dialogue with larger groups, the benefits of conversation require full Inclusion of students, and that cannot be achieved in whole-group settings. Like any dialogue, IC is a pleasurable event for both the students and teacher, all of whom enjoy the lively exchange of ideas and reaching shared understandings. Instruction conducted through conversation brings with it many advantages: a variety of participation formats, enhancement of students' active involvement, students' experience of Inclusion, and the teacher's opportunity to be responsive to and supportive of each student.

In content areas where text is the dominant medium—literacy, social sciences, humanities—the IC is most often conducted over a text, the analysis, criticism, or appreciation of which is the instructional goal. In mathematics, the conversation may be quite similar, although the accompanying activity may be joint problem solving or application of mathematical concepts. In science, the IC may be scheduled during a collaborative experiment or over the analysis of a data set. In theater, the conversation can be interspersed among readings or brief performances, and in art the conversation can be over a potter's wheel or while putting paint on a mural. In fact, like all activity settings, IC is most effective when it accompanies or leads to a joint product. What distinguishes IC from other activity settings is the role of the teacher, who, through the medium of dialogue, assists and guides each student through the next stage of cognitive development.

The implementation of IC transforms the Phase 4 classroom into a fully functioning learning community. The teacher has students arrayed in a variety of groups, including large groups at times, for experiences at multiple activity settings. The students attend activity settings established in the classroom according to their schedules, which can include a choice contract that they keep in their folders. The distinguishing feature of these groups, however, is that they form and reform for the different activity settings with every transition. This routing plan varies students' membership in groups and is changeable whenever the teacher chooses. This is accomplished through use of the grouping worksheet in the Appendix (Table A.3).

Designing Phase 5

Roles and Relating.

- Apply Standard V: Teaching Through Instructional Conversation daily.
- Teach the Subject Area Content.
- Assess students' knowledge, experience, and preferences through academic conversation about activity.

In IC, teachers guide students to express their ideas, reasoning, logic, and theories about content topics using specific language of a content area. On the surface, this strategy may appear simple and merely social. In fact, it is a powerful form of assistance for students and teachers for conceptual learning. Because students' participation in conversation stimulates them to use language to share their experience and thoughts, learning is socially motivated. Teachers use social influence to encourage students' conversation, but student learning in IC depends on its clear instructional goal and plan for guiding students, through thoughtful dialogue, to the goal of understanding.

If students have little common knowledge on a selected topic (as may be the case in diverse classrooms), a teacher will provide appropriate direct or indirect experience in the form of hands-on activities; field trips; complex, real-world problems; or resource books, media, or other sources. Such an experience provides all participants with similar knowledge of the intended IC topic, which is the basis for initiating IC. While any good conversation exhibits some latitude and drift from the topic, the teacher continuously guides the conversation to the topic goal. While the goal remains firm, the route to the goal is responsive to student participation and developing understanding.

Instructional Conversation can accommodate a variety of student participation formats, depending on teacher and student preferences and the conventions and courtesies of conversation in different cultures. In any format, teachers can combine ordinary conversation's responsive and inclusive features with assessment and assistance to motivate students' interaction toward an instructional goal. Although the IC format typically produces vigorous student participation, the teacher selectively elicits and responds to student talk to ensure full Inclusion and Equity and restricts his or her own speech to no more than 50 percent of the dialogue. To be as responsive as possible to students' need for guidance, teachers make on-the-spot decisions to modify their planned questions, comments, or directions. Although the teacher respectfully accepts students' best available expressions in their own language codes and genres, informal language, or everyday vocabulary, the teacher's goal is to model and elicit precise use of the language of instruction in grammar, syntax, and content lexicon. This is assisted by questioning, modeling, and praising. More precise and complex student language expression enables more precise and complex thinking.

Grouping and Routing.

- Activate the power of the community of learners.
- Offer students choice contracts, when needed (Figure 6.9).

For today's mostly large (30–40 students) kindergarten through twelfth-grade classrooms, it usually takes an organization of five or six groups to reduce student numbers enough for student interaction around complex activity to be inclusive and substantive. Guidelines for grouping in small, direct instructional settings have been the subject of considerable dispute. In classrooms or schools where groups are fixed and tracked across all activities, such constant use of homogeneous groups—particularly if sorted by ability—are hardly defensible on any count, academic, social, or ethical. In other classrooms, where the only small-group activity is the direct instruction with the teacher, students are frequently grouped by ability to "expedite" learning, a vestige of the scientific management model.

But consider a classroom such as Cynthia's Phase 4. The Frame we discussed there contained six activity settings, each the same length. We have surprised many teachers and program designers by urging them to use—against a background of rich and insistent diversity—some small groups of the same culture, language group, gender, friendship, or ability. In an urban classroom in interior British Columbia, five Chilcotin Indian students were carefully and "correctly" mixed in with the majority students of British or Polish descent, with the effect that almost never, across the entire school day, did they speak a word. Native American sociolinguistic patterns involve long wait times; by the time a courteous interval has passed, majority culture students and the teacher have already taken the floor again. Gaining participation in majority-dominated conversations remains a problem even for Native American college students (Leacock 1976). We urged that the teacher meet separately with the Chilcotin students at least once a week to make sure that their concerns and difficulties with learning English as a second language were recognized and given voice.

If students do not talk, they will not learn language. So, in California and Texas we have counseled teachers in bi- or multilingual classrooms to include in their Frame of activities some opportunity for the teacher to interact with groups of Mexican heritage or Hmong immigrant students and to schedule groupings in the independent activities so that at least pairs of same-language students are present to help one another with problems of vocabulary and translation. Again we repeat: This guideline, though important, is subordinate to the general value of Inclusion. But it is equitable, too, that those Chilcotin and Hmong students have an opportunity to say their say, ask their specific questions, and get tailored guidance in their preferred patterns.

But what of ability grouping? It is an option for the Instructional Conversation. Disparities in knowledge and cognitive development can produce dominance and inhibition as surely as can language and social class differences. Grouping students by skill compatibilities or complements for ICs can challenge every student, from learning disabled to gifted/talented, to develop within his or her zone of proximal development. But a range of ability in any grouping enriches the conversation and provides student models for thinking and language. Ability is rarely so clearly an assessment that grouping cannot be improved by considering student qualities of participation, interests, and classroom sociometrics.

Whatever grouping decisions teachers make, the goal is to ensure Inclusion and Equity across the Frame of activity. We do not recommend any criterion alone as a sole guideline for any grouping decision. Almost all sets of students are fuzzy sets, and on the margins, other considerations can make for better functioning groups—other issues of affinity, or new propinquity opportunities, or other capacity differences such as differential capacities of multiple intelligences.

In summary, we must acknowledge that classrooms contain such complexities of need and opportunity that every option cannot be taken. Of all the potential groupings, which? Equity and Inclusion are good guidelines; they will produce diversity. A part of diversity of grouping is some like-with-like or matched on some feature. Diversity produces Excellence. And a classroom designed on those values will be a community of Harmony—at least, as harmonious as a human society is likely to be.

Routing students for Phase 5 takes on new dimensions as a community of learners is fully achieved. Many variations are possible. Routing can be assigned or include choice contracts, in which students fill out a form to display which activity settings they will attend and how long they will spend there. (See Figure 6.9.) In choice contracts, students continue to participate in AS 1 and 2/3 but select other ASs to attend in the unassigned slots, as shown in Figure 6.9. The teacher negotiates with students for these contract arrangements to make sure they continue to work in a variety of roles with a variety of students on appropriate activities.

Even in choice contracts, some activity settings will be required; AS 1 (the Instructional Conversation) and AS 2/3 (follow-up activities from the IC) make up the heart of the instructional system and are the teacher's main connection for influencing and staying apprised of students' work directions. For example, students may be expected to attend some activity settings once a week such as keeping a journal, computing, student-generated activities, library, and vocabulary. The other openings in the routing are the students' choices guided by the teacher. For example, secondary students may be working on research projects and will spend many rotations in the school library and on the Internet. Time on the computer for writing, e-mailing, and Internet researching may require some students to use hardware outside the classroom in the computer lab. Younger students may have a garden project that needs concentrated work at certain times of the year and will spend many rotations there. But students are encouraged to make thoughtful choices about their activities, considering both their interests and needs. The choice contract is a powerful tool for developing students' responsibility for their own learning.

The options in this design are unlimited. Because the Instructional Frame is steered from AS 1 where students meet regularly with the teacher, students' other activity is continuously reported and assessed. Teachers may have to reschedule or relocate ASs 1 and 2/3 to meet students' peripatetic activities, but they do not cancel participation in the exchange of AS 1, which is critical for learning.

Tasks and Products.

- Collect representative samples of student work for Inclusion in students' portfolios.

In Phase 5, the classroom functions on a rich diet of activity and inter-action from implementation of all the Standards. The teacher who has be-come adept at leveling tasks for every student is at the center, guiding and continuously refining students' learning experiences at activity set-tings. The teacher stocks the tasks in the activity settings for students to complete, using student-generated tasks wherever possible. Groups can be assigned these tasks so that, for example, all the Blue Group members will do the same task at an activity setting even though they do not visit the activity setting at the same time. Simple logistics such as clipping all of Blue Group's tasks and activities together with blue paper clips, clothespins, or in some other blue holder make materials easy to find. Within the materials, the teacher may individualize tasks for particular students, labeling the material with the student's name, or enclosing the material in a see-through plastic bag or other container that is easy to spot. The individualized tasks are certainly discussed at AS 1, and stu-dents are alerted to look for them at activity settings during Briefing.

This system's greatest strength lies not only in the quality of tasks and activities tailored to students' needs and the instructional goals that stu-dents perform at independent activity settings, but also in the opportuni-ties presented for the regular, academic dialogue of the Instructional Conversation. As the instructional expert, the teacher is allowed by this system to direct the power of more teaching contexts than have ever be-fore been activated in classrooms. In addition, the regular addition of the IC activity (AS 1) involves students in academic discussion of abstract text and complex problems.

Organizationally, the IC itself is an academic activity (AS 1) with fol-low-up tasks in AS 2/3 to reinforce emerging understanding. Activity setting 2/3 is used for follow-up to allow for differentiated activities for students. For example, if the home group (which may be a matched or a mixed group depending on instructional goals) is used for IC, it may re-flect a broad range of ability, and the follow-up activities may be individ-ualized at AS 2/3. The students may have different tasks for relearning, practice, enrichment, or research. Activity setting 2/3 provides the op-portunity for a variety of tasks and breakouts for the students as follow-up or, occasionally, as a prelude to IC. It is important to note that in the routing schedule the follow-up AS 2/3 will occasionally occur before some students have rotated to AS 1. In this case, teachers provide tasks that are appropriate to the work at AS 1, taking advantage of this opportunity to prepare students for academic instruction.

Getting Started in Instructional Conversation

A teacher begins Instructional Conversation by simply asking students to talk about a selected activity, text, or experience from their point of view, that is, based on their available knowledge from home, community, or school. The teacher encourages every student to talk specifically about personal and school experiences that relate to the text and the concepts the teacher plans to develop. This conversation can appear informal and casual, but the teacher has a clear goal and intends to assess and assist. For example, student contributions reveal their level of language proficiency and their existing level of topic knowledge, two major considerations in selecting (and adjusting) topics for the group discussion.

As students share their knowledge and understanding, the teacher has an ideal opportunity to assess their oral language proficiency. Thus even the initial stages of the Instructional Conversation provide a uniquely meaningful context for authentic assessment of students' language proficiency. When the Instructional Conversation is fully developed and all students are included, teachers observe and note the level of content-related conceptual knowledge. The teacher uses this assessment information, on the spot, to decide how to develop, modify, lengthen, shorten, or supplement the IC content to attain the instructional goal. Assessment information also guides the design of follow-up tasks, other Instructional Conversations, and the teacher's reflection on the success of the lesson for students' academic achievement.

Instructional Conversation provides unique opportunities for the teacher to give responsive assistance. In literacy topics, teachers can assist students with plot, character, setting, and style, but also to understand narratives as expressions of human ideals, dreams, and dilemmas. When teacher/student dialogue builds from individual experience to text analysis, students can comprehend the text's complex meanings. When Instructional Conversation is focused on science or mathematics, the goals include an understanding of concepts and lexicon and a developed ability to apply them to problem solving or research inquiry. As students are drawn into Instructional Conversation, teachers respond to individual learning needs by tailoring or "sheltering" their language and by active questioning and modeling of speech and thought. This dialogue provides opportunities for students to explain their rationales; validate their positions based on text, experiments, observations, or logic; and negotiate with the group about what meaning to construct about the topic.

Seventh-Grade Social Studies.   In an all-girl, small-group Instructional
Conversation, the teacher, Stacey, guides discussion about "Freedom Not
to Go to School." As part of the study of the U.S. Constitution and its
guaranteed liberties, Stacey divided the class into five groups, each attempting to write a constitution for its fictitious country. Stacey rotates to
each table, challenging each group to think more deeply about its constitution's guaranteed liberties. She accepts every student's comment, even
the freedom of "no school," but she then challenges them to consider the
consequences by asking direct questions: "What's good about it?" and
"Why do you want it?" She also asks them to consider possible negative
effects. Since they say it would be bad if they didn't learn to read, she
asks why they value reading. She probes further: "What else?" The students eventually reveal the value they place on reading, knowledge of
other cultures, and access to information about the larger world.

Stacey challenges and assists them to think precisely about concepts such
as literacy, work, and culture, and to explain their reasoning in more depth
than they could on their own. Her success is manifested by the level of students' participation and the quality of their responses. This rich, complex
student talk shows English Language Learners engaging in solid academic
conversation, exercising logic, and using the lexicon of the content area.

Sixth-Grade Literature Class.   Cynthia discusses a novel, Places like Durango Street, with a small group of sixth graders. They are seated around
a kidney-shaped table while the rest of the class works independently at
activity settings. Her goal in this lesson is for the students to understand
a very complex idea: Literature works by using language that evokes
readers' memories, which in turn create impressions of setting, atmosphere, and character. If they are to succeed, she will have to lay some
careful groundwork. That work began on the previous day. After reading
some of the book, the students listed all their impressions of Durango
Street for the chart on the wall chart. After summarizing them, Cynthia
begins: "Do you think a place like this really exists?"

Cynthia's discussion elicits the students' own experiences of "mean
streets" like those in the book in the real, nearby cities of Gallup and Albuquerque. Cynthia presses them for details and for precise language
that expresses their perceptions and feelings about those intimidating
streets. Because she relates the text to the students' personal experiences,
they will understand the Durango Street book much better. This connecting activity promotes achievement of Cynthia's higher goal: to analyze
the author's use of language.

Instruction Conversation Indicators

There are indicators that describe what IC does in instruction. They are specific, concrete actions that bring this Standard to life in a classroom accord-

ing to the criteria that support academic learning. In Phase 5, Instructional Conversation is suitable for any grade level, subject, and students, including non-English-speaking students. IC with English Language Learners uses many forms of communication such as drawing and labeling to build sight vocabulary, pattern sentences to learn syntactic patterns, music, math, and hands-on science experiments. The indicators are that the teacher:

- Arranges the classroom to accommodate conversation between the teacher and a small group of students on a regular and frequent schedule, preferably daily.
- Has a clear academic goal that guides conversation with students.
- Ensures that student talk occurs at higher rates than teacher talk.
- Guides conversation to include students' views, judgments, and rationales, using text evidence and other substantive support.
- Ensures that all students are included in the conversation according to their preferences.
- Listens carefully to assess levels of students' understanding.
- Assists students' learning throughout the conversation by questioning, restating, praising, encouraging, and so forth.
- Guides the students to prepare a product that indicates the Instructional Conversation's goal was achieved.

Transcript of an Instructional Conversation

Cynthia's goal with her sixth-grade literacy class is to teach issues of setting and the use of language in the creating of setting and atmosphere. She is seated at one table of four students and is involved in an Instructional Conversation with her group of three male (MS) and one female student (FS).

> CYNTHIA: OK, last time we were together we talked about Rufus. So we did a character analysis. This time we're going to talk about the setting. Who knows what the setting is? When you read a story, what's the setting?
> FS IN WHITE SHIRT: [unintelligible].
> CYNTHIA: Yes, it's Durango Street. What is the setting, when you say the setting of …
> FS: Where it's at.
> CYNTHIA: Exactly. Where it's at. And like Elvira said, it's Durango St. So we're going to talk about the setting, you guys are doing great already, we're going to talk about the setting of Durango St. So what is Durango St. like?
> MS: All dirty.

CYNTHIA [writes "dirty" on chart paper.]: OK, what else? What else is Durango St. like? What is it?

MS: Junky.

CYNTHIA: Boy, you guys have good words.

FS: Messed up.

CYNTHIA: Why is it messed up?

FS: Because they're doing projects, they are building houses.

CYNTHIA: Because they're building houses? It's messed up because they're building houses? Are they building houses on Durango St?

STUDENTS: No.

CYNTHIA: They're taking houses ...

FS: They're breaking houses ...

FS: They're making brand new ones.

CYNTHIA: They're building brand new houses on Durango St.? What does Durango St. look like? You've said it's dirty, messy, junky ... what do the people look like?

FS: Mean.

FS: Bessies.

CYNTHIA: They're mean, they're bessies. What do they look like?

MS: They wear dirty clothes.

MS: They're bums.

CYNTHIA: They're bums? OK, why do the places look junky? What do the buildings look like? Why do they look junky?

MS: They're torn.

MS: They don't wash themselves.

MS: They have graffiti on them.

MS: And they put bad words on them.

CYNTHIA: OK, graffiti and bad words. And you said about the houses, they're torn? What do you mean by that?

MS: They're broken down.

MS: They hang out in it.

MS: No, they sleep in it.

CYNTHIA: Who sleeps in the broken down houses?

MS: BUMS!

CYNTHIA: OK, so bums sleep where?

MS: In broken houses.

CYNTHIA: OK, are there plants on Durango St., or animals?

MS: Dogs, cats.

CYNTHIA: OK, what are the dogs and cats like who live there?

FS: Skinny.

STUDENT: Scrawny.

CYNTHIA: Skinny, scrawny dogs and cats? OK. You guys have good imagination. What are the buildings like? Are they like schools? What kind of buildings are there?

MS: They're tall and derelict.

CYNTHIA: They're tall and what else?

FS: Broken.

CYNTHIA: What part of them is broken?

FS: Windows.

CYNTHIA: Broken windows and they're tall. Broken windows and doors. OK, now, you guys have done very well. You've talked about all these different things that Durango St. is like. Now let's read over them. Start from the top. You said, graffiti, bad words, junky, messy, tall buildings, skinny, scrawny dogs and cats, dirty, the people are skinny and dirty, there are broken windows doors and lights, bums sleep in the broken houses, there are bums, and the houses are broken down. Good. Now, do you think a place like this can really exist? Can there really be a place like this?

STUDENTS: YES!

CYNTHIA: Like where?

MS: Like Albuquerque.

MS: Gallup.

CYNTHIA: Like Albuquerque or Gallup, OK. So, do you think there are other places besides Albuquerque or Gallup that could be like that?

MS: San Antonio.

CYNTHIA: San Antonio, OK. Now, how is Albuquerque like this? Like, who's been to Albuquerque before?

MS: I have. [Five students raise hands.]

CYNTHIA: Have you guys seen this area that's like that? 'Cause I haven't, I've only been to the shops.

MS: Yeah, and homeless.

CYNTHIA: They're homeless in Albuquerque? OK, what part of Albuquerque looks like this? The downtown?

MS: No. Not the downtown.

MS: No, it's that one place on …

MS: Central.

MS: Central, yeah.

CYNTHIA: Central? So, have you driven through there? What's it like? When you drove through there, what did it look like? What was there?

FS: Scary.

CYNTHIA: It was scary? Why was it scary?

MS: All those bums. Yeah, and gangs that hang out in dark places.

CYNTHIA: Gangs that hang out in dark places? OK, what about Jocelyn?

FS: [unintelligible] a gang and they were all walking across and we almost hit them because they were all wearing black.

CYNTHIA: Oh, they were in a gang? So what happened when you got near them?

FS: My dad just stopped 'cause he almost hit them.

CYNTHIA: OK, what did the people in the gang do?

FS: Nothing.

CYNTHIA: Did they just stand there or did they get on the sidewalk or what?

FS: They just [unintelligible].

CYNTHIA: OK, and [unintelligible] said Gallup was like this. What parts of Gallup are like this?

MS: Alleys.

CYNTHIA: Alleys? OK.

MS: Um, what's that place ...

CYNTHIA: What's that local place near the Round-Up Saloon. Near the 7-Eleven? That place is like this? Really? How?

MS: There's burnt houses.

MS [joking]: Skinny dogs.

CYNTHIA: There's skinny dogs? OK, so you say Albuquerque is like this? And you've been to Albuquerque and you've been to Albuquerque, Francesca? And you say Gallup is like this near, what's the name of that saloon? Round-Up Saloon? OK, well, now ... when you were reading Durango St., which is kind of like Gallup and kind of like Albuquerque, like you said ... Let's see who wrote this book. What's this guy's name?

MS: Frank Bonham.

CYNTHIA: Frank Bonham. OK, when Frank Bonham wrote this book, what you just read, there was nowhere in the book where he said there were bums on the street. He didn't say there were skinny and scrawny cats, and he didn't even say there were tall buildings, or graffiti. But, somehow he got you to see that, and he got you to see the right thing. How did he get you to see that?

MS: He was talking about it.

CYNTHIA: Right, and what words did he use when he was talking about it so you could see it in your mind?

MS: Strong language.

CYNTHIA: Strong language. Let's turn to page 18 and look at that and find what words he used to help you think of all of these things that you got in your mind. OK, let's start at the top of page 18. And let's look for words that made you see that in your mind. Let's see what words. "The street Durango Street speared

through a small, doomed area of grimy stores." What words in
there make you think of that stuff?

MS: Stores.

CYNTHIA: Stores? What kind of stores were they?

MS: Messed up.

CYNTHIA: Messed up? What's the word they used?

MS: Grimy.

CYNTHIA: OK, good. We have one word already, grimy. What are
some other words that made you think of Durango Street?

MS: Bars.

CYNTHIA: OK, bars. Church? Does church make you think of bad
stuff? That's true, some people throw stuff around churches.
Should we put that one? OK, what else? What other words did
the author use? Shabby houses. Should we use the word shabby or
the word houses? OK, now I'm going to show you our next task.
We're going to make a poster, a poster of all those words we
found. [Gives them supplies for poster making.]

Instructional Conversation:
The Ultimate Academic Activity Setting

When instruction has a clear goal, conducting it through conversation
brings many advantages to students: a variety of participation formats and
a (perhaps new) experience of being included. The format allows students
to negotiate with the teacher and peers to meet their social and academic
needs. Advantages to the teacher include the opportunity to explore the
students' worlds of experience and knowledge in responsive ways. In IC,
teachers combine ordinary conversation's responsive and inclusive features with assessment and assistance to motivate students' interaction toward an instructional goal.

Students are not discouraged from using language forms and styles
that are comfortable for them. Those forms and styles vary enormously;
after all, whole cultures have very different styles for how they talk
with each other and how children talk with adults. By accepting students' preferred participation formats, teachers can elicit more student
speech. That gives teachers more opportunities to promote precise and
complex student language expression. Precise and complex thought is
developed simultaneously.

Cynthia's classroom, in Phase 5, demonstrates cooperation and support for task accomplishment, an expression of the community's value
for academic learning. Such valuing of quality teaching and maximized
opportunity for learning in a Phase 5 classroom rely to a great extent on
the capacity of the classroom to function as a community. As such, in

Phase 5, the conditions are present for teaching with IC to engage academic discourse leading to complex learning.

Conclusion

The challenge to current classrooms, in meeting contemporary academic standards, is this: Teachers must increase rates of all students' participation in complex tasks and extended discourse about content concepts. This means engaging students in academic activity with more frequency and for more sustained periods. Classrooms of the common tradition cannot support the frequency and multiplicity of activities and higher rates of student participation required for academic Excellence. Phase 5 classrooms provide this capacity, because they exponentially extend the communication surfaces available in the classroom that promote students' independence for active learning.

We have traced the development of a classroom from yesterday's format through Phase 5, from one of the common tradition to the fully implemented design and application of the five pedagogy Standards that can assure teaching and learning Excellence, Fairness, Inclusion, and Harmony. The developmental process provides a systematic guide that can be valuable for the novice or the expert in mastering a new craft or refining practice. Vygotsky (1978) described the utility of the developmental approach, explaining how examining any fully achieved, completed practice reveals little about its dynamics, the process of its emergence, or its origins. We can improve or employ capacity effectively only if we understand how it develops.

In the case of Phase 5 classrooms, what would the first-time observer perceive? The increased surfaces of communication will be noticed in the lively engagement of the students, and so will their good mood. But the first-time visitor is unlikely to comprehend the classroom's specialized capacity to teach or to grasp its essential components. The careful, step-by-step building of students' self-confidence through frequent, early successes on academic tasks and its maintenance by a competent teacher are not readily discernible. The ownership of the shared community values will not be evident from the short, apparently casual Briefings and Debriefings of a well-functioning Phase 5 classroom. The gradual building of the community value for the daunting work of academic learning may not even be mentioned, but it will permeate and undergird the activities invisibly.

In our final chapter, prepared by this developmental analysis, we turn to the vision of the fully transformed classroom to examine its potentials, justifications, and prospects for vitality and proliferation.

7   Classrooms of Phase 5: Evidence, Vision, and Future

As the morning opens, the first-grade students, on the floor and in chairs, cluster around the teacher, who chats quietly with them about things personal or general. They are soon calm and attentive; the teacher then opens the daily flag and anthem ceremonies. Immediately after, she explains to the whole group the new tasks for the day. She asks whether there are any special things that they should think about during the morning. Two talk about doing a better job of task completion than they did the day before. Another suggests improving clean-up, another noise level. Then, the students get their individual folders that contain their personal schedules for the next two-and-one-half-hour block, showing their activity settings during each of the six rotations.

The students quickly disperse into some of the ten or twelve stations of the room—most are tables, but some consist of floor pillows or cubicles with computers or listening devices or other hands-on tools. One to five students share these stations, so not all stations are occupied at all times. In each of these activity settings there is a careful grouping of students to ensure a good mix of interests and abilities and to assure that during the instructional unit each student has the experience of working with every other one. The Instructional Conversation table is always filled. That is where the reading lesson takes place. The teacher is seated so that she can easily view every activity, but her attention is focused on the semi-circle of five or six students before her. The composition of the reading groups is adjusted every six weeks based on performance in the discussions and on criterion-referenced tests specific to current objectives. As the teacher passes out the text materials for the lesson, students at other stations are sorting out the materials they have found there and are getting to work. Students at the nearest stations often keep an ear half-cocked to the lesson of the Instructional Conversation, but they are never allowed to interrupt or join the discussion. The teacher is concentrating on teaching each reading group in turn, maximizing inclusive academic participation.

In teaching reading, the Instructional Conversation involves the discussion of a story's elements or themes. If the day's story is a new one, the teacher's questions draw out the children's previous experience, through life or text, which they can bring to bear in achieving comprehension of the new material. "This story is about a frog. Has anyone ever seen a frog?" "Yes!" the students may chorus. "Have you even touched a frog?" "Ick!" or "Yeah!" Some students may volunteer frog-touching incidents. "What did it feel like?" As students offer responses such as "cold" or "soft," the teacher probes to develop students' language, using "What else?" and "How?" questions; eliciting or, if necessary, introducing key words from the story. The teacher then leads students on a "picture walk," asking questions that help students predict what the story might be about as they examine each picture for clues. (By the third-grade level, a teacher would connect the children's experience to the upcoming text at more abstract levels such as forms of government or themes of jealousy or loyalty.) Then the teacher, based on or prompted by the discussion, sets a reason to read, a general question to bear in mind during the silent reading to come. "Why does Freddie want to have a frog? Read page one to page three to find out, and then look up at me."

As the students read silently for perhaps two or three minutes, the teacher scans the room, where there is a high rate of engagement in all the independent activity settings. There is a hum of muted conversation as the students discuss their work, assist each other, or chat socially. She praises them for their productive engagement. She responds to infractions by praising a diligent group nearby. If the disrupter continues, she writes the name on the board as a warning of consequences to come at recess. All the students know what these are from their Briefing and Debriefing discussions. Only on rare occasions of extreme boisterousness does the teacher call out the transgressor's name.

Now the students have read to page three and the teacher begins the group discussion. Questions often begin at a recall-of-detail level: "What is the boy's name, Malia? Where is he when the story begins? Who is the man he's working with?" Of course the thematic question previously set is reviewed: "Why does Freddie want a frog?" As the discussion continues, it becomes more vigorous, with some overlapping and volunteered speech. The students supplement one another's remarks; several students contribute before the teacher refocuses with another question. The teacher encourages this pattern but ensures full Inclusion over a week's period by inviting contributions from more reticent students. The teacher's questions are preponderantly of a higher order: "Can Freddie really hide that frog? How could he do that? How do you think he feels now? Why is his uncle taking the frog? What do you think he will do now?" Her questions frequently return to the child's own experience in ways that relate to the text materials and can be woven into deeper understanding: "Does anyone have an uncle like that? Do you remember last month's science lesson? What will Freddie's frog want to eat? What would you do if you were Freddie?" She then sets another theme question, the students silently read the next text segment, and the teacher again scans the other stations.

After about fifteen minutes of alternating reading and discussion, the books are closed and other aspects of reading skills are taught: phonics; drill in sight vocabulary; and, at higher grades, instruction in skills for information retrieval, vocabulary development, writing, or literary analysis. The teacher may work at the blackboard, use chart paper, or work from printed material. This part of the lesson is brisk, and choral responses are characteristic (although some touch-up individual work is frequently inserted). The content of this part of the lesson is drawn whenever possible from words or issues in the current story.

The reading lesson has now lasted about twenty minutes, and the teacher sets off a signal—often a bell or chimes—that cues the whole class to prepare to rotate. The first reading group disperses to the stations specified in their folders; ordinarily this group all goes to Station 2, where they find follow-up work directly drawn from that morning's reading instruction. During later rotations, the Instructional Conversation group members scatter according to their individual schedules, perhaps to the listening station, the art station, or the library corner. Among the most popular activity settings are those where students are designing crossword puzzles to be solved later by students in the puzzle-solving activity setting.

Within one minute, the students have all relocated. The next group is at the Instructional Conversation table with the teacher. In fifteen to twenty-five minutes another rotation will occur. By lunchtime, every student will have been in face-to-face, active dialogic instruction with the teacher. Every day.

When the bell rings for the final session, the teacher calls for everyone's attention, and asks how the morning went. "Good!" the students chorus. "We followed directions," they say. "You certainly did," the teacher agrees. "You stayed focused and solved problems on your own. Good work!" She signals that they can line up for the cafeteria.

At the beginning of the book, we proposed a solution to the problem of achieving Excellence, Fairness, Inclusion, and Harmony, simultaneously and seamlessly, by the operation of a coherent system for designing and organizing instructional activity, adaptable across grades and subject matters. That solution is the Phase 5 classroom. The defining elements of

Phase 5 classrooms are (1) diversified, simultaneous activity settings; (2) organized to provide meaningful contact with like and diverse others; (3) purposeful, integrated instructional tasks; and (4) the enactment of the Five Standards for Effective Pedagogy. To judge our claim that this classroom solves the problem of achieving Excellence, Fairness, Inclusion, and Harmony, let us briefly review our arguments and the evidence.

The Organizational System for Instructional Activity

Our discussion of the design and organization of activity has been guided by sociocultural theory, an integrated set of concepts that clarifies how society organizes and reproduces itself from generation to generation through patterned activity and patterning of participants. We have demonstrated how those same concepts clarify the activity patterns in conventional classrooms and how those classrooms play their role in reproducing the society in which they are embedded. By understanding how those forces work, we can envision alternatives, and by redirecting those forces, use them to achieve the high goals of our educational ideals.

We know now that the activities in which students engage, and the language and problem solving that accompany them, determine students' thinking, perceiving, and valuing. To design and organize those activities requires careful attention to a few central dimensions, among them: Who works with whom? and How are teachers and students in classrooms sorted out? The structure of society extends itself into classrooms, and if unimpeded, operates conservatively to perpetuate itself in each of its new classroom cells. Maximizing teaching and learning requires that instructional activity be designed and organized to some degree against those forces, because education itself means change and growth from present status, as do Excellence, Fairness, Inclusion, and Harmony.

We have discussed how activity affects relationships and minds. The qualities of peer and teacher relationships have profound consequences for learning and development and for the attainment of academic Excellence. Activity patterns of collaboration, reflection, and involvement foster positive relationship development among all members of the classroom community, teachers, and students. It is within the power of the teacher to mobilize the enormous educative power of classroom activity to improve children's intellectual, social, and moral development.

Students' local cultural communities and families build familiarity and preferences for certain aspects of activity patterns. Consequently, students vary in their comfort with and capacities to manage different roles, power relationships, and language codes and in their valuation of individualist or collectivist patterns. Schools may work with students' present capacities and work to expand them. To ignore existing capacities is unwise and unkind and prevents the development of students' full potential; to allow cultural and familial habits to totally determine classroom activity will limit learning, both academic and social. Thus, we have recommended a variety of activities and interactions. Contextualizing classroom activity in the patterns of the surrounding community will motivate students by employing their repertoires and providing the comforts of familiarity. Challenging them to acquire new competencies will give them the pleasures of mastery.

We have seen that effective classrooms require multiple, diverse, and simultaneous activity settings; in the mix there are activities in which every student receives assistance, from the teacher and also from peers more expert in the task at hand. Teacher assistance must also be regularly available in a context of intense, responsive, and sustained dialogue.

We have outlined the best available research-and-practice-derived Standards for Effective Pedagogy and demonstrated how those standards are enabled by a more complex design of instructional activity. And finally, we presented a developmental process for transforming classrooms of the common tradition into a differentiated organization containing varied, simultaneous, related, and appropriate activity settings.

Theory and Dynamics

The new school year opens, and students pour into the empty classroom, replicating their histories and communities by sorting themselves in their seating and interactions according to friendships and affinities or, lacking that, into groups and cliques of like-perceiving-like. Social sorting is not abstract; it is physical, palpable, and interactional. Maps of friendship groups, cliques, and crowds are not only people maps; they are geographical maps of territories, in the schoolyard and in the classroom. Thus existing affinities draw students together in the classroom, and the old patterns are printed out again in classroom propinquities, which make joint activity more likely—and the conservative Great Cycle of Social Sorting continues to roll.

Absent active teacher design, the pattern of classroom instructional activity will be determined by these affinity/propinquity patterns. The dominant group's preferences (likely also to be the teacher's) in roles, power, language use, and individualism/collectivism will dominate activity settings. Our review of research and theory has demonstrated that teacher initiatives to change seating patterns alone are impotent for fostering cognitive and intersubjective value growth. Propinquity across affinity boundaries, without joint activity, merely produces discomfort and centripetal aversions that will shortly dissolve any form of forced propinquity. However, when joint activity is introduced among unfamiliar associates, it transforms relationships because the joint products, the common goals, and the sharing of skills produce the conditions by which common understanding develops. What are these conditions? The simple ones of talking together over work and problem solving, of developing a common terminology for shared events, of sharing the same emotions for the same reasons over the same experience. Thus, even after the bell ends the Phase 5 classroom of Ms. Young, students who would otherwise never share a hallway conversation talk together naturally and unselfconsciously, the sure sign of intersubjectivity. These are the conditions for new affinity development, and when students enter Ms. Young's classroom the next day, their propinquity maps have more to do with their recent project affiliations than they do with language, culture, race, or social status. Of course, the Phase 5 classroom does not produce totally homogeneous sociometry, with perfect friendships with everyone. But the Phase 5 classroom is harmonious, new appreciations develop, and respect is more widespread and is distributed in patterns not merely mirroring the surrounding community. And everyone's academic potential is fostered.

In the developmental sequences proposed in Chapter 6, we showed that Phase 5's complex simultaneous joint activity cannot be immediately implemented unless there is already a rare condition of near-total intersubjectivity in the classroom. That is why Phase 2 is necessary, because joint activity will not necessarily be productive unless there is already present the shared values of productivity and the productive values of sharing. Phase 2 classrooms begin by engaging in the joint productive activity of creating shared values for work, mutual respect, and mutual support. Being human as we are, the work of the Briefing/Debriefing handles is never complete, because the system of shared values is continually being strengthened, shored up, and modified in the light of the community's developing experiences.

The teacher's role is key and indispensable. The teacher has the vision, the experience, and the skill to envision a Phase 5 condition and to assist the community to create it. The teacher has the responsibility and the potential. It is the teacher who encourages, assists, and ultimately enforces the democratic and Excellence values that characterize Phase 5.

Fundamentally, the purpose of education is to prepare students who are able to take a productive role in creating a society for Excellence, Fairness, Inclusion, and Harmony. We must suppose that it is the teacher who understands these goals and will guide students toward them. It is the teacher who possesses the advanced subject matter knowledge and cognitive capacities toward which we want students to strive. For this reason, the creation of intersubjectivity between student and teacher takes precedence. This is why it is vital that the Instructional Conversation, over shared work, among teacher and students, be recognized as the centerpiece of instructional activity. Instructional Conversation is required not only to develop intersubjectivity but also to develop cognition and academic achievement. Teachers are not fulfilling the potential for student development if they merely orchestrate activities among "cooperative learning groups" or only float among activity settings, touching down briefly and randomly to answer some student need. Fulfillment comes when intersubjectivity is built from sustained, unrelenting effort to assure joint work with conversation and the building of a shared language, values, and understanding. These are the conditions in which teacher assistance and guidance can be offered in cognitively challenging activities for maximizing academic achievement. They are the conditions in which the teacher can be the source of academic and social support, with all the felicitous consequences for school achievement discussed in Chapter 4. This is why the Instructional Conversation is the capstone of a Phase 5 education.

Do Phase 5 Classrooms Achieve Excellence, Fairness, Inclusion, and Harmony?

Excellence

Phase 5 classrooms maximize Excellence. They do not compromise it in favor of Inclusion or Fairness; they do not subordinate productive work to Harmony. They achieve Harmony through inclusive participation in work toward shared goals. Phase 5 classrooms, so far as we now know, are the best route toward academic Excellence: All else being equal, Phase 5 classrooms provide the best-known design of instructional activity, for all, for each. These are strong claims, but we know of no disconfirming evidence, and the consensus encompasses the major theoretical systems of our time: cognitive science, critical theory, and sociocultural theory.

Oakes and Lipton say: "Interactions that promote learning must build on the knowledge, language, and cultures that students bring with them to school. In this way, teaching that is informed by sociocultural theory is teaching that is socially just" (p. 370). They go on to quote Dewey:

> Learning which develops intelligence and character does not come about when only the textbook and the teacher have a say; ... every individual becomes educated only as he has an opportunity to contribute something from his own experience, no matter how meager or slender that background of experience may be at a given time; and finally ... enlightenment comes from the give and take, from the exchange of experiences and ideas (Dewey 1938, p. 296, quoted in Oakes and Lipton 1998, p. 371).

Fairness

Phase 5 classrooms are fair. Equity of opportunity means assuring that each student has equal access to each other, to the teacher's close attention and assistance, and to activities that require a variety of roles and goals. Equity classrooms accommodate cultural needs and cultural strengths and simultaneously give every student the benefit of challenging them to learn to their limits. Classrooms provide equity by letting the low-status student not only learn but lead. Fairness consists of allowing students the comforts of sometimes working with friends, while also teaching all students, equally, to work harmoniously with every member of the classroom community and thus to explore a broader screen of friendship than that projected by their own neighborhoods.

Inclusion

Phase 5 classrooms are inclusive, both academically and socially. They eliminate the dreadful, familiar pattern of the excluded and resistant cadre in the back rows. Every student participates; every student is present and responsible in instructional activity settings. Every student's strength is included, whether this is a capacity to work cooperatively or to display an unusual pattern of multiple intelligences. Inclusion is explicit and implicit, academic and social. Every student is included in the classroom's circle of respect because curriculum is contextualized in the experiences and problems of each student's family and community.

Harmony

Phase 5 classrooms are as harmonious as human society can be. Harmony is created through explicit, formalized, regular, and frequent discussion and revision of community rules, values, and goals. These sessions are the handles by which every Instructional Frame is carried, and ad hoc sessions are held whenever an extraordinary problem appears. Although every classroom's value set will vary to some degree, other elements of the Phase 5 classroom are predictable and universally necessary: respect for one another; facilitation and lack of interference with others' work; the valuation of learning, productivity, and quality; belief that all members have valuable capacities to contribute; and the expectation and tolerance of multiple perspectives; and the necessity of finding underlying unities. These are the presumptions, the challenges, and the necessities of democracy, and Phase 5 classrooms prepare students for citizenship in the classroom's microcosmic version. Langer has described this phenomenon in a literature class: "a classroom culture where the literary environment exemplifies as well as considers issues of ethics, civic and social responsibility, cultural identity, aesthetics, and reasoning—as they relate to literature, self, and others" (Langer 1995, p. 60). This is what Oakes and Lipton (1998) call "doing democracy."

Supporting Evidence

Existence Proof

Can such classrooms exist at all? Yes, they do exist, and include classrooms in Santa Cruz High School, Santa Cruz, California (Sirota et al. 1999); Half Moon Bay High School, Half Moon Bay, California; Fenger Academy, a public high school in inner-city Chicago (Lee 1995); Wai'anae High School, Wai'anae, Hawai'i; elementary classrooms at Starlight Elementary School, Watsonville, California; and Bullit County and two adjacent counties in Kentucky. They exist in a private school for the gifted, Satori School in Tucson, Arizona; and in a multilingual, multicultural public school, Hazeltine Elementary in Los Angeles Unified School District (Saunders and Goldenberg 1999). They are in many schools for Native Americans, particularly in the Southwest Region School District of Alaska (Blum n.d.); at Rough Rock Demonstration School, Rough Rock, Arizona (Dick, Estell, and McCarty 1994; Begay et al. 1995); and at Zuni Middle School, Zuni, New Mexico (Tharp et al. 1999). The most fully realized Phase 5 schools known to us are two in The Netherlands developed in association with faculty at the Hogeschool Alkmaar Department of Education. At De Kring School in the small middle-class town of Alkmaar and in De Willibrord, an inner-city school in Zaandam serving a multi-ethnic, multilingual population, instructional activities are creatively integrated with community and even business organizations (Bok and Conihn 1994, 1996; Borst and Kempenaar 1998; van Brandwijk et al. 1998).

Proof of Effectiveness

The journey to the vision of Phase 5 classrooms has been sinuous, with byways and alternate routes. The vision has revealed itself gradually, by lifting one scrim, then another. Evidence of its effectiveness comes from classrooms of several types. Some are largely unsupported efforts by individual teachers. Many more are from systematic programs of three general types. The first are hand-crafted small programs, often designed by educator/researcher teams, many in out-of-the-way villages or ghettos, in which schools of the common tradition were failing to teach local populations. Second are several long-term programs with systematic evaluation data, tending to focus on various combinations of Phase 5 elements but not emphasizing them all. The third type includes the full Phase 5 implementation, with evaluation/experimentation data of various depths.

Descriptions of fine examples of individually created classrooms have been published in Alaska by Lipka (1990) and in Florida by Lee and Fradd (1996a). Our own study of multicultural classrooms in the Monterey and San Francisco Bay area has discovered that Phase 4 or Phase 5 classrooms are very rare in fourth grade, but up to one-fourth of first-grade teachers use substantial portions of the Phase 5 elements. Classrooms with these elements foster higher student performance compared to those without (Estrada, Sayavong, and Guardino 1998). Informal observation also indicates that in these classrooms, in which there is a good mixing of students in grouping, peer relationships are more inclusive and harmonious. Further investigation of this issue will be conducted for two additional years.

Handcrafted programs that exemplify one or more key elements of Phase 5 are far too numerous to list here; the interested reader can consult virtually any compendium of exemplary practices or any subject matter's new professional standards for effective teaching and find exemplars. More extensive lists of programs participating in the emerging consensus of Standards for Effective Pedagogy can be found in Tharp (1989, 1994, 1997; Yamauchi and Tharp 1995; Dalton 1998a; Dalton and Youpa 1998). Here there is space only to call attention to a few exemplars, illustrating a wide range of ages, subject matters, and cultural/linguistic groups. They include the Inuit science program based on community whaling, reported by Lipka (1994); Carol D. Lee's classrooms that are teaching literary criticism to African-American adolescents (Lee 1993, 1995); and Sophie Haroutunian-Gordon's (1991) teachers who work with similar high school populations in teaching through conversation. They can be seen in the classrooms of the research teachers working with González et al. (1995) in translating Mexican heritage students' families "funds of knowledge" into classroom activities (Moll et al. 1992) and in many Canadian schools for native students controlled by native communities (e.g., Gardner 1986; Harrison 1986). Excellent examples are the classrooms of Palincsar, Anderson, and David (1993) that teach scientific literacy in middle grades through collaborative problem solving. Many classrooms following the Foxfire Approach reflect the culture of the school and community, and emphasize joint activity and the needs and interests of the students served (Starnes and Paris in press).

Programs that emphasize some Phase 5 elements include several well-known sustained research and development models. We mention here six programs notable for their clarity of program description, explanatory integrity, and effectiveness data. Each has contributed to the growing consensus that has produced the Five Standards for Effective

Pedagogy, and each has developed detailed procedures for enacting Phase 5 elements. While not developed specifically for culturally and linguistically diverse students, there is evidence of effectiveness across student populations.

Cognitively Guided Instruction (Carpenter, Fennema, and Franke 1996) is a program that assists teachers to create elementary mathematics classes that are rich with the use of mathematics language, are activity focused, and are characterized by "figuring out" how mathematics relates to the solving of problems.

Complex Instruction (Cohen and Lotan 1997; Bower 1997) features cognitively challenging activities that require varied abilities in a small-group, multiple-activity format. Cohen and Lotan's recommendations for social organization and activity design are especially notable, corresponding to many elements of Phase 4.

Authentic Instruction, by contrast, focuses on the role of the teacher. Teachers help to construct knowledge using disciplined inquiry (connecting students' previous knowledge to their expressions of current material). Authentic Instruction also emphasizes contextualizing instruction in values and issues beyond the classroom (Newmann 1996; Newmann, Secada, and Wehlage 1995).

Reciprocal Teaching employs small-group discussion as a basis for teaching reading. Students conduct discussions that are not scripted, but rather employ consistent strategies, such as asking for assistance when stumped, regular summarization, and prediction (Palincsar and Brown 1985; Brown, Metz, and Campione 1996).

Instructional Congruence (Lee and Fradd 1998) interweaves science and literacy teaching but is a more general approach emphasizing contextualization, language, and literacy development and challenging instruction.

The Cooperative Integrated Reading and Comprehension (CIRC) program has shown consistent positive effects on academic achievement through its emphases on joint productive activity, language development, and cognitive challenge (e.g., Stevens et al. 1987). Its bilingual version (BCIRC) adds contextualization and accelerates the attainment of exit criteria for bilingual education (Calderón and Carreón 1994; Calderón, Herta-Lazarowitz, and Slavin 1998).

Our characterizations of these programs are drawn from the emphases in their own program descriptions, but as teachers and schools adapt these programs according to their own locales and experiences, there are undoubtedly instances of each that do reach Phase 5.

In studies of exemplary practices, schools, and/or teachers, those ped-agogical factors that are mentioned by researchers are in consistent align-ment with one or more of the Five Standards. For example, research by the Center for the Improvement of Early Reading Achievement (CIERA) (Taylor and Pearson 1999; Taylor et al. 1998; see also www.ciera.org), studying schools and teachers that are "beating the odds" in teaching all children to read, emphasizes more time spent in small-group and less time in whole-group instruction; the use of a "coaching" versus "telling information" interaction style by teachers; and contextualizing of word recognition teaching by coaching during the reading of books. Thirty-seven percent of teachers in most effective schools asked highest-level questions of students; no such questions were asked by teachers in the least-effective schools. The presence of home liaison materials linking school instruction to the family context is emphasized by Hiebert et al. (1992).

The degree to which the Five Standards are enacted is associated with student achievement. Estrada and Imhoff (1999) conducted six case stud-ies of elementary bilingual and multilingual classrooms. Teachers who were stronger implementers of the Five Standards produced significantly greater gains in reading performance, regardless of whether the students spoke English only, were fully English proficient, or were English Lan-guage Learners.[1]

Full Phase 5 Implementation

The most extensive, long-term demonstration of Phase 5 has been the Kamehameha Elementary Education Program (KEEP), a program for at-risk kindergarten through third-grade Native Hawaiian students, oper-ated from 1970 through 1988 with fidelity to its original self-description. Scores of publications have described that program (e.g., Tharp 1982; Au et al. 1986; Tharp et al. 1984). In the National Academy of Sciences report on educational programs for English-language-learning minorities, KEEP was listed as the only available such study with true experimental design (August and Hakuta 1998, p. 87). Pronounced improvement in reading achievement (Tharp 1982) and in student industriousness (Antill and Tharp 1974) resulted from the program. Through many years of upscal-ing into fifteen multicultural public schools of Hawai'i, evaluation results remained above non-KEEP programs' academic achievement. These ef-fects continued until too-rapid expansion and reduction of resources had, by 1992, cost the program its fidelity of implementation. In 1997, it was formally terminated (Gallimore et al. 1982; Calkins et al. 1989; Klein 1988; Klein and Calkins 1988; Tharp 1982; Yap, Estes, and Nickel 1988).

As a test of the model in a different locus and population, the KEEP program was extended into Rough Rock Elementary School (Navajo),

Arizona, in 1984 (Jordan 1995; Vogt, Jordan, and Tharp 1992). The program took root, "naturalized" in the Navajo locale (Sells 1994), and became the Rough Rock English-Navajo Language Arts Program (Dick, Estell, and McCarty 1994; Begay et al. 1995). The program now has a ten-year history. Its operations are fully congruent with Phase 5, and literacy in both English and Navajo is significantly higher than comparison groups.

While KEEP remains the best example of wide-scale, long-term enactment of Phase 5, it is by no means a complete demonstration of its potential. KEEP retained a primary focus on literacy, was less well developed in mathematics and science, and was confined to the lower elementary grades. Many examples of local, handcrafted models (see above) have extended Phase 5 into a variety of grades, subject matters, and educational settings. Among those with published evaluation data are the Southwest Region School District of Alaska's cross-curriculum high school programs (Blum 1998, n.d.) and the middle school programs of the Center for Research in Education, Diversity & Excellence (Hilberg 1998).

Shall We Improve Our Schools?

L. Scott Miller's (1995) An American Imperative, the highly acclaimed[2] call for accelerating minority educational advancement, concludes with a series of social welfare and educational policy recommendations, each thoughtful, well analyzed, and clear eyed:

> From a long-term perspective, some of the most important research and development work must be concerned with expanding our understanding of educationally important cultural differences and developing professional practices and strategies responsive to them. Much of this work should look at cultural differences defined simultaneously in terms of race/ethnicity and social class in order to gain a better understanding of how ethnic and social class factors interact. A number of studies should be launched that examine home, school, and community experiences of groups defined in these terms. With regard to the school-oriented studies, special interest should be taken in assessing the impact of different types of school organization, classroom organization and instructional strategies on different subpopulations (pp. 370–371).

We too would prioritize this work, and have done so in our own careers. However, for the eventual success of Miller's proposals, there is good news: The instructional strategies and classroom organization needed for students at risk of educational failure are not different from those most effective for any other students.

It is true that much of the research that has built the consensus on the principles and standards for instructional activity has been conducted in classrooms for cultural, racial, ethnic, and linguistic minorities. But those principles and standards are not applicable to at-risk students alone; they are the foundational conditions for the effective education of all students, mainstream as well as diverse. Research in the "at-risk" field should be understood as the foundation for research on education for all students because it is based on the full range of variance necessary for full generalizability. Research that is conducted on mainstream students, schools, teachers, and policies alone provides a far too narrow range to establish universal principles.

Mainstream middle-class families and communities continue to provide their students with developmental opportunities outside of school that are characterized by the Five Standards, and so schools get by with offering those students the recitation script of the common tradition. This masks the universal desirability of Phase 5 classrooms. Contextualized teaching; Instructional Conversation; joint productive activity with literate discourse; the development of scientific, commercial, and professional language conventions—these are provided in the bedtime stories, the car-pool driving, the dinner table conversations, the family homework projects, the little league coaching, scouting, and the myriad activities of the middle class that prepare students with the cognitive skills and expectations needed for the literacy activities of school. These sociocultural activities occur much less often in typical at-risk students' families and communities. Therefore, the school must provide equivalent instructional activities if equity of opportunity is to be reached. Those equivalent instructional activities are those that provide for the enactment of the Five Standards. Schools for middle-class students can be careless about these ideal conditions because they rely on families and communities to do the work of cognitive development. Miller's (1995) thorough review of the relevant literature has convincingly detailed the relevant differences in primary socialization in lower- and middle-social class families; Hart and Risley (1995) have shown how social class differences in quantity of verbal interaction are closely linked to academic readiness and eventual success.

Although mainstream students can prosper in schools of the common tradition, designing effective instructional activities in schools can enhance every student's performance. Rueda (1998a) has recounted the design process for the OLE! (Optimal Learning Environment) program for special education language minority students. After years of frustration, the developers looked to classes for the gifted and talented, found there the complex instructional activities of Phases 4 and 5, adapted them to their own students, and produced one of the outstanding special education programs on record.[3] For gifted, for needful, for minority, for majority—a national policy of Inclusion and Excellence does not require different medicine for different groups. We suffer a common educational disorder.

But is it worth it? Are schools good enough for most, and an investment in reform of value only to a few? Underachievement is not only the problem of somebody else's students. We need look no further than the well-documented reports from the Carnegie Corporation (1996), the National Education Goals Panel (1995), and the Third International Mathematics and Science Study (TIMMS) report (National Center for Education Statistics 1996) to understand that U.S. educational underachievement is everyone's problem:

> Students from all backgrounds face obstacles to successful learning—native speakers of English as well as second-language learners; students in regular classrooms as well as pupils in special education; students from middle-income families as well as those who live in poverty; students in the suburbs as well as those in the cities. If their approaches to learning are at odds with the approaches that characterize most classrooms, and their strengths and needs go unnoticed, they are at special risk of having educational experiences that are at best unsatisfactory, and at worst deeply scarring.... By the time they reach fourth grade, the great majority of today's students have not met the standards for proficiency in reading, writing, and mathematics that have been set in this country (Carnegie Corporation 1996, p. 14).

Comparisons of U.S. students' achievement with that of other nations show a similar underachievement pattern. A ten-year longitudinal study comparing schools in Minneapolis and Chicago with schools in three East Asian cities showed that underlying aptitude for mathematics is not different among U.S. and Asian students, but over time the performance of U.S. students falls steadily behind (Stevenson and Stigler 1992, cited in Carnegie Corporation 1996). For the first grade the highest-scoring U.S. school was lower than any of the Chinese schools and was at about the median of the Taiwanese and Japanese schools. For the fifth grade, the highest-scoring U.S. school scored similarly to the lowest-scoring East Asian schools. Lamentations over students ill prepared for higher education are heard everywhere, in newspapers, in the teachers' lounge, and at faculty meetings. All too often, our "top" students have difficulty in a variety of fields with conceptualizing, analyzing, and solving problems and with writing coherently and convincingly. In educational reform, the stakes and payoffs are common to us all. "Cuando uno se levanta, todos se levantan." "When one rises, all rise."[4]

The Image of Schools in the Eyes of Educators and the Public

The schools of the common tradition are by no means restricted to North America. There is sharp similarity among classrooms in different parts of the world (Erickson 1987; Ost 1991; Sharan and Sharan 1987), a phenomenon we have labeled the "trans-national culture of the school" (Jordan and Tharp 1979). The ubiquity of the model makes it more difficult to envision alternatives.

In Greenland, educational policy makers currently envisioning Phase 5 classrooms are encountering the same resistance, from some teachers, administrators, parents, and legislators: Schools with such classrooms cannot be real schools. Everyone knows that real schools, even for Greenlanders, should operate in the common tradition. The deep dialogue between the two visions continues as of this writing.

The Saami Minority in Arctic Norway

Höem concluded that low pupil achievement (for the Saami) was due to the inappropriateness of the Norwegian cultural system of education set in a different cultural milieu. The school system was well funded, the quality of facilities and equipment were adequate and were of a high quality. Teachers were well trained by high Norwegian standards. All that was needed for a good education had been provided by the government, but to little avail. Since the time of this study, inadequate (Saami) pupil performance compared with the achievements of the majority population has remained the norm. Moreover, education officials, arguing that the best school system possible is in place, continue to ponder the question of why performance is so low. In terms of what they accept is the best, their argument is correct. It is not only the best system known to them, it is the only one. The question, What would the system look like if the present one was changed to reflect the environment and culture of the people where it is located? goes unasked (Darnell and Höem 1996, p. 232).

Whatever conservatism operates in the minds of teachers and administrators, and it is considerable, professional educators do experience unease at seeing too many students fail. Of course, they often resist the radical transformation that Phase 5 represents. But educators feel that there must be something better than current practice, so they search in the catalogs of fads, for this and that new program that can, like a small plug-in, enliven their traditional classrooms without fundamentally changing them.

For the public, who know the common tradition recitation script from their own childhoods and from observations of the same pattern in classrooms of their own children, a Phase 5 classroom is a radical transformation indeed: so noisy! so chaotic! so undisciplined! Of course, it is not undisciplined chaos, but the patterns of activity and organization are complex. Noisier it is indeed; Phase 5 is full of talk, as education requires. But without guides to their observations, many parents and board members and legislators can flee from this complex activity back to the security of the basics and the quiet of the common tradition.

Not all parents resist. In communities where schools are clearly failing their students, parents are anxious for and can even be demanding a more relevant education. At a parent-teacher working seminar that we conducted in a remote minority community, many parents took vacation time from work to attend. One such mother, hearing teacher objections to the Phase 5 vision, protested, "What's wrong with teaching them like that? It's just like we work at the highway department!"

But how can this new vision of transformed teaching and classrooms be communicated and justified to parents whose students are succeeding reasonably well by the standards of current schools? Exemplars proving that Phase 5 is effective are essential and should be encouraged and spotlighted. But observation of any complex phenomenon, without guidance and explanation, is a guarantee of misunderstanding. The research and development community of educators has a responsibility to communicate this vision and explain its justifications in all possible arenas, to local school boards and PTAs, to commissions and policy makers, and to concerned parents in groups large and small.

Preparing Teachers for Phase 5

The transformations from classrooms of the common tradition to those of Phase 5 are radical, comprehensive, liberating, vigorous, satisfying—and difficult. Teachers who effect this transit on their own are miracle workers. It would be absurd to expect the current American teaching corps to reinvent itself and begin performing at expert levels without assistance, support, models, and coaching. Preparation of the next generation of teachers will require an equally radical transformation of teacher education programs. Institutions of higher education are just as conservative and slow to change as are primary through secondary schools. Such reform will not take place unless there is a consensual subscription to a vision of transformed teaching, so strong that faculties and administrators will themselves be motivated to embark on the complex and difficult journey. Do that consensus and will to change exist?

Almost; there is certainly an emerging general sense of the quality teacher. The influential report of the National Commission on Teaching and America's Future (1996) proposed major departures from status quo teaching and preparation for teaching. We are in full accord with the Commission's belief that all students deserve to have teachers who are qualified in their subject matter, understand their students' needs, and have skills to enliven teaching and learning for academic goals. The report also speaks to aspects of classroom teaching that have been relatively unexplored in teacher preparation and professional development (and are the foci of this book): classroom organization to support greatly increased levels of students' activity and interaction and a pedagogy to guide those active and expressive students.

The report premises that "School reform cannot succeed unless it focuses on creating the conditions in which teachers can teach, and teach well" (p. vi). The report acknowledges that "most schools are still not structured to support high-quality teaching: Teachers do not have enough sustained time with their students each day and over the years to come to know them well and to tackle difficult kinds of learning with them ... " (p. 9). It is clear that quality teaching only occurs in settings designed to support the process. "Successful schools have found that they need to create communities that work toward shared standards, where students are well known both personally and academically, where parents are involved as partners, and where a variety of teaching approaches are used" (p. 9).

The Commission is confident about the potential of standards to improve all students' mastery of challenging content, because teaching that draws on today's standards and assessments frameworks attempts much more than "covering the curriculum" and basic skills. The report describes quality teaching as activity based, thus engaging students in becoming speakers, writers, problem solvers, historians, and mathematicians (p. 27). We view our own work as the implementation of much of the Commission's general vision.

In assessing the will of the nation to reform, it is a positive sign that there is consensus among general educators about the broad outlines of quality teaching; it is also highly positive that there is strong agreement about effective pedagogy and activity design in the research-and-development community of researchers. It is not at all clear, however, that there is any full awareness of what it would require to prepare teachers for this transformation.

Most experience of preparing teachers for Phase 5 classrooms has come from the work itself in developing the programs listed above. Teachers and researchers working together in a process of self-transformation have created many of the "handcrafted" programs. Others, notably the KEEP program, have developed systematic teacher training specifically for their own programs (Sloat, Tharp, and Gallimore 1977). In any event, virtually all teacher preparation for Phase 5 has been a process of retraining because teacher education has no distinguished record in professional development for reformed classrooms.

Oakes and Lipton, immediately following their remarks and their quotation of Dewey, say about teacher preparation:

> Enlightenment does, indeed, come "from the give and take, from the exchange of experiences and ideas." This, perhaps, explains a great frustration for beginning teachers. Too often, the training of teachers is plagued by the same myth of efficiency as the teaching of the young, with too little opportunity for give and take and exchange. Teacher education institutions ... pass along just enough of the bits and pieces of "practical" teacher knowledge that add up to professional training (Oakes and Lipton 1998, p. 371).

One way of describing this issue is that teachers are not taught in Phase 5 classrooms themselves, nor for that matter have they even seen Phase 5 practiced, so they are doubly handicapped; not only are they denied Dewey's "enlightenment," they are not taught to implement Phase 5 for the benefit of their future students. The appropriate socioculturally valid principles and standards for education of primary and secondary students are not different from those for adults, and therefore they are the appropriate principles and standards for the education of educators (Tharp and Gallimore 1988). Rueda (1998b) has summarized the arguments for using the Five Standards for Effective Pedagogy as the basis for conducting professional development, both in-service and preservice. At the present time, there are glimmers of enlightening teacher education programs. An underground grapevine in the profession shares experiments and experiences. Systematic efforts to expand such training to the programmatic level are active at California State University, Chico, in their Special Education Teacher Education Program. We may be optimistic that the new experimental teacher education program at the University of California, Los Angeles, led by Jeannie Oakes, may well provide a national model. Internationally, Israel's Mofit Institute is a source of ideas and inspiration.

We cannot predict the exact appearance of reformed teacher education programs. There will almost certainly be as much surface variation as we find in Phase 5 classrooms for kindergarten through twelfth grade, but the variation will be over the same firm underlying structure of the Five Standards for Effective Pedagogy. The Instructional Conversation will be there—an opportunity for aspiring teachers to mull, to consider, to formulate and exchange thoughts, in dialogue with an experienced instructor; to learn "from the give and take, from the exchange of experiences and ideas." We conclude this book with an excerpt of such a conversation. Audrey Sirota, a master of Instructional Conversation herself, teaches introductory classes in the subject matter of this book to first-year teachers-in-training. Here she is demonstrating the Instructional Conversation with five students in a fishbowl activity observed by the other twenty students in the class, which meets in the library of an elementary Professional Development School. The subject of the discussion is the Instructional Conversation itself.

AUDREY: During the Instructional Conversation [IC], I'm going to ask the participants to actually read an excerpt from Rousing Minds to Life.[5] There's two excerpts, it's page 108 to page 111, and the other section is page 134 to 136, if you have your books with you. Don't start reading yet! I'm going to ask the people in the Instructional Conversation to speak really loudly and clearly, because yesterday we had a problem with people in the audience hearing. People in the audience: We're doing this as a fishbowl activity so that you can gain access to some of the skills needed to do an Instructional Conversation with your students. Any questions about the goal? Okay, so let's start. Let's talk about what's your understanding at this time about what IC is. So, what do you guys know about an IC?

LILY: They're small groups of students with the teachers.

ANN: It takes the form of a dialogue.

RUTH: The teacher asks the questions?

BELEM: Students contribute what they already know to the conversation.

AUDREY: Anything else?

BELEM: The dialogue would be based around … I would think that the teacher would have an idea of something she's trying to teach that the conversation is being revolved around, maybe not directly, but that it's hopefully going to evolve to. There's an instructional component to the Instructional Conversation! [Laughs.]

AUDREY: See I knew there was something else.… I could see it in your brain! Anything else? Okay, let's talk about what you want to learn about an Instructional Conversation. What do you want to learn about it? How do you plan one?

TARA: Well, sometimes maybe how do you bridge a gap from what students know to what you want them to learn in the dialogue. How do you make bridges, connections, or weave together knowledge?

ANN: I want to know how do you structure it, but also be able to be inclusive, like how do you do those dual jobs of why you're holding the conversation, and making sure to allow all the students to contribute.

AUDREY: So it sounds like two things. One is how do you structure it, and then another is how do you include everyone?

ANN: Well how do you mediate both of those at the same time. When you're the teacher, what tools can you use to make sure you're doing it? I guess I would worry that I'd have a tendency to focus on one thing and leave something out. So ...

AUDREY: Oh! Inclusive as far as curriculum, what you're trying to teach. So how do you keep it structured and include everything you're trying to get across.

ANN: Right.

LILY: And how do you know if the students have learned?

AUDREY: How do you know if the students have learned what you want them to know. Okay, I think that's enough! Those are big goals to accomplish for this first time. Now at this point what I'd like you to do, the people who have page 108, you go ahead and read your section. So take about five minutes to go ahead and read that section. Feel free to take notes.

[Five-minute pause while students read.]

AUDREY: So, given the things that you read in your passage, plus the things that you already had an idea about, think about whether you've ever experienced anything that resembles an IC. Think about what you experienced and what you learned from that experience. It can be school or a non-school ...

LILY: When we were at the Earth First camp up at Headwaters, we were learning about backwoods action—you know, protesting logging. There were ten of us, and two were obviously more experienced in backwoods action and nonviolent action, and they led a discussion and helped us to learn about safety in the woods, and safety in demonstrations. But they led us through it, we weren't just sitting there listening to them preach, they were using our experiences a lot and asking us to talk about where we'd been and what we had done previously. That was a really good instruction. I got a lot out of it. It was very strong. I still think about it a lot.

AUDREY: Okay, thanks. Other examples?

RUTH: Just regular Instructional Conversations that we may have had?

AUDREY [nods]: And keep in mind, too, on page 134 it says "some teachers for some purposes in some classrooms may refer to this conversation as the reading lesson. Others may describe it as the language development lesson. For others it is the writing group, and for older students, it might be the science lesson."

RUTH: Well I can tell what I'm doing. Usually the first couple of days I ask the students, "What is science?" That's how we start off, with this dialogue trying to weave in physical science, or chemistry or life science. They may or may not know what those words are. So we have a dialogue or conversation of—I guess we would call it "schooled language"—and what they perceive it to be, and what I may think it is, and how it relates to the community and the world and their assignments in the class. That's how we just start off these conversations.

ANN: I can only think of something I was wanting to try when I lead my TA [Teaching Assistant] sections. For instance, last time I wanted to elicit some depth reflection on what they were reading. So we talked about it—what they wrote in their journals, they would always write about facts but they wouldn't go beyond that to reflection. So in our discussion, I started by asking them to reflect. Just asking them to think and talk about what they knew so far—and then maybe allowing their voices to cause them to reflect somewhat more. Then I would know by listening to the conversations if they'd reflected more or not.

So I would be guiding it somewhat ... I would be guiding it, wouldn't I? Somewhat?

The lesson did not end there, but this is a fine question on which to leave them. Phase 5 teachers work, plan, design, support, trust, urge, assist, and orchestrate. They guide the Instructional Conversation—somewhat. We will leave this group of soon-to-be teachers, establishing their own community, coming to understand how community is conversation, where guiding and following are not separable. That is a mystery not to be solved, but to be lived. Although it is much like melody or magic, it can be conveyed.

Notes

1. Performance was based on the percentage of students reaching grade level or higher and the amount of progress from fall to spring using running records of reading.

2. Winner of the American Educational Research Association Outstanding Book of the Year Award 1997 and of the Grawemeyer Prize in Education 1998.

3. In a program where students typically make extremely slow academic progress as shown by statewide achievement figures, more than a third of the OLE! students jumped in academic achievement by more than two years' equivalence (Ruiz and Figueroa 1995).

4. A teaching of Jose Estrada, Peggy Estrada's father.

5. Tharp and Gallimore 1988.

Appendices

TABLE A.1 Phasing into Simultaneous, Differentiated, Multiple Activity Settings (ASs) in Support of Phase 5 Instructional Conversation (IC)

	Phase 1 1–4 weeks	Phase 2 2–3 weeks	Phase 3 1–2 weeks	Phase 4 2–3 weeks	Phase 5 on-going
Pedagogy Standards, Grouping, and Routing	• Enact standards I, II, III. • Use Frame, handles. • Build community. • Assure success. • Apply SCIPP. • Provide feedback. • Whole group formal at homeroom seats.	• Enact standards I, II, III. • Use Frame, handles. • Encourage peer support. • Develop students' independence. • Mix students in groups. • 1/2, 1/3, 1/4, 1/5 group formats. • Round-robin routing.	• Enact standards I, II, III. • Use Frame, handles. • Introduce activity settings (AS). • Group students to match and mix strengths and talents. • Transition to AS-driven routing.	• Enact standards I, II, III, IV. • Use Frame, handles. • Routinize ASs. • Select home groups. • Route students to ASs in mixed and matched groupings. • Offer choice contracts.	• Introduce as AS. • Enact all Standards. • Schedule daily IC. • Stabilize home groups. • Route students to ASs as mixed and matched. • Offer choice contracts.
Content, Tasks, and Activities	• Early Content Theme (ECT) is lesson/task basis and bridge to SAC. • Community building. • Review skills in ECT. • Design independent-level tasks and JPA. • Create tasks leveled and timed accurately for completion in Frame.	• ECT review and reteach. • Assure student success by accurately leveling and timing tasks and activities. • Assess skill levels in ECT. • Provide feedback on match to pedagogy Standards and community values.	• Complete ECT review and reteaching. • Preview SAC skills, concepts. • Plan tasks and activities in SAC. • Check accuracy of task and activity leveling. • Assess student content and skill knowledge for progress in SAC.	• Teach SAC. • Provide more complex tasks at ASs. • Tailor tasks for groups, individuals. • Provide feedback on match to pedagogy content Standards.	• Teach SAC. • Provide activity basis for IC. • Use context lexicon and concepts to solve problems in dialogue. • Assure student success by accurately leveling tasks and activities to student capacity at ASs.
AS#1 Teacher teaches	• Teach ECT topics in Frame in large group. • Float to review skills in large-group follow-ups.	• Reteach concepts and skills in ETC in large-group and smaller-group follow-ups. • Float to review skills in follow-ups.	• Teaching is conversational involving students' responses that are extended (more than yes/no or nonverbal responses).	• Teach content in small groups. • Teaching is conversational. • Teacher and students use content lexicon.	• Introduce AS. • Teacher and students dialogue and produce together at AS#1. • Early ICs on issues of community, contracts, grouping, and SAC.
AS#2/3 Apply/Extend IC Follow-up	• Provide AS#1-related independent-level tasks that apply/extend. • Assess skill levels.	• Teacher monitors instructional level. • Relates skill practice to ECT.	• Introduce as AS. • Teacher monitors instructional level.	• Complete AS#1 follow-up and extension tasks.	• IC preparation, application, and/or extension.

Activity Setting					
AS#4 Library	• Reading about ECT.*	• Read silently and with companion.*	• Introduce as AS with new books and reading log.*	• Read silently and with companion.*	• Community decides library activity.*
AS#5 Vocabulary	• Provide motivating tasks relating to ECT.*	• Provide independent tasks relating to ECT.*	• Students prepare independent vocabulary tasks.*	• Introduce as AS#5. Students prepare and check peers' work.*	• Students prepare vocabulary visual displays to post.*
AS#6 Journaling	• Draw or write about experience and ECT in large group.*	• Draw, write about ECT.* • Teacher responds.	• Introduce as AS. Students respond to teachers' remarks.*	• Teacher and students interact in writing.*	• Open journaling for peers and teachers.*
AS#7 Research	• Use materials to research ECT topics.*	• Use materials to research SAC topics.*	• Introduce AS#7 with informational resources and technology.	• Use choice contract to increase time for research projects.*	
AS#8 Games and Listening				• Introduce AS#8 by purpose, materials.	
AS#9 Technology	• Assess computer literacy skills.	• Introduce AS#9 by purpose, materials.	• Route students to computer AS.	• Use choice contract for computer work.	
AS#10 Experiments / Observation	• Design and stock for experiments and observation.*			• Introduce AS#10 by purpose, materials when needed.	
AS#11 Peer-Designed Tasks	• Students design tasks, activities for peer use.*			• Introduce AS#11 by purpose, materials.	
AS#12 Portfolio/ Student Assessment	• Students organize their portfolio format.*	• Students check peers' work and record results.*	• Students and teacher select evidence to go into students' portfolios.*	• Introduce AS#12 testing when ready for assessment after 6–8 weeks teaching.	

ECT=Early Content Theme; SAC=Subject Area Content; AS=Activity Settings
Pedagogy Standards: #1 JPA=Joint Productive Activity; #2 LD=Language Development; #3 CX=Contextualization; #4 CC=Cognitive Complexity; #5 IC= Instructional Conversation.
*=Activity can be used during early Phase-In for teaching and follow-up, which previews later activity setting installation.

Appendix A. 2 Organizing Classrooms for Multiple, Simultaneous Activity Settings (ASs)

The following guidelines are to help you arrange your classroom furniture for multiple and simultaneous activity settings. The guidelines are designed to meet students' needs as independent learners and members of the learning community and teachers' needs to interact with students in a variety of formats, particularly Instructional Conversation (IC). Each classroom will have special features to consider in addition to the guidelines listed here. Every teacher will have arrangements for student travel and materials management that are unique to the local situation and the teacher's preference.

- Assign every student a homeroom seat.
- Decide how students will store and carry their materials (folder, writing equipment).
- Make an AS available for large-group instructional activity. For early elementary students, this may be a rug area. In other classrooms, students must be able to look at the teacher easily from their seats. Avoid seating students with their backs to the place the teacher will occupy for large-group or other interactions.
- Arrange an AS for the teacher to work with a small group (3–7) of students regularly that has writing display areas (boards, charts) and storage space for materials. This instructional setting is in addition to and separate from the teacher's desk.
- Make ASs available for small group work, dyads, and individual instructional activity.
- Assure that every AS's work area is visible from any position the teacher will occupy to facilitate monitoring of student activity. The teacher must be able to see every student's activity at all times.
- Place quiet ASs away from potentially noisy ones, like games or experiments.
- Provide equipment for each AS such as task cards, bins, boxes for placing individual/group assignments, storing students' folders and texts.
- Match furniture to requirements of ASs:
- Most ASs need seating for 3 or more students.
- Each AS needs easily accessible storage space for materials. This may be as simple as the middle of the table.
- Art, listening, other hands-on activities need sink, electric plugs, or other prep/clean-up areas.
- Games may be placed on the floor, preferably carpeted.

(continues)

(continued)

- Technology needs electricity, hook-ups, supplies, ease of access for all students.
- Check that traffic patterns provide easy movement between ASs, especially for students with disabilities.
- Arrange for space to post materials or use equipment like charts, stands, oversized materials.
- Provide students with folders to house their work in progress and their routing plan or contract for the week.
- Designate a storage place for student folders.
- Designate a place for student work to be turned in daily for review.
- Provide mailboxes, folder system, or other arrangement for returning work to students. Students retrieve their teacher- and/or peer-reviewed work from this system daily.

TABLE A.2   Sample Grouping and Routing to Eight Activity Settings (ASs)
Activity Settings: Simultaneous and Differentiated Routing for Matched
(#1, 2 & 3) and Mixed (#4–9) Groups

Week of: _____

10 ROTATIONS OF 20 MINUTES EACH TO 8 ASs

GROUPS	A	B	C	D	E	F	G	H	I	J
BLUE GROUP										
1. S	1	2/3	4	5	9	1	2/3	6	8	7
2. S	1	2/3	6	7	8	1	2/3	4	5	9
3. S	1	2/3	7	4	5	1	2/3	8	6	9
4. S	1	2/3	8	5	4	1	2/3	9	7	6
5. S	1	2/3	4	6	5	1	2/3	8	9	7
6. S	1	2/3	5	9	4	1	2/3	6	8	7
ORANGE GROUP										
7. S	4	1	2/3	6	5	8	1	2/3	9	7
8. S	6	1	2/3	4	7	5	1	2/3	8	9
9. S	7	1	2/3	8	4	6	1	2/3	5	9
10. S	5	1	2/3	9	6	4	1	2/3	7	8
11. S	8	1	2/3	4	5	9	1	2/3	6	7
12. S	9	1	2/3	5	8	7	1	2/3	4	6
YELLOW GROUP										
13. S	7	4	1	2/3	9	6	5	1	2/3	8
14. S	4	5	1	2/3	6	9	8	1	2/3	7
15. S	6	7	1	2/3	4	5	9	1	2/3	8
16. S	5	4	1	2/3	7	8	6	1	2/3	9
17. S	4	8	1	2/3	5	9	7	1	2/3	6
18. S	6	8	1	2/3	7	5	9	1	2/3	4
19. S	8	6	1	2/3	4	5	9	1	2/3	7
GREEN GROUP										
20. S	6	7	4	1	2/3	5	8	9	1	2/3
21. S	4	6	8	1	2/3	7	5	9	1	2/3
22. S	7	5	9	1	2/3	6	8	4	1	2/3
23. S	5	9	8	1	2/3	4	6	7	1	2/3
24. S	8	5	9	1	2/3	4	7	6	1	2/3
RED GROUP										
25. S	2/3	5	6	4	1	2/3	9	8	7	1
26. S	2/3	5	4	9	1	2/3	6	7	8	1
27. S	2/3	4	5	6	1	2/3	7	8	4	1
28. S	2/3	6	7	8	1	2/3	5	4	9	1
29. S	2/3	5	4	9	1	2/3	6	7	8	1
30. S	2/3	7	8	6	1	2/3	5	9	4	1

Activity Settings
1 = Teaching
2/3 = Teaching follow-up
4 = Library
5 = Vocabulary and process building
6 = Journaling

7 = Information retrieval/research
8 = Games/Listening
9 = Observation/Experiment (not included)
10 = Computing (not included)

TABLE A.3 Grouping, Rotation, and Routing Worksheet

Week of:
Sample ASs: 1 = Reading; 2 = Reading Follow-up; 3 = Reading Follow-up;
4 = _____ ; 5 = _____; 6 = _____; 7 = _____; 8 = _____

SCHEDULE: Suggest 20 minute center times regularly. Students repeat center to increase time on task. Teaching (1) and follow-up (2 & 3) scheduled to maximize teaching.

GROUPS/AS*	A	B	C	D	E	F	G	H	I	J
BLUE GROUP										
1.	1	2/3				1	2/3			
2.	1	2/3				1	2/3			
3.	1	2/3				1	2/3			
4.	1	2/3				1	2/3			
5.	1	2/3				1	2/3			
6.	1	2/3				1	2/3			
ORANGE GROUP										
7.		1	2/3				1	2/3		
8.		1	2/3				1	2/3		
9.		1	2/3				1	2/3		
10.		1	2/3		.		1	2/3		
11.		1	2/3				1	2/3		
12.		1	2/3				1	2/3		
YELLOW GROUP										
13.			1	2/3				1	2/3	
14.			1	2/3				1	2/3	
15.			1	2/3				1	2/3	
16.			1	2/3				1	2/3	
17.			1	2/3				1	2/3	
18.			1	2/3				1	2/3	
19.			1	2/3				1	2/3	
GREEN GROUP										
20.				1	2/3				1	2/3
21.				1	2/3				1	2/3
22.				1	2/3				1	2/3
23.				1	2/3				1	2/3
24.				1	2/3				1	2/3
RED GROUP										
25.	2/3				1	2/3				1
26.	2/3				1	2/3				1
27.	2/3				1	2/3				1
28.	2/3				1	2/3				1
29.	2/3				1	2/3				1
30.	2/3				1	2/3				1

Activity Settings
1 = Teaching
2/3 = Teaching follow-up
4 = Library
5 = Vocabulary and process building
6 = Journaling

7 = Information retrieval/research
8 = Games/Listening
9 = Observation/Experiment (not included)
10 = Computing (not included)

References

Aguirre, A. 1988. Code switching, intuitive knowledge, and the bilingual classroom. In Ethnolinguistic issues in education, edited by H. S. Garcia and R. Chavez. Lubbock, TX: Texas Tech University, Lubbock College of Education.

Allport, G. 1954. The nature of prejudice. Cambridge, MA: Addison-Wesley.

Alvarez, C. M., and O. Pader. 1979. Cooperative and competitive behavior of Cuban-American children. Journal of Psychology 101(1): 265–271.

American Association for the Advancement of Science. 1993. Benchmarks for science literacy. New York: Oxford University Press.

Andrade, R., M. A. Callanan, C. A. Cervantes, G. Guardino, R. Hilberg, D. Kyle, E. McIntyre, H. Rivera, R. G. Tharp, and R. Rueda. 1999. Parents as intellectuals, parents as experts. Symposium at the annual meeting of the American Education Research Association, Montreal, Canada.

Antill, E., and R. G. Tharp. 1974. A comparison of the industriousness levels of KEEP and public school students. Honolulu: Kamehameha Schools.

Apple, M. W. 1979. Ideology and curriculum. London: Routledge and Kegan Paul.

Applebee, A. N. 1996. Curriculum as conversation: Transforming traditions of teaching and learning. Chicago: University of Chicago Press.

Asher, S. R., and J. G. Parker. 1989. Significance of peer relationship problems in childhood. In Social competence in developmental perspective: Vol. 51, edited by B. H. Schneider, G. Attili, J. Nadel, and P. Weissberg. Dordrecht, Netherlands: Kluwer Academic Publishers.

Asher, S. R., J. T. Parkhurst, S. Hymel, and G. A. Williams. 1990. Peer rejection and loneliness in childhood. In Peer rejection in childhood, edited by S. R. Asher and J. D. Coie. New York: Cambridge University Press.

Asher, S. R., S. Hymel, and P. D. Renshaw. 1984. Loneliness in children. Child Development 55: 1456–1464.

Au, K. H. 1979. Using the Experience-Text-Relationship method with minority children. Reading Teacher 32(6): 677–679.

Au, K. H., D. C. Crowell, C. Jordan, K. C. M. Sloat, G. E. Speidel, T. W. Klein, and R. G. Tharp. 1986. Development and implementation of the KEEP reading program. In Reading comprehension: From research to practice, edited by J. Orasanu. Hillsdale, NJ: Lawrence Erlbaum Associates.

August, D., and K. Hakuta, eds. 1998. Educating language-minority children. Washington, DC: National Academy Press.

Avellar, J., and J. Kagan. 1976. Development of competitive behaviors in Anglo-American and Mexican-American children. Psychological Reports 39: 191–198.

Bakhtin, M. M. 1981. The dialogic imagination. Austin: University of Texas Press.

_____. 1986. Speech genres and other essays. Austin: University of Texas Press.

Barnhardt, C. 1982. Tuning-in: Athabaskan teachers and Athabaskan students. In *Cross-cultural issues in Alaskan education*, edited by R. Barnhardt. Fairbanks, AL: Center for Cross-Cultural Studies.

Beals, D. E. 1998. Reappropriating schema: Conceptions of development from Bartlett and Bakhtin. *Mind, Culture and Activity* 5(1): 3–24.

Begay, S., G. S. Dick, D. W. Estell, J. Estell, T. L. McCarty, and A. Sells. 1995. Change from the inside out: A story of transformation in a Navajo community school. *Bilingual Research Journal* 19(1): 121–139.

Benham, M. K., and R. H. Heck. 1998. *Culture and educational policy in Hawai'i.* Mahwah, NJ: Lawrence Erlbaum Associates.

Berndt, T. J., and J. A. Hawkins. 1987. The contribution of supportive friendships to adjustment following the transition to junior high school. Unpublished manuscript.

———. 1988. Adjustment following the transition to junior high school. Unpublished manuscript.

Berndt, T. J., and K. Keefe. 1995. Friends' influence on adolescents' adjustment to school. *Child Development* 66: 1312–1329.

Berscheid, E., and H. T. Reis. 1998. Attraction and close relationships. In *Handbook of social psychology: Vol. 2*, edited by D. T. Gilbert and S. T. Fiske. Boston: Mcgraw-Hill.

Bianchini, J. A. 1997. Where knowledge construction, equity, and context intersect: Student learning of science in small groups. *Journal of Research in Science Teaching* 34(10): 1039–1065.

Birch, S. H., and G. W. Ladd. 1997. The teacher-child relationship and children's early school adjustment. *Journal of School Psychology* 35: 61–79.

Blum, R. 1998. *Closing the gap: Alaska.* Portland, OR: Northwest Regional Educational Laboratory.

———. n.d. *Lessons from Alaska and more.* Portland, OR: Northwest Regional Educational Laboratory.

Blumenfeld, P. C., V. L. Hamilton, S. T. Bossert, K. Wessel, and J. Meece. 1983. Teacher talk and student thought: Socialization into the student role. In *Teacher and student perceptions: Implications for learning.* Hillsdale, NJ: Lawrence Erlbaum Associates.

Bochner, S. 1994. Cross-cultural differences in the self-concept: A test of Hofstede's individualism/collectivism distinction. *Journal of Cross-Cultural Psychology* 25: 273–283.

Boggs, S. T. 1985. *Speaking, relating and learning: A study of Hawaiian children at home and at school.* Norwood, NJ: Ablex.

Bok, A., and P. Conihn. 1994. *De klas als Optisch Laboratorium, De kunst van het Leerlandschap.* Alkmaar, The Netherlands: Drukkerij Hogeschool.

———. 1996. *Een kleine stad van wereldformaat, De kunst van het Leerlandschap.* Alkmaar: Drukkerij Hogeschool.

Borst, K., and R. Kempenaar. 1998. *Groep 7 beheert een Uitgeverij.* Alkmaar: Drukkerij Hogeschool.

Bossert, S. T. 1977. Tasks, group management, and teacher control behavior: A study of classroom organization and teacher style. *School Review* 85: 552–565.

———. 1979. *Tasks and social relationships in classrooms.* New York: Cambridge University Press.

Bower, B. 1997. Effects of the multiple-ability curriculum in secondary social studies classrooms. In Working for equity in heterogeneous classrooms: Sociological theory in practice, edited by E. G. Cohen and R. A. Lotan. New York: Teachers College Press.

Braddock, J. H., and J. M. McPartland. 1993. Education of early adolescents. Review of Research in Education 19: 135–170.

Brislin, R. 1993. Conceptualizing culture and its impact. In Understanding culture's influence on behavior. Fort Worth, TX: Harcourt Brace.

_____. 1994, August. Education and cultural diversity: Suggestions for classroom and community. Paper read at the annual meeting of the American Psychological Association at Los Angeles, CA.

Brody, J., and C. Evertson. 1981. Student characteristics and teaching. New York: Longman.

Bronfenbrenner, U. 1979. The ecology of human development: experiments by nature and design. Cambridge: Harvard University Press.

Brown, A. D. 1980. Cherokee culture and school achievement. American Indian Culture and Research Journal 4: 55–74.

Brown, A. L., K. E. Metz, and J. C. Campione. 1996. Social interaction and individual understanding in a community of learners: The influence of Piaget and Vygotsky. In Piaget-Vygotsky: The social genesis of thought, edited by A. Tryphon and J. Voneche. East Sussex, UK: Psychology Press.

Bruer, J. T. 1993. Schools for thought: A science of learning in the classroom. Cambridge, MA: MIT Press.

Calderón, M., and A. Carreón. 1994. Educators and students use cooperative learning to become biliterate and bilingual. Cooperative Learning 14(3): 6–9.

Calderón, M., R. Herta-Lazarowitz, and R. Slavin. 1998. Effects of bilingual cooperative integrated reading and composition on students making the transition from Spanish to English reading. Elementary School Journal 99: 153–165.

Calkins, R., T. W. Klein, C. Guili, K. Au, L. Cunningham, and R. Springer. 1989. Kamehameha Elementary Education Program: An evaluative summary. Honolulu: The Kamehameha Schools Center for the Development of Early Education.

Carnegie Corporation of New York. 1996. Years of promise: A comprehensive learning strategy for America's children. New York: Carnegie Corporation of New York.

Carpenter, T., E. Fennema, and M. Franke. 1996. Cognitively guided instruction: A knowledge base for reform in primary mathematics instruction. Elementary School Journal 97: 3–20.

Cauce, A. M. 1986. Social networks and social competence: Exploring the effects of early adolescent friendships. American Journal of Community Psychology 14: 607–628.

Cauce, A. M., C. Mason, N. Gonzales, Y. Hiraga, and G. Liu. 1994. Social support during adolescence: Methodological and theoretical considerations. In Social networks and social support in childhood and adolescence, edited by F. Nestmann and K. Hurrelmann. New York: Walter de Gruyter.

Cauce, A. M., and D. S. Srebnick. 1989. Peer social networks and social support: A focus for prevention efforts. In Primary prevention in the schools, edited by L. A. Bond and B. Compas. Newberry Park, CA: Sage.

Cauce, A. M., K. Hannan, and M. Sargeant. 1987. Negative events, social support, and locus of control in early adolescence: Contributions to well-being. Paper read at the annual meeting of the American Psychological Association at New York.

Cauce, A. M., R. D. Felner, and J. Primavera. 1982. Social support in high-risk adolescents: Structural components and adaptive impact. *American Journal of Community Psychology* 10: 417–428.

Cazden, C. 1998, January. The language of African American students in classroom discourse. Paper read at the Language Diversity and Academic Achievement in the Education of African American Students Conference at New York.

Cazden, C. B. 1983. Peekaboo as an instructional model: Discourse development at school and at home. In *The sociogenesis of language and human conduct: A multidisciplinary book of readings*, edited by B. Bain. New York: Plenum.

Cheon, H., J. McClelland, and J. Plihal. 1995. Korean immigrant parents' experiences with their children's schooling in the United States. Paper read at the annual meeting of the American Educational Research Association at San Francisco, CA.

Chisholm, I. M. 1994. Preparing teachers for multicultural classrooms. *Journal of Educational Isues of Language Minority Students* 14: 3–70.

_____. 1995–1996. Computer use in a multicultural classroom. *Journal of Research on Computing in Education* 28(2): 162–174.

Ciofalo Lagos, N. 1994. Achievement motivation: Cross cultural research in a developing vs. a developed society (Mexico vs. Germany). Paper read at the meeting of the Hawaii Educational Research Association at Honolulu, HI.

Coburn, J., and S. Nelson. 1989. *Teachers do make a difference: What Indian graduates say about their school experience*. Portland, OR: Northwest Regional Educational Laboratory.

Cohen, E. G. 1986. *Designing groupwork: Strategies for the heterogeneous classroom*. New York: Teachers College Press.

_____. 1994a. *Designing groupwork: Strategies for the heterogeneous classroom*. 2d ed. New York: Teachers College Press.

_____. 1994b. Restructuring the classroom: Conditions for productive small groups. *Review of Education Research* 64(1): 1–35.

Cohen, E. G., and R. A. Lotan. 1995. Producing equal status interaction in the heterogeneous classroom. *American Educational Research Journal* 32: 99–120.

_____. 1997. *Working for equity in heterogeneous classrooms*. New York: Teachers College Press.

Cohen, E. G., R. A. Lotan, and C. Leechor. 1989. Can classrooms learn? *Sociology of Education* 62: 75–94.

Coie, J. D., and K. A. Dodge. 1983. Continuities and changes in children's social status: A five-year longitudinal study. *Merrill-Palmer Quarterly* 29: 261–282.

Comer, J. P. 1980. *School power: Implications of an intervention project*. New York: Free Press.

Cook, H., and C. Chi. 1984. Cooperative behavior and locus of control among American and Chinese-American boys. *Journal of Psychology* 118: 169–177.

Csikszentmihalyi, M., K. Rathunde, and S. Whalen. 1993. *Talented teenagers*. New York: Cambridge University Press.

Dalton, S. S. 1989. Teachers as assessors and assistors: Institutional constraints on interpersonal relationships. Paper read at the American Education Research Association annual meeting at San Francisco, CA.

_____. 1998a. Pedagogy matters: Standards for effective teaching practice. Santa Cruz, CA: University of California, Center for Research on Education, Diversity & Excellence.

_____. 1998b. Teaching Alive! Interactive CD-ROM disc. Santa Cruz, CA: University of California, Center for Research on Education, Diversity & Excellence.

Dalton, S. S., and D. G. Youpa. 1998. Standards-based teaching reform in Zuni Pueblo middle and high schools. Equity and Excellence in Education 31(1): 55–68.

Dalton, S. S., and J. Sison. 1995. Enacting instructional conversations with Spanish-speaking students in middle school mathematics. Santa Cruz: University of California, National Center for Research on Cultural Diversity and Second Language Learning.

D'Amato, J. D. 1988. "Acting": Hawaiian children's resistance to teachers. The Elementary School Journal 88: 529–542.

Darling-Hammond, L., and B. Falk. 1997. Using standards and assessments to support student learning. Phi Delta Kappan 79(3): 190–199.

Darnell, F., and A. Höem. 1996. Taken to extremes: Education in the far north. Cambridge, MA: Scandinavian University Press North America.

Dewey, J. 1938. Essays. New York: Society for Ethical Culture.

Deyhle, D., and M. Le Compte. 1994. Cultural differences in child development: Navajo adolescents in middle schools. Theory into Practice 33: 156–166.

Dick, G. S., D. W. Estell, and T. L. McCarty. 1994. Saad Naakih Bee'enootihji Na'alkaa: Restructuring the teaching of language and literacy in Navajo community school. Journal of American Indian Education 33: 31–46.

DiGiulio, R. 1995. Positive classroom management. Thousand Oaks, CA: Corwin Press.

Domino, G. 1992. Cooperation and competition in Chinese and American children. Journal of Cross Cultural Psychology 23: 456–467.

Dyson, A. H., and C. Genishi. 1991. Visions of children as language users: Research on language and language education in early childhood. Berkeley, CA: Center for the Study of Writing.

Echevarria, J. 1995. Interactive reading instruction: A comparison of proximal and distal effects of instructional conversations. Exceptional Children 61(1): 536–552.

Epstein, J. L. 1983a. Examining theories of adolescent friendships. In Friends in school: Patterns of selection and influence in secondary schools, edited by J. L. Epstein and N. Karweit. New York: Academic Press.

_____. 1983b. The influence of friends in achievement and affective outcomes. In Friends in school: Patterns of selection and influence in secondary schools, edited by J. L. Epstein and N. Karweit. New York: Academic Press.

_____. 1983c. Selection of friends in differently organized schools and classrooms. In Friends in school: Patterns of selection and influence in secondary schools, edited by J. L. Epstein and N. Karweit. New York: Academic Press.

_____. 1986. Friendship selection: Developmental and environmental influences. In Process and outcome in peer relationships, edited by E. Mueller and C. Cooper. New York: Academic Press.

_____. 1989. The selection of friends. In Peer relationships in child development, edited by G. Ladd and T. Berndt. New York: John Wiley & Sons.

Epstein, J. L., and J. M. McPartland. 1976. Classroom organization and the quality of school life. Baltimore: Center for Social Organization of Schools, Johns Hopkins University.

Erickson, F. 1980. Timing and context in everyday discourse: Implications for the study of referential and social meaning. Austin, TX: Southwest Educational Development Lab.

_____. 1987. Conceptions of school culture: An overview. Educational Administration Quarterly 23: 11–12.

Esmailka, W., and C. Barnhardt. 1981. The social organization of participation in three Athabaskan cross-cultural classrooms. Fairbanks, AL: University Center for Cross Cultural Studies.

Estrada, P. 1996a. Support from best friends during the transition to middle school and its relation to educational functioning in poor urban youth. Paper read at the annual meeting of the Society for Research on Adolescence at Boston, MA.

_____. 1996b. Teacher support during the transition to middle school and its relation to education functioning in poor urban youth. Paper read at the annual meeting of the American Educational Research Association at Atlanta, GA.

_____. 1997. Patterns of social organization in a sample of nine culturally and linguistically diverse schools. Technical Report No. 1, Project 5.8. Santa Cruz, CA: University of California, Center for Research on Education, Diversity and Excellence (CREDE) and the Office of Educational Research and Improvement.

Estrada, P., and B. Imhoff. 1999. Patterns of language arts instructional activity and excellence, fairness, inclusion and harmony: Six first grade case studies. Technical Report No. 3, Project 5.8. Santa Cruz, CA: University of California, Center for Research on Education, Diversity & Excellence.

Estrada, P., P. Sayavong, and G. M. Guardino. 1998. Patterns of language arts instructional activity in first and fourth grades: Pedagogy, simultaneity/diversification of activity, diversification of persons, and student performance. Technical Report No. 2, Project 5.8. Santa Cruz: University of California, Center for Research on Education, Diversity and Excellence (CREDE) and the Office of Educational Research and Improvement.

Feldlaufer, H., C. Midgley, and J. S. Eccles. 1988. Student, teacher, and observer perceptions of the classroom environment before and after the transition to junior high school. Journal of Early Adolescence 8: 133–156.

Foster, M. 1989. It's cooking now: A performance analysis of the speech events of a Black teacher in an urban community college. Language in Society 18: 1–29.

_____ 1992. Sociolinguistics and the African-American community: Implications for literacy. Theory in Practice 31(4): 303–311.

_____. 1995. Talking that talk: The language of control, curriculum, and conflict. Linguistics and Education 7: 129–150.

Foster, M., and T. Peele. In press. Teaching and learning in contexts of African American English, community and culture. Claremont, CA: Claremont Graduate University.

Fradd, S. H., and P. Larrinaga McGee. 1994. Instructional assessment: An integrative approach to evaluating student performance. Reading, MA: Addison-Wesley.

Fránquiz, M. E. 1995. Transformations in bilingual classrooms: Understanding opportunity to learn within the change process. Ph.D. diss., School of Education, University of California, Santa Barbara.

Fraser, B. J., and D. L. Fisher. 1982. Predicting students' outcomes from their perceptions of classroom psychosocial environment. *American Education Research Journal* 19: 498–518.

Gabriel, S. L., and I. Smithson, eds. 1990. Gender in the classroom. Urbana and Chicago: University of Illinois Press.

Gallimore, R., J. W. Boggs, and C. Jordan. 1974. Culture, behavior and education: A study of Hawaiian-Americans. Beverly Hills, CA: Sage.

Gallimore, R., R. G. Tharp, K. C. Sloat, T. W. Klein, and M. E. Troy. 1982. Analysis of reading achievement test results for the Kamehameha Early Education Project: 1972–1979. Technical Report 95. Honolulu: Kamehameha Early Education Project, Kamehameha Schools/Bishop Estate.

Gallimore, R., R. G. Tharp, and R. Rueda. 1989. The social context of cognitive functioning of developmentally disabled students. In *Cognitive approaches in special education*, edited by D. Sugden. London: Falmer Press.

Gallimore, R., T. S. Weisner, D. Guthrie, L. P. Bernheimer, and K. Nihira. 1993. Family responses to young children with developmental delays: Accommodation activity in ecological and cultural context. *American Journal on Mental Retardation* 98 (2): 185–206.

Garcia, E. E. 1991. "Hispanic" children: Theoretical, empirical and related policy issues. *Educational Policy Review* 4(1): 69–93.

Gardner, E. B. 1986. Unique features of a band-controlled school: The Seabird Island community school. *Canadian Journal of Native Education* 13: 15–32.

Goldenberg, C. 1992–1993. Instructional conversations: Promoting comprehension through discussion. *Reading Teacher* 46(4): 316–326.

Goldenberg, C., and G. Patthey-Chavez. 1995. Discourse processes in instructional conversations: Interactions between teacher and transition readers. *Discourse Processes* 19(1): 57–74.

González, N., L. Moll, M. Tenery, A. Rivera, P. Rendon, R. Gonzales, and C. Amanti. 1995. Funds of knowledge for teaching in Latino households. *Urban Education* 29 (4): 444–471.

Goodenough, W. 1971. Culture, language, and society. Reading, MA: Addison-Wesley.

Goodenow, C. 1993. Classroom belonging among early adolescent students: Relationships to motivation and achievement. *Journal of Early Adolescence* 13: 21–34.

Graybill, S. W. 1997. Questions of race and culture: How they relate to the classroom for African American students. *Clearing House* 70(6): 311–318.

Greenfield, P. M. 1994. Independence and interdependence as developmental scripts: Implications for theory, research, and practice. In *Cross-cultural roots of minority child development*, edited by P. M. Greenfield and R. R. Cocking. Hillsdale, NJ: Lawrence Erlbaum Associates.

Gudykunst, W. B., and S. Ting-Toomey. 1988. The influence of cultural variability on affective communication. *American Behavioral Scientist* 31: 384–400.

Gudykunst, W. B., Y. C. Yoon, and T. Nishida. 1987. The influence of individualism-collectivism in ingroup and outgroup relationships. *Communication Monographs* 54: 295–306.

Gumperz, J. J. 1982. Discourse strategies. Cambridge, England: Cambridge University Press.

Gumperz, J. J., and E. Hernandez-Chavez. 1971. Cognitive aspects of bilingual communication. In *Language use and social change*, edited by W. H. Whiteley. London: Oxford University Press.

Haleck, P. 1996. Student voices: Samoan perspectives of ideal student and ideal teacher. Ph.D. diss., University of Hawai'i, Honolulu.

Hallinan, M. T. 1976. Friendship patterns in open and traditional classrooms. Sociology of Education 49: 254–265.

_____. 1980. Patterns of cliquing among youth. In Friendship and social relations in children, edited by H. C. Foot, A. J. Chapman, and J. R. Smith. New York: John Wiley & Sons.

_____. 1982. Classroom racial composition and children's friendships. Social Forces 61(1): 56–72.

Hallinan, M. T., and A. B. Sorensen. 1985. Ability grouping and student friendships. American Education Research Journal 22: 485–499.

Hallinan, M. T., and R. A. Williams. 1989. Interracial friendship choices in secondary schools. American Sociological Review 54(1): 67–78.

Hallinan, M. T., and S. S. Smith. 1989. Classroom characteristics and student friendship cliques. Social Forces 67: 898–919.

Hansell, S., and N. Karweit. 1983. Curricular placement, friendship networks, and status attainment. In Friends in school: Patterns of selection and influence in secondary schools, edited by J. L. Epstein and N. Karweit. New York: Academic Press.

Haroutunian-Gordon, S. 1991. Turning the soul: Teaching through conversation in high school. Chicago: University of Chicago Press.

Harrison, B. 1986. Manokotak: A study of school adaptation. Anthropology & Education Quarterly 17: 100–110.

Hart, B., and T. R. Risley. 1995. Meaningful differences in the everyday experience of young American children. Baltimore: P. H. Brookes.

Hatch, A. 1994. Appropriate practices in non-mainstream settings: Perspectives on inner-city early childhood educators. Paper read at annual meeting of the National Association for the Education of Young Children at Atlanta, GA.

Heath, S. B. 1983. Research currents: A lot of talk about nothing. Language Arts 60: 999–1007.

Hertz-Lazarowitz, R., and S. Sharan. 1984. Enhancing prosocial behavior through cooperative learning in the classroom. In Development and maintenance of prosocial behavior, edited by E. Staub, D. Bartal, J. Karylowski, and J. Reykowski. New York: Plenum Press.

Hiebert, E. H., J. M. Colt, S. Catto, and E. Gury. 1992. Reading and writing of first-grade students in a restructured Chapter 1 program. American Educational Research Journal 29: 545–572.

Hilberg, R. 1998. The effectiveness of CREDE's standards-based method of mathematics instruction for American Indian students. Master's thesis, Education Department, University of California, Santa Cruz, CA.

Hilberg, R., R. W. Doherty, S. S. Dalton, D. Youpa, and R. G. Tharp. In press. Standards for effective mathematics education for American Indian students. In Changing the faces of mathematics: North American indigenous people's perspective: Vol. 5, edited by J. T. Hankes and G. R. Fast. Reston, VA: National Council of Teachers of Mathematics.

Hirsch, J. B., and B. D. Rapkin. 1987. The transition to junior high school: A longitudinal study of self-esteem, psychological symptomatology, school life, and social support. Child Development 58: 1235–1243.

Hoetker, J., and W. P. Albrand, Jr. 1969. The persistence of recitation. American Education Research Journal 6(2): 145–164.

Hofstede, G. 1980. Culture's consequences: International differences in work-related values. Beverly Hills, CA: Sage.

_____. 1986. Cultural differences in teaching and learning. International Journal of Intercultural Relations 10: 301–320.

Horton, M., and P. Freire. 1990. We make the road by walking. Edited by B. Bell, J. Gaventa, and J. Peters. Philadelphia: Temple University Press.

Hvitfeldt, C. 1986. Traditional culture, perceptual style, and learning: The classroom behavior of Hmong adults. Adult Education Quarterly 36(2): 65–77.

Jacob, E. 1999. Cooperative learning in context: An educational innovation in everyday classrooms. Ithaca, NY: State University of New York Press.

Jamieson, D. W., and K. W. Thomas. 1974. Power and conflict in the student-teacher relationship. Journal of Applied Behavioral Science 10(3): 321–336.

John-Steiner, V. 1985. Notebooks of the mind: Explorations in thinking. Albuquerque: University of New Mexico Press.

John-Steiner, V., and L. Smith. 1978, July 10–14. The educational promise of cultural pluralism: What do we know about teaching and learning in urban schools? Paper read at the Urban Education Program, CEMREL, Inc.'s National Conference on Urban Education at St. Louis, MO.

John-Steiner, V. P., and H. Osterreich. 1975. Learning styles among Pueblo children: Final report to the National Institute of Education. Albuquerque: College of Education, University of New Mexico.

Johnson, D. W., and R. T. Johnson. 1983. Social interdependence and perceived academic and personal support in the classroom. Journal of Social Psychology 120(1): 77–82.

Johnson, D. W., R. T. Johnson, L. A. Buckman, and P. S. Richards. 1985. The effect of prolonged implementation of cooperative learning on social support within the classroom. Journal of Social Psychology 119(1): 405–411.

Johnston, P. 1999. Documenting literacy achievements in integrated instruction: Conceptual and methodological issues. Paper presented at the Reading Research 1999 Conference, International Reading Association, San Diego, CA.

Jordan, C. 1978. Peer relationships among Hawaiian children and their educational implications. Paper read at the annual meeting of the American Anthropological Association at Los Angeles, CA.

_____. 1995. Creating cultures of schooling: Historical and conceptual background of the KEEP/Rough Rock Project. Bilingual Research Journal 19(1): 83–100.

Jordan, C., and R. G. Tharp. 1979. Culture and education. In Perspectives in cross-cultural psychology, edited by A. J. Marsella, R. G. Tharp, and T. Ciborowski. New York: Academic Press.

Jordan, C., R. G. Tharp, and L. Vogt. 1985. Compatibility of classroom and culture: General principles with Navajo and Hawaiian instances. Honolulu: Kamehameha Schools/Bishop Estate Center for the Development of Early Education.

Jorgensen, J. N. 1992. Children's code switching in group conversations. ERIC Document #ED 363 125.

Kagan, S., G. L. Zahn, and J. Gealy. 1977. Competition and school achievement among Anglo-American and Mexican-American children. Journal of Educational Psychology 69: 432–441.

Karweit, N. 1983. Extracurricular activities and friendship selection. In Friends in school: Patterns of selection and influence in secondary schools, edited by J. L. Epstein and N. Karweit. New York: Academic Press.

Karweit, N., and S. Hansell. 1983. School organization and friendship selection. In Friends in school: Patterns of selection and influence in secondary schools, edited by J. L. Epstein and N. Karweit. New York: Academic Press.

Kim, M. S., J. E. Hunter, A. Miyahara, A. M. Horvath, M. Bresnahan, and H. J. Yoon. 1996. Individual- vs. culture-level dimensions of individualism and collectivism: Effects on preferred conversational styles. Communication Monographs 63: 29–49.

King, A. 1990. Enhancing peer interaction and learning in the classroom through reciprocal questioning. American Educational Research Journal 27(4): 664–687.

Klein, T. W. 1988. Program evaluation of the Kamehameha Elementary Education Program's reading curriculum, in Hawai'i public schools: The cohort analysis 1978–1986. Honolulu: Center for the Development of Early Education, Kamehameha Schools/Bishop Estate.

Klein, T. W., and R. Calkins. 1988. The typical pattern of student achievement in KEEP from grade one to grade three: A look at different achievement measures across the years. Honolulu: Center for the Development of Early Education, Kamehameha Schools/Bishop Estate.

Kluckhohn, F., and F. Strodtbeck. 1961. Variations in value orientations. New York: Row.

Knight, G. P., S. Kagan, and R. Buriel. 1982. Perceived parental practices and prosocial development. Journal of Genetic Psychology 141: 57–65.

Kupersmidt, J. B. 1983. Predicting delinquency and academic problems from childhood peer status. Paper read at the biennial meeting of the Society for Research in Child Development at Detroit, MI.

Ladd, G. W. 1990. Having friends, keeping friends, making friends, and being liked by peers in the classroom: Predictors of children's early school adjustment. Child Development 61(1): 1081–1100.

Ladd, G. W., and B. J. Kochenderfer. 1996. Linkages between friendship and adjustment during early school transitions. In The company they keep: Friendships in childhood and adolescence, edited by W. M. Bukowski, A. F. Newcomb, and W. W. Hartup. New York: Cambridge University Press.

Ladd, G. W., B. J. Kochenderfer, and C. C. Coleman. 1996. Friendship quality as a predictor of young children's early school adjustment. Child Development 67(1): 1103–1118.

Ladd, G. W., and C. C. Coleman. 1997. Children's classroom peer relationships and early school attitudes: Concurrent and longitudinal associations. Early Education and Development 8(1): 51–66.

LaFrance, M., and C. Mayo. 1978. Cultural aspects of nonverbal communication. International Journal of Intercultural Relations 2: 71–89.

Lamb, J. C. 1998. Cross-age, paired, interactive tutoring: Personal agency, literate behaviors, and metacognition of Hmong-American fifth graders. Ph.D. diss., School of Education, University of Colorado.

Langer, J. A. 1995. Envisioning literature: Literary understanding and literature instruction. New York: Teachers College Press.

Lave, J., and E. Wegner. 1991. Situated learning: Legitimate peripheral participation. New York: Cambridge University Press.

Leacock, E. 1976. The concept of culture and its significance for school counselors. In Schooling in the cultural context, edited by J. I. Roberts and S. K. Akinsanya. New York: David McKay.

Lebra, T. S. 1976. Japanese patterns of behavior. Honolulu: University of Hawai'i Press.

_____. 1994. Mother and child in Japanese socialization: A Japan-U.S. comparison. In Cross-cultural roots of minority child development, edited by P. M. Greenfield and R. R. Cocking. Hillsdale, NJ: Lawrence Erlbaum Associates.

Lee, C. D. 1993. Signifying as a scaffold for literary interpretation: The pedagogical implications of an African American discourse genre. Urbana, IL: National Council of Teachers of English.

_____. 1995. A culturally based cognitive apprenticeship: Teaching African American high school students skills in literacy interpretation. Reading Research Quarterly 30: 608–630.

Lee, O., and S. H. Fradd. 1996a. Interactional patterns of linguistically diverse students and teachers: Insights for promoting science learning. Linguistics and Education: An International Research Journal 8: 269–297.

_____. 1996b. Literacy skills in science performance among culturally and linguistically diverse students. Science Education 80: 651–671.

_____ 1998. Science for all, including students from non-English-language backgrounds. Educational Researcher 27(4): 12–21.

Lee, V. E., J. B. Smith, and R. G. Croninger. 1995. Another look at high school restructuring: More evidence that it improves student achievement, and more insight into why. In Issues in restructuring schools. Madison: Wisconsin Center for Educational Research.

Lehrer, R., and D. Chazan, eds. 1998. Designing learning environments for developing understanding of space and geometry. Hillsdale, NJ: Lawrence Erlbaum Associates.

Lehrer, R., and L. Schauble. 1998. Reasoning about structure and function: Children's conception of gears. Journal of Research in Science Teaching 35(1): 3–25.

Lehrer, R., and T. Romberg. 1996. Exploring children's data modeling. Cognition and Instruction 14(1): 69–108.

Leith, S., and K. Slentz. 1984. Successful teaching strategies in selected northern Manitoba schools. Canadian Journal of Native Education 12: 24–30.

Lemke, J. L. 1990. Talking science: Language, learning, and values. Norwood, NJ: Ablex Publishing.

Leont'ev, D. A. 1989. Joint activity, communication, and interaction (toward well-grounded "Pedagogy of Cooperation"). Journal of Russian & East European Psychology 30(2): 43–58.

Levitt, M. J., J. L. Levitt, N. Franco, and M. E. Silver. 1995. Social support networks and achievement: The role of network member attitudes. Paper read at the meeting of the American Educational Research Association, New York.

Linder-Scholer, B. 1996. Industry's role in standards-based systemic reform, for K–12 mathematics, science and technology education. A look at industry and community commitment to educational systemic reform. A handbook. College Park, MD: Triangle Coalition for Science and Technology Education.

Lipka, J. 1986. School-community partnerships in rural Alaska. Rural Educator 7(3): 11–14.

_____. 1990. Integrating cultural form and content in one Yup'ik Eskimo classroom: A case study. Canadian Journal of Native Education 17: 18–32.

_____. 1994. Culturally negotiated schooling: Toward a Yup'ik mathematics. Journal of American Indian Education (Spring): 14–30.

Lucas, T., R. Henze, and R. Donato. 1990. Promoting the success of Latino language minority students: An exploratory study of six high schools. Harvard Educational Review 60(3): 315–340.

MacDonald, S., and R. Gallimore. 1971. Battle in the classroom. Scranton, PA: Intext.

Mann, L., M. Radford, and C. Kanagawa. 1985. Cross-cultural differences in children's use of decision rules: A comparison between Japan and Australia. Journal of Personality and Social Psychology 49: 1557–1564.

Markus, H. R., and S. Kitayama. 1991. Culture and the self: Implications for cognition, emotion, and motivation. Psychological Review 98: 224–253.

McClelland, F. M., and J. A. Ratliff. 1947. The use of sociometry as an aid in promoting social adjustment in ninth grade homeroom. Sociometry 19: 147–153.

McIntyre, E., ed. In press. Classroom diversity: Connecting students' cultures to instruction. Portsmouth, NH: Heinemann Books.

McLaren, P. 1999. A pedagogy of possibility: Reflecting upon Paulo Freire's politics of education. Educational Researcher 28(2): 9–54.

McLaughlin, M. W., and L. A. Shepard. 1995. Improving education through standards-based reform: A report by the National Academy of Education Panel on Standards-Based Education Reform. Washington, DC: National Academy of Education.

McPartland, J. M. 1991. How departmentalized staffing and interdisciplinary teaming combine for effects on middle grade students. Paper read at the meeting of the American Educational Research Association at Washington, DC.

Megargee, E. I. 1969. Influence of sex roles on the manifestation of leadership. Journal of Applied Psychology 53: 377–382.

Mehan, H. 1979. "What time is it, Denise?": Asking known information questions in classroom discourse. Theory into Practice 18: 285–294.

Meier, T. 1996. Never so truly free: Reading and writing about Malcolm in the community college. In Teaching Malcolm X, edited by T. Perry. New York: Routledge.

_____. 1998, January. The case for Ebonics as part of exemplary teacher preparation. Paper read at the Language Diversity and Academic Achievement in the Education of African American Students Conference at New York.

Midgley, C., E. Anderman, and L. Hicks. 1995. Differences between elementary and middle school teachers and students: A goal theory approach. Journal of Early Adolescence 15(1): 90–113.

Midgley, C., H. Feldlaufer, and J. S. Eccles. 1989. Student/teacher relations and attitudes toward mathematics before and after the transition to junior high school. Child Development 60(1): 981–992.

Miller, A. G., and R. Thomas. 1972. Cooperation and competition among Blackfoot Indian and urban Canadian children. Child Development 43: 1104–1110.

Miller, K. E., and T. J. Berndt. 1987. Adolescent friendship and school orientation. Paper read at the Society for Research in Child Development Conference at Baltimore, MD.

Miller, L. S. 1995. An American imperative: Accelerating minority educational advancement. New Haven, CT: Yale University Press.

Miltenburg, R., and E. Singer. 1999. Culturally mediated learning and the development of self-regulation by survivors of child abuse: A Vygotskian approach to the support of survivors of child abuse. Human Development 42(1): 1–17.

Moll, L. C., C. Amanti, D. Neff, and N. González. 1992. Funds of knowledge for teaching: Using a qualitative approach to connect homes and classrooms. Theory into Practice 21: 132–142.

Morgan, S. W., and B. Mausner. 1973. Behavioral and fantasized indicators of avoidance of success in men and women. Journal of Personality 41: 457–470.

Mussen, P., and N. Eisenberg-Berg. 1977. Roots of caring, sharing, and helping. San Francisco: Freeman.

National Center for Education Statistics. 1996. Pursuing excellence: Initial findings from the third international mathematics and science study. A Synthesis Report. Washington, DC: National Center for Education Statistics.

National Commission on Teaching and America's Future. 1996. What matters most: Teaching for America's future. New York: National Commission on Teaching and America's Future.

National Council of Teachers of Mathematics. 1991. Professional standards for teaching mathematics. Reston, VA: National Council of Teachers of Mathematics.

National Education Goals Panel. 1995. National education goals report: Building on a nation of learners. Washington, DC: National Education Goals Panel.

National Research Council. 1996. National science education standards. Washington, DC: National Academy Press.

Newmann, F. M., ed. 1996. Authentic achievement: Restructuring schools for intellectual quality. San Francisco: Jossey-Bass.

Newmann, F. M., W. G. Secada, and G. Wehlage. 1995. A guide to authentic instruction and assessment: Vision, standards, and scoring. Madison: Wisconsin Center for Educational Research at the University of Wisconsin.

Nickerson, J. R., and R. S. Prawat. 1981. Affective interactions in racially diverse classrooms: A case study. Elementary School Journal 81(1): 290–303.

Ninio, A., and J. Bruner. 1978. The achievement and antecedents of labelling. Journal of Child Language 5: 1–15.

Nye, B. 1993. Some questions and answers about multiage grouping. ERS Spectrum 11(3): 38–45.

Nystrand, M., and A. Gamoran. 1991. Instructional discourse, student engagement, and literature achievement. Research in the Teaching of English 25: 261–290.

———. 1992. From discourse communities to interpretive communities. In Exploring texts: The role of discussion and writing in the teaching and learning of literature, edited by G. Newell and R. Durst. Norwood, MA: Christopher-Gordon.

Oakes, J. 1990. Tracking and ability grouping: A structural barrier to access and achievement. In Access to knowledge: An agenda for our nation's schools, edited by J. I. Goodlad and P. Keating. New York: College Entrance Examination Board.

Oakes, J., and M. Lipton. 1998. Teaching to change the world. New York: McGraw-Hill College.

O'Donnell, C. R., and R. G. Tharp. 1990. Community intervention guided by theoretical development. In *International handbook of behavior modification and therapy*, edited by A. S. Bellack, M. Hersen, and A. E. Kazdin. New York: Plenum Press.

Okabe, R. 1983. Cultural assumptions of East and West. In *Intercultural communication theory*, edited by W. Gudykunst. Newbury Park, CA: Sage.

Okamura, J. 1981. Situational ethnicity. *Ethnic and Racial Studies* 4: 452–463.

Ost, D. H. 1991. The culture of teaching: Stability and change. In *Current perspectives on the culture of schools*, edited by N. Wyner. Cambridge, MA: Brookline Books.

Oyserman, D., L. Gant, and J. Ager. 1995. A socially contextualized model of African American identity: Possible selves and school persistence. *Journal of Personality and Social Psychology* 69: 1216–1232.

Palincsar, A., and A. Brown. 1985. Reciprocal teaching: A means to a meaningful end. In *Reading education: Foundations for a literate America*, edited by J. Osborn, P. Wilson, and R. C. Anderson. Lexington, MA: D. C. Heath.

Palincsar, A. S., and A. L. Brown. 1989. Classroom dialogues to promote self-regulated comprehension. In *Advances in research on teaching*, edited by J. Brophy. New York: JAI.

Palincsar, A. S., C. Anderson, and Y. M. David. 1993. Pursuing scientific literacy in the middle grades through collaborative problem solving. *Elementary School Journal* 93(5): 643–658.

Parker, J. G., and S. R. Asher. 1987. Peer relations and later personal adjustment: Are low-accepted children at risk? *Psychological Bulletin* 102(1): 357–389.

_____. 1993. Friendship and friendship quality in middle childhood: Links with peer group acceptance and feelings of loneliness and social dissatisfaction. *Developmental Psychology* 29(1): 611–621.

Peplau, L. A. 1976. Impact of fear of success and sex-role attitudes on women's competitive achievement. *Journal of Personality and Social Psychology* 34: 561–568.

Perry, D. G., S. J. Kusel, and L. D. Perry. 1988. Victims of peer aggression. *Developmental Psychology* 24: 807–814.

Phelan, P., Y. H. Cao, and A. L. Davidson. 1994. Navigating the psychosocial pressures of adolescence: The voices and experiences of high school youth. *American Educational Research Journal* 31(1): 415–447.

Philips, S. U. 1972. Participant structures and communicative competence: Warm Springs children in community and classroom. In *Functions of language in the classroom*, edited by C. B. Cazden, V. P. John, and D. Hymes. New York: Teachers College Press.

Pianta, R. C., M. S. Steinberg, and K. B. Rollins. 1995. The first two years of school: Teacher-child relationships and deflections in children's classroom adjustment. *Development & Psychopathology* 7(1): 295–312.

Pratt, D. 1986. On the merits of multiage classrooms. *Research in Rural Education* 3(3): 111–116.

Preston, V. 1991. Mathematics and science curricula in elementary and secondary education for American Indian and Alaska Native students. Washington, DC: U.S. Department of Education, Indian Nations at Risk Task Force.

Pukui, M. T., E. W. Haertig, and C. A. Lee. 1972. *Nana ike kumu* (Look to the source). Vols. 1–2. Honolulu: Hui Hanai.

Ramsey, S. J. 1979. Nonverbal behavior: An intercultural perspective. In *Handbook of intercultural communication*, edited by M. K. Asante, E. Newmark, and C. A. Blake. Newbury Park, CA: Sage.

Rhodes, R. W. 1989. Native American learning styles. *Journal of Navajo Education* 7: 33–41.

Richmond, G., and J. Striley. 1996. Making meaning in classrooms: Social processes in small-group discourse and scientific knowledge building. *Journal of Research in Science Teaching* 33(8): 839–858.

Rogoff, B. 1990. *Apprenticeships in thinking: Cognitive development in social context.* New York: Oxford University Press.

_____. 1991. Social interaction as apprenticeship in thinking: Guidance and participation in spatial planning. In *Perspectives on socially shared cognition*, edited by L. B. Resnick, J. M. Levine, and S. D. Teasley. Washington, DC: American Psychological Association.

Rosenholtz, S. 1982. Treating problems of academic status. In *Status, attributions, and justice*, edited by J. Berger and M. Selditch. New York: Elsevier.

Rothenberg, J. 1982. Peer relations and activity structures in elementary school classrooms. Ph.D. diss., University of Michigan, Ann Arbor.

Rowan, B. 1995. Focusing reform: How the Lee, Smith and Croniger Report can enhance school restructuring. In *Issues in restructuring schools*. Madison: Center on Organization and Restructuring of Schools, University of Wisconsin.

Rubin, M. 1991. *Corpus Christi: The Eucharist in late medieval culture.* New York: Cambridge University Press.

Rueda, R. 1998a. Principles of professional development. Paper read at the Bueno Institute Conference, invited address, August, at Vail, CO.

_____. 1998b. *Standards for professional development: A sociocultural perspective.* Santa Cruz, CA: University of California, Center for Research on Education, Diversity & Excellence.

Rueda, R., C. Goldenberg, and R. Gallimore. 1992. *Rating instructional conversations: A guide.* Santa Cruz, CA: University of California, National Center for Research on Cultural Diversity and Second Language Learning.

Ruiz, N. T., and R. A. Figueroa. 1995. Learning-handicapped classrooms with Latino students: The Optimal Learning Environment (OLE) Project. *Education in Urban Society* 27(4): 463–483.

Sadker, M., and D. Sadker. 1986. Sexism in the classroom: From grade school to graduate school. *Phi Delta Kappan* 67: 512–515.

_____. 1994. *Failing at fairness: How America's schools cheat girls.* New York: Macmillan.

Saunders, W., and C. Goldenberg. 1992. Effects of instructional conversations on transition students' concept development. Paper read at the annual meeting of the American Education Research Association at San Francisco, CA.

Saunders, W. M., and C. Goldenberg. 1999. *The effects of instructional conversations and literature logs on the story comprehension and thematic understanding of English proficient and limited English proficient students.* Santa Cruz, CA: University of California, Center for Research on Education, Diversity & Excellence.

Savin-Williams, R. C., and T. J. Berndt. 1990. Friendships and peer relations. In *At the threshold: The developing adolescent*, edited by S. S. Feldman and G. R. Elliott. Cambridge: Harvard University Press.

Schaefer, W., and C. Olexa. 1971. Tracking and opportunity. Scranton, PA: Chandler.

Schuncke, G. M. 1978. Social effects of classroom organization. Journal of Educational Research 7(1): 303–307.

Scribner, S., and M. Cole. 1973. Cognitive consequences of formal and informal education. Science 182: 553–559.

Sells, A. 1994, April. Initiating and sustaining positive change: Navajo tribal perspective on the KEEP-Rough Rock experience. Paper read at the annual meeting of the American Educational Research Association at New Orleans, LA.

Shackleton, V. J., and A. H. Ali. 1990. Work-related values of managers: A test of the Hofstede model. Journal of Cross-Cultural Psychology 21: 109–118.

Sharan, Y., and S. Sharan. 1987. Training teachers for cooperative learning. Educational Leadership 45(3): 20–25.

Sirota, A. J., W. B. Rutherford, L. Ianacone, and J. Mallory. 1999. Pedgaogy, research, and practice: A video documentary case study of change. Paper read at the annual meeting of the American Education Research Association at Montreal, Quebec, Canada.

Slavin, R. 1994. Cooperative learning: Theory, research, & practice. 2d ed. Boston: Allyn & Bacon.

Slavin, R. E. 1979. Effects of biracial learning teams on cross-racial friendships. Journal of Educational Psychology 71(1): 381–387.

_____. 1985. Cooperative learning: Applying contact theory in desegregated schools. Journal of Social Issues 41(1): 45–62.

_____. 1987. A theory of school and classroom organization. Educational Psychologist 22(1): 89–108.

_____. 1995. Enhancing intergroup relations in schools: Cooperative learning and other strategies. In Toward a common destiny: Improving race and ethnic relations in America, edited by W. D. Hawley and A. W. Jackson. San Francisco: Jossey-Bass.

_____. 1996. Research for the future: Research on cooperative learning and achievement: What we know, what we need to know. Contemporary Educational Psychology 21(1): 43–69.

Sleeter, C., and C. A. Grant. 1988. Making choices for multicultural education: five approaches to race, class, and gender. Columbus, OH: Merrill.

Sloat, K. C. M., R. G. Tharp, and R. Gallimore. 1977. The incremental effectiveness of classroom-based teacher-training techniques. Behavior Therapy 8: 810–818.

Speidel, G. E. 1987a. Conversation and language learning in the classroom. In Child language, edited by K. E. Nelson and A. van Kleeck. Hillsdale, NJ: Lawrence Erlbaum Associates.

_____. 1987b. Language differences in the classroom: Two approaches for developing language skills in dialect-speaking children. In Sociocultural perspectives of language acquisition and multilingualism, edited by E. Oksaar. Tübingen: Gunter Narr Verlag.

Spencer-Oately, H. 1997. Unequal relationships in high and low power distance societies: A comparative study of tutor-student role relations in Britain and China. Journal of Cross-Cultural Psychology 28: 284–302.

Springer, L., M. E. Stanne, and S. S. Donovan. 1999. Effects of small-group learning on undergraduates in science, mathematics, engineering, and technology: A meta-analysis. Review of Educational Research 69: 21–51.

St. Clair, R. N., and G. Valdés-Fallis. 1980. The sociology of code-switching. Language Sciences 2: 205–221.

Stacey, K. 1992. Mathematical problem solving in groups: Are two heads better than one? Journal of Mathematical Behavior 11: 261–275.

Stairs, A. 1994. Indigenous ways to go to school: Exploring many visions. Journal of Multilingual and Multicultural Development 15: 63–76.

Starnes, B., and C. Paris. In press. Choosing to learn: Learning to choose. Phi Delta Kappan.

Steinberg, L., and N. Darling. In press. The broader context of social influence in adolescence. In Adolescence in context, edited by R. Silbereisen and E. Todt. New York: Springer.

Stevens, R. J., N. A. Madden, R. E. Slavin, and A. M. Farnish. 1987. Cooperative Integrated Reading and Composition: Two field experiments. Reading Research Quarterly (22): 433–454.

Stevens, R. J., and R. E. Slavin. 1995. The cooperative elementary school: Effects on students' achievement, attitudes, and social relations. American Educational Research Journal 32(1): 321–351.

Stevenson, H. W. , and J. W. Stigler. 1992. The learning gap: Why our schools are failing and what we can learn from Japanese and Chinese education. New York: Summit Books.

Stone, S. J. 1995. Teaching strategies: Strategies for teaching children in multiage classrooms. Childhood Education 71: 102–105.

Strube, M. J. 1981. Meta-analysis and cross-cultural comparison: Sex differences in child competitiveness. Journal of Cross-Cultural Psychology 12: 3–20.

Suina, J. H., and L. B. Smolkin. 1991, July. From natal culture to school culture to dominant society culture: Supporting transitions for Pueblo Indian students. Paper read at the Continuities and Discontinuities in the Cognitive Socialization of Minority Children Conference at Washington, DC.

Swing, S. R., and P. L. Peterson. 1982. The relationship of student ability and small-group interaction to student achievement. American Educational Research Journal 19(2): 259–274.

Swisher, K., and D. Deyhle. 1987. Styles of learning and learning of styles: Educational conflicts for American Indian/Alaskan Native youth. Journal of Multilingual and Multicultural Development 8: 345–360.

Tata, S. P., and F. T. L. Leong. 1994. Individualism-collectivism, social-network orientation, and acculturation as predictors of attitudes toward seeking professional psychological help among Chinese-Americans. Journal of Counseling Psychology 41: 280–287.

Taylor, B., and D. Pearson. 1999, May. A national study of effective schools and accomplished teachers of reading in the primary grades. Paper presented at the Reading Research 1999 Conference, International Reading Association, San Diego, CA.

Taylor, B. M., P. D. Pearson, K. Clark, and S. Walpole. 1998, December. Beating the odds in teaching all children to read: Lessons from effective schools and exemplary primary grade teachers. Paper presented at the annual meeting of the National Reading Conference, Austin, TX.

Tharp, R. G. 1963. Psychological patterning in marriage. Psychological Bulletin 60: 97–117.

_____. 1982. The effective instruction of comprehension: Results and description of the Kamehameha Early Education Program. Reading Research Quarterly 17(4): 503–527.

_____. 1989. Psychocultural variables and constants: Effects on teaching and learning in schools. American Psychologist 44(2): 349–359.

_____. 1991. Cultural diversity and treatment of children. Journal of Consulting & Clinical Psychology 59(6): 799–812.

_____. 1994. Research knowledge and policy issues in cultural diversity and education. In Language and learning: Educating linguistically diverse students, edited by B. McLeod. Albany: State University of New York Press.

_____. 1997. From at-risk to excellence: Research, theory, and principles for practice. Santa Cruz, CA: University of California, Center for Research on Education, Diversity and Excellence.

_____. 1999. Therapist as teacher. Human Development 42(2): 18–25.

Tharp, R. G., C. Jordan, G. E. Speidel, K. H. Au, T. W. Klein, R. P. Calkin, K. C. M. Sloat, and R. Gallimore. 1984. Product and process in applied developmental research: Education and the children of a minority. In Advances in developmental psychology, edited by M. E. Lamb, A. L. Brown, and B. Rogoff. Hillsdale, NJ: Lawrence Erlbaum Associates.

Tharp, R. G., H. Lewis, R. Hilberg, C. Bird, G. Epaloose, S. S. Dalton, D. G. Youpa, H. Rivera, M. Riding In-Feathers, and W. Eriacho. 1999. Seven more mountains and a map: Overcoming obstacles to reform in Native American schools. Journal of Education for Students Placed at Risk 4(1): 5–26.

Tharp, R. G., H. Rivera, D. G. Youpa, S. S. Dalton, G. M. Guardino, and S. Lasky. 1998. Activity setting observation system (ASOS) coding rulebook. Santa Cruz: University of California, Center for Research on Education, Diversity & Excellence.

Tharp, R. G., and M. Note. 1988. The triadic model of consultation: New developments. In School consultation: Interdisciplinary perspectives on theory, research, training, and practice, edited by F. West. Austin: Research and Training Project on School Consultation, University of Texas at Austin & the Association of Educational and Psychological Consultants.

Tharp, R. G., and R. Gallimore. 1988. Rousing minds to life: Teaching, learning, and schooling in social context. New York: Cambridge University Press.

Tharp, R. G., S. Dalton, and L. A. Yamauchi. 1994. Principles for culturally compatible Native American education. Journal of Navajo Education 11: 33–39.

Thomas, D. R. 1975. Cooperation and competition among Polynesian and European children. Child Development 46: 948–953.

Tizard, B., and M. Hughes. 1984. Young children learning: Talking and thinking at home and at school. Cambridge: Harvard University Press.

Tobin, J. J., D. Wu, and D. Davidson. 1989. Preschool in three cultures: Japan, China, and the United States. New Haven, CT: Yale University Press.

Toole, D. 1990. Discourse analysis in ethnographic research. Annual Review of Applied Linguistics 11: 42–56.

Treichler, P. A., and C. Kramarae. 1983. Women's talk in the ivory tower. Communication Quarterly 31: 118–132.

Triandis, H. C., R. Bontempo, M. J. Villareal, M. Asai, and N. Lucca. 1988. Individualism and collectivism: Cross-cultural perspectives on self-ingroup relationships. Journal of Personality and Social Psychology 54: 323–338.

Trickett, E. J., and R. H. Moos. 1974. Personal correlates of contrasting environments: Student satisfactions in high school classrooms. American Journal of Community Psychology 2(1): 1–12.

Valdés-Fallis, G. 1978. Code switching and the classroom teacher. Arlington, VA: Center for Applied Linguistics.

Vallo, N. H. 1988. Traditional instructional strategies of Pueblo Indian parents: An exploratory study. Ph.D. diss., University of New Mexico, Albuquerque.

van Brandwijk, D., B. Pompert, P. Conijn, M. Uylings, N. Fijma, and E. de Geus-Dorgelo. 1998, June 7–11. From play activity to learning activity: Developmental education for young children (4–8 years). Paper presented at the Fourth Congress of the International Society for Cultural Research and Activity Theory at Aarhus, Denmark.

Vogt, L. A., C. Jordan, and R. G. Tharp. 1992. Explaining school failure, producing school success: Two cases. In Minority education: Anthropological perspectives, edited by E. Jacob and C. Jordan. Norwood, NJ: Ablex.

Vygotsky, L. 1978. Mind in society. Translated by A. R. Luria. Edited by M. Cole, V. John-Steiner, S. Scribner, and E. Souberman. Cambridge: Harvard University Press.

_____. 1981. The genesis of higher mental functions. In The concept of activity in Soviet psychology, edited by J. V. Wertsch. Armonk, NY: M. E. Sharpe.

_____. 1987. Collected works of L. S. Vygotsky: Vol. 1: Problems of general psychology. Translated by N. Minick. Edited by R. W. Rieber and A. S. Carton. New York: Plenum Press.

Warren, B., A. Rosebery, and F. R. Conant. 1994. Discourse and social practice: Learning science in language minority classrooms. In Adult biliteracy in the United States, edited by D. Spener. Washington, DC: Center for Applied Linguistics.

Warring, D., D. W. Johnson, G. Maruyama, and R. Johnson. 1985. Impact of different types of cooperative learning on cross-ethnic and cross-sex relationships. Journal of Educational Psychology 77(1): 53–59.

Waxman, H. C., Y. N. Padron, and S. L. Knight. 1991. Risks associated with students' limited cognitive mastery. In Handbook of special education research and practice, edited by M. C. Wang, M. C. Reynolds, and H. J. Walberg. New York: Pergamon Press.

Webb, N. M., J. D. Troper, and R. Fall. 1995. Constructive activity and learning in collaborative small groups. Journal of Educational Psychology 87(3): 406–423.

Webb, N. M., and S. Farivar. 1994. Promoting helping behavior in cooperative small groups in middle school mathematics. American Educational Research Journal 31(2): 369–395.

Weisfeld, C. C., G. E. Weisfeld, and J. W. Callahan. 1982. Female inhibition in mixed-sex competition among young adolescents. Ethology and Sociobiology 3: 29–42.

Weisfeld, C. C., G. E. Weisfeld, R. A. Warren, and D. G. Freeman. 1983. The spelling bee: A naturalistic study of female inhibition in mixed-sex competition. Adolescence 18: 695–708.

Wertsch, J. V. 1985. Vygotsky and the social formation of mind. Cambridge: Harvard University Press.

Wyatt, J. D. 1978–1979. Native involvement in curriculum development: The native teacher as cultural broker. Interchange 9: 17–28.

Yamauchi, L. A. 1993. Visions of the ideal Zuni classroom: Multiple perspectives on Native American education. Ph.D. diss., University of Hawai'i, Honolulu.

_____. 1994, August. Video reflexive interviewing in a Zuni Indian school. Paper read at the annual meeting of the American Psychological Association at Los Angeles, CA.

Yamauchi, L. A., and K. O'Neil. 1994, January. Cultural differences in college students' expectations of teacher and student roles in the classroom. Paper read at the annual meeting of the Hawai'i Educational Research Association at Honolulu, HI.

Yamauchi, L. A., and R. G. Tharp. 1995. Culturally compatible conversations in Native American classrooms. *Linguistics and Education* 7: 349–367.

Yap, K. O., G. D. Estes, and P. R. Nickel. 1988. *A summative evaluation of the Kamehameha Early Education Program.* Honolulu, HI: Northwest Regional Educational Laboratory.

Zabel, R. H., and M. K. Zabel. 1996. *Classroom management in context.* New York: Houghton Mifflin.

Zajonc, R. B., and I. C. Marin. 1967. Cooperation, competition, and interpersonal attitudes in small groups. *Psychonomic Science* 7(8): 271–272.

Index

Teaching Transformed

RENEWING AMERICAN SCHOOLS:
THE EDUCATIONAL KNOWLEDGE BASE

SERIES EDITORS: Henry M. Levin, Stanford University, and
Jeannie Oakes, University of California–Los Angeles

Teaching Transformed

Achieving Excellence, Fairness, Inclusion, and Harmony

Roland G. Tharp
University of California, Santa Cruz

Peggy Estrada
University of California, Santa Cruz

Stephanie Stoll Dalton
U.S. Department of Education

Lois A. Yamauchi
University of Hawai'i, Mānoa

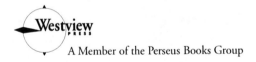
A Member of the Perseus Books Group

Renewing American Schools

Copyright © 2000 by Westview Press, A Member of the Perseus Books Group

Published in 2000 in the United States of America by Westview Press, 5500 Central Avenue, Boulder, Colorado 80301-2877, and in the United Kingdom by Westview Press, 12 Hid's Copse Road, Cumnor Hill, Oxford OX2 9JJ

Find us on the World Wide Web at www.westviewpress.com

Library of Congress Cataloging-in-Publication Data
Teaching transformed : achieving excellence, fairness, inclusion, and
    harmony / Roland G. Tharp . . . [et al.].
      p.   cm. — (Renewing American schools)
    Includes bibliographical references and index.
    ISBN 0-8133-2268-5 (hc) — ISBN 0-8133-2269-3 (pb)
    1. School improvement programs—United States.   2. Educational
equalization—United States.   3. Inclusive education—United States.
I. Tharp, Roland G., 1930–   . II. Series.
LB2822.82.T44   2000
371.2′00973—dc21   99-42077
                                                                                      CIP

The paper used in this publication meets the requirements of the American National Standard for Permanence of Paper for Printed Library Materials Z39.48-1984.

PERSEUS
POD
ON DEMAND   10   9   8   7   6   5   4   3   2

Contents